BRIEF PSYCHOTHERAPY

BRIEF PSYCHOTHERAPY

Brief Encounters

By

KARL KAY LEWIN, M.D.

Clinical Assistant
Professor of Psychiatry
University of Pittsburgh
School of Medicine
Pittsburgh, Pennsylvania

With a Foreword by
VAN BUREN O. HAMMETT, M.D.

WARREN H. GREEN, INC.
St. Louis, Missouri, U.S.A.

Published by

WARREN H. GREEN, INC.
10 South Brentwood Blvd.
St. Louis, Missouri 63105, U.S.A.

Library of Congress Catalog Card Number 78-96987

Printed in the United States of America
2-A   (160)

To Rose and The Doctor

FOREWORD

FROM time to time in the history of modern psychiatry, at irregular intervals, there have appeared individuals who, by providing some fresh perception of great value, have deserved the designation "original." With the writing of this volume, Karl Lewin has earned his place among this select coterie. This book is destined, I believe, to have a significant impact upon psychiatry.

The contemporary situation contains a combination of factors which create a mood of receptivity to the message of this book. In the first place there has been a growing impatience with the cumbersome aspect of psychoanalysis and the intensive and extensive method of therapy derived from it. The public—or at any rate that segment which is informed and affluent enough to seek psychoanalysis—is satisfied with its efficacy. But this treatment does take a long time, too long to escape criticism on that account, which may be one of the main reasons for its waning popularity. Other important factors in the current situation are the rapid growth of the population and ever-increasing awareness of emotional illness as a form of disease which requires treatment; the combined effect of these factors is to increase greatly the demand for therapy. This demand cannot be met through the application of methods of treatment which require hundreds of hours for each indivdual—there simply are not enough psychiatrists, nor is it likely that there ever will be. Finally, there is the development of community mental health centers, which is so prominently a feature of the contemporary psychiatric scene. Assisted by governmental subsidies these centers are coming into being on a nation-wide scale, especially in the larger cities. Offering treatment for mental and emotional illness to those who need help, regardless of whether or not they can pay for it, they are attempting to deliver good psychiatric care to a large segment of society which was heretofore unattended. This development has already brought to psychiatry's doorstep many thousands of new patients, and the number will continue to increase. The community centers are committed to the goal of providing quality care for their patients, but this will be almost impossible to achieve by the use of traditional methods of psychoanalytic therapy.

For all of these reasons, psychiatrists have recognized the need for a brief method of therapy which would be nonetheless effective. Many men of good intention have worked to solve this problem; various techniques have been devised, but none has been altogether satisfactory. In the context of this "hour of need," Dr. Lewin has come forward with this book, which contains a clear exposition of a method of therapy which is both brief and, from all appearances, effective.

Lewin's work is based upon an understanding of human nature which is firmly rooted in psychoanalytic theory, from which he deviates in just two particulars; these are, however, quite important to the technique which he has developed. His understanding of the psychosexual development of females differs from the traditional analytic theory significantly, and the reader will do well to study this difference carefully. Also—and this is crucial to his method—he strongly emphasizes the importance of the role played by conscience, with a corresponding de-emphasis of instinct and its vagaries.

It is in his *method of therapy* that he takes his departure from psychoanalysis: in just about every way, his method is almost the opposite of analytic technique. The following outline of the basic principles of Lewin's brief therapy will enable the reader to grasp readily how much, and in what ways, the two procedures differ.

1. Before beginning treatment, Lewin and the patient agree upon the goals of their work.

2. Right from the beginning—indeed, especially in the beginning—the doctor is very active in confronting the patient with the evidence of his self-punitive role. Hopefully, the first session will produce in the patient realization that much of his distress is self-induced.

3. There is early interpretation of transference, especially the negative aspects.

4. The therapist focuses the patient's attention in each session, in order to obtain continuity.

5. The patient is asked to do "homework—24 hours a day, 7 days a week."

6. The therapist actively makes available to the patient a more normal, less punitive conscience—his own—by means of his comments and behavior.

We can arrive at the essence of this method if we paraphrase a deathless line from the classical literature of the theater. Hamlet says: "Conscience doth make cowards of us all." Lewin says: "Warped conscience makes neurotic sufferers of many of us." The keystone of his method is recognition of conscience-gone-awry as the principal adversary of patient and doctor in the therapy. The hallmark of his therapeutic style is his use of active, even bold interpretation and confrontation, to bring the patient rapidly—in the first session preferably—to a feeling recognition of his own role in his illness.

The question: How active should a therapist be in the transactions between him and the patient? has been and continues to be difficult to answer to everyone's satisfaction. The traditional model for the therapist's behavior, and the one which continues to dominate in the training of the psychiatrist, emphasizes that he should require the patient to take the initiative in their dialogue, should not "steer" the patient's thoughts beyond the asking of questions, should limit his comments to interpretations of the patient's words and behavior, should refrain from expressing his opinions or emotional reactions, should keep his own personality from "intruding" upon the situation, and in general should preserve a neutral position towards the patient's ideas and behavior.

Those who favor this model for the therapist are apt to bridle whenever it is spoken of as passive, a term which has—in almost any context—a pejorative implication for most humans. They are right to object, for strictly speaking the model of behavior outlined above is not synonymous with passivity. However, it is in the actual application of this model in the treatment situation that the real nub of the question lies. The guidelines expressed above are clear enough, but in practice they tend to become fuzzy and uncertain. Strict neutrality is the half-brother of passivity, and it is quite easy for the therapist with a latent tendency towards inactivity to cross over the indistinct border that separates the one attitude from the other. To be active requires more work of the therapist; he must concentrate more intensely, and think harder about what the patient is saying and doing. Being active involves more risk to the therapist, such as the risk of making mistakes. A more passive role is easier: it minimizes the chance for error by delaying comment until more information is obtained; it allows a more relaxed state of receptive attention, while waiting for the patient's communications to make clear their point. This book challenges this latter model of therapist behavior and finds it unsuited to brief therapy.

It requires many qualities to be a good therapist, but there are two things which are certainly essential: a plentiful supply of intuition, fortified by knowledge of the dynamics of human nature in health and in sickness. It has been my observation that many psychiatrists possess both of these requisites in full measure, but some of them, at least, seem to be somewhat inhibited when it comes to using them in therapy; they tend to be cautious, even somewhat timid. This is in striking contrast to Lewin's style, as described in this book; he is quite active, even daring. He confidently uses his intuition, his knowledge of dynamics, and his own associations in his communications to the patient. To be sure, his communications tend to be selective, favoring his focus upon guilt and self-punishment, but we must keep in mind that he is not doing open-ended, long-term treatment. He is concentrating his and the patient's efforts upon achieving a therapeutic goal in a relatively short time.

I thoroughly agree with Lewin's statement that "psychiatrists as a general rule underestimate what is tolerable for a patient." One of the persistent myths in psychiatry is the scary idea that the therapist may drive his patient over the brink of madness by overly penetrating interpretations. After a quarter-century of experience I have come to believe that there is very little subtance to this notion. It is not plain speaking or penetrating comments which cause patients to worsen; it is something unhealthy in the psychiatrist, interacting with the patient's pathology. The psychiatrist, if he is himself free of sarcasm, sadism, seduction, and fear, need never hesitate to speak directly to the true facts without euphemistic sugarcoating. Indeed, doing just that will help the patient to get on with the work.

A special feature of this book is the case material, presented for the most part in the form of detailed reproductions of interviews between doctor and patient. One of the greatest difficulties which complicate our efforts to study psychotherapy has to do with the problem of obtaining reliable and accurate records of what takes place during the sessions. Such records bear the same relation to psychotherapy as do x-rays, blood counts, and tissue sections to clinical medicine. They are the evidence necessary for retrospective analysis of the process. Without them, we are reduced to conjecture. But such records are very hard to come by because of the extreme difficulty of conducting an interview and recording it at the same time. Within recent years, investigators have made use of electronic devices such as tape recorders, videotapes, and motion pictures in combination with sound tracks, in order to obtain objective recordings of the process of psychotherapy *in vivo*. Records thus obtained have yielded much valuable material for study. There are, however, two difficulties in the use of these devices: considerable technical skill is necessary, and the recordings contain such a profusion of detail as to require a great amount of time for analysis. Lewin experimented with tape recordings of interviews but discarded this technique because of the amount of time and labor necessary for transcription. He evolved his own technique, consisting of his own brand of "shorthand," so that he could record the interviews as they occurred. I have discussed this point with him, because of its special significance. The reproductions of interviews in the book are, first of all, extremely interesting, but of far greater importance is the fact that they serve as examples of his method and documentation of the results. The reader will want to be satisfied that he is receiving an accurate account of the transactions of these interviews. Lewin assures me that his notes, taken during the course of the interview, are in sufficient detail to enable him to reproduce the dialogues as presented in the text.

I said in the beginning that I think this book will have an impact upon psychiatry. It has something definite to say, and the message is delivered with a clout. The author has conviction about his method of brief therapy and the theoretical considerations upon which it is based, and his statements are unequivocal and forthright. I anticipate that there will be considerable reaction, and that in addition to favorable response there will also be adverse criticism. Some advocates of psychoanalysis may feel that Lewin is attempting to disparage that method of therapy. I do not think this is the case. To be sure, he makes comparisons between the techniques of his brief therapy and those of psychoanalysis, and does not hesitate to point out that the latter is a much more protracted affair. But nowhere does he say that his method is better. He does emphasize that it is *different*, and that is precisely the point. It is done *differently*, with *different* objectives in mind.

There will be, almost for a certainty, criticism on the grounds that the conceptual basis for this therapy is overly simplistic. Lewin takes his stand, so to speak, on the premise that conscience —excessively strict, warped conscience as distinct from the healthy kind—is the primary *agent provocateur* of neurotic emotional distress, and the main thrust of his method of treatment is aimed at vitiating its harmful effects. Critics may challenge his relative disregard of instinct—deviant or immature instinct, that is—as a factor in the etiology of emotional illness. I will leave it to Lewin to defend his thesis against this criticism. If I have read him correctly, he considers bad conscience to be the principal villain— the "heavy," so to speak—and assigns to instinct a role analogous to that of the "straight man" who only sets up the situation, leaving the definitive action to the star. A significant portion of the book is devoted to an exposition of Lewin's reasons for thus formulating the genesis of neurotic suffering.

Some readers, as they study the text's detailed reproduction of dialogues between therapist and patient, may wonder at Lewin's seeming neglect of that familiar *bete noire* of interpretation, resistance; they will note that he often cuts across presumed ego resistances to make direct statements of his interpretations and confrontations, and they will question how this can succeed in truly reaching the patient's affective consciousness. It is a fair question. I will say only this: perhaps we psychiatrists have tended somewhat to overcautiousness in this matter, thus prolonging therapy. Certainly no one would deny the fact and the force of ego resistance to unwelcome self-perception, but may it not be that the very challenging of this resistance is a potent force towards its dissolution? After all, a straight line *is* the shortest distance between two points.

This foreword would be incomplete without some comment upon Lewin's style as an author. It is excellent. Quite apart from its provocative and valuable content, this book is a pleasure to read because of its good syntax, its lucidity, and its adept use of appropriate analogy and metaphor. Lewin has a happy facility for finding the phrase that makes clear his point. For example, when discussing the therapeutic inadequacy of intellectual insight he concludes with: "There is no prize for being the best informed neurotic on the block." And in his discussion of introjection we find this: "The memorial to the dead is not the slab of marble or granite that stands on his grave, but rather that part of him that lives on in the minds and hearts of those who admired, respected, and loved him."

One final comment, not about his style of writing but about his personality as it is revealed in this book: he comes across as confident, committed and unafraid to criticize the shibboleths of traditional psychotherapy, yet at the same time he presents his ideas with modesty and humor.

VAN BUREN O. HAMMETT, M.D.

ACKNOWLEDGMENTS

I AM indebted to Dr. Lewis E. Etter, Professor of Radiology at the University of Pittsburgh, without whose encouragement this book would never have been written. I would like also to thank Dr. Henry Brosin, who stimulated my interest in psychiatry in the first place, and Doctors Frederick Weniger, Edward Carroll, James T. McLaughlin and the late Leroy William Earley for their training and preceptorship.

The staff of the Staunton Clinic, Department of Psychiatry of the School of Medicine, University of Pittsburgh, was the whetstone for most of this work. Doctors William Browne, Paul Blastos, Ralph Coppola, Victor Freeman, Joseph Hinchliffe, Monte Joseph, Rex Pittenger, Marvin R. Plesset, Walter Reis, Richard Russell, Elliott Shinn, Ralph Zabarenko, and especially C. Glenn Cambor, who often served as my interpreter to the staff, have helped me to sharpen both my method and its description.

Under the supervision of Mrs. Harold Glasser, the Staunton Clinic secretarial staff: Mrs. Harold J. Collins, Jr., Mrs. Jay W. Simon, Mrs. Edward C. Alko, and Miss Barbara Zambon assisted in the preparation of this manuscript, for which I am grateful.

Finally, and most important, were it not for the tranquility and buoyancy provided by my wife, Gayle, and our children, the writing of this book would have been impossible.

* * *

The case illustrations presented in this book are from my private practice. While they are entirely accurate, the identity of the patients has been concealed, so that only each of them will be able to recognize himself.

K.K.L.

CONTENTS

BRIEF PSYCHOTHERAPY

Chapter I

THE NEED FOR BRIEF PSYCHOTHERAPY

IN our anxiety-ridden age the need for effective brief psychotherapy is desperate. Current treatment methods cannot possibly fill the ever-increasing demand for psychiatric care. The 19,000 practicing psychiatrists[18] in the United States are woefully inadequate to provide mental health care for a country in which ten percent of the population require psychiatric treatment at some point in their lifetime.[5] Almost one-half of all hospital beds in the United States are occupied by patients with emotional disorders. The shortage of psychiatrists exceeds that of any other medical specialty. Regionally, the shortage is outrageous, for *five states have more than one half of all the practicing psychiatrists in the nation.*[5] (New York 21%, California 13%, Pennsylvania and Massachusetts each 6%, Illinois 5%). Since this country's population increases more rapidly than a proportionate number of new psychiatrists can be trained, the personnel shortage must inevitably continue and worsen. Each year, approximately one thousand new psychiatrists complete their training, while the population expands by three million! Even if the number of able students going to colleges, medical schools, and eventually into psychiatric residencies were increased through scholarship grants, improved recruitment, encouragement, stimulation, and better teaching, the number of psychiatrists would be supplemented by merely one-tenth.[10]

Little assistance can be expected from physicians other than psychiatrists, except in dispensing record numbers of tranquilizer and antidepressant pills. Physicians have otherwise been reluctant to assume the responsibility that is logically and morally theirs, the treatment of emotional illnesses.[12, 14, 15, 23] In an unpublished study at a typical medical outpatient clinic, thirty consecutive psychiatric referrals from within the clinic were followed up. After psychiatric consultations that were designed specifically to

3

assist the referring doctors in their continued care of these patients, not a single patient had been given a return appointment by the referring clinics.[16] Patients with emotional illnesses are dumped at the psychiatrist's doorstep. Unless we are willing to leave the treatment of emotional disorders to non-medical people (hopefully social workers, psychologists, and clergymen, but unfortunately also faith-healers, newspaper sob sisters, and bartenders), the burden must be borne by psychiatrists.

Against the rising tide of emotional illness, psychiatrists have fared poorly. The fate of most community mental health clinics illustrates the predicament. When a new psychiatric facility opens, enthusiasm reigns, and referrals pour in for evaluation. Within a few months, the "treatment waiting list" carries the names of most of these referrals, the rest having been referred to social agency personnel, to religious counselors, or back to their own physicians. A handful of patients rapidly consumes the staff treatment time for a prolonged period. Meanwhile, the clinic's schedule is glutted with an unending supply of evaluation cases, and the treatment waiting list grows. Moreover, the long wait for treatment has insured that only the most regressed and dependent people remain, since those with any ego strengths have made arrangements for therapy elsewhere. This unintentional distortion of case selection almost guarantees therapeutic failures. Under all these conditions, the clinic cannot fulfill its function, and the community becomes disillusioned.

If psychotherapy could be shortened and still remain effective, many of the problems of community health care would be ameliorated. Regardless of any other benefits, the number of patients receiving therapy could be doubled or tripled. The question is: who will offer new methods of psychotherapy? Two conceptual approaches, neuropsychiatry and psychoanalysis, have dominated psychotherapy and psychiatric research in the United States. If any new methods for brief therapy are forthcoming, one or both of those two philosphies must supply them.

Neuropsychiatry, the older approach based on neuroanatomy and neurology, views symptoms as being synonymous with illness. Symptomatic relief is the goal of treatment for the neuro-psychiatrist. Although he may allow that an unconscious exists, he does not feel that unconscious conflicts cause symptoms, nor does he view emotional illness as a recurrence of an infantile neurosis. The interpretation of dreams is not an essential part of his treatment method. Most important, the patient-doctor relationship is not analyzed. Instead, the neuropsychiatrist deals actively with the patient in his current life situation, giving advice quite directively and often dispensing medications. An unspoken contract fixes their roles; the patient is passive and submissive, the therapist, active, aggressive, and dominant. Frequently, the neuropsychiatrist manipulates the patient's environment or uses special devices such as hypnosis, electroconvulsive treatment, or deconditioning. The neuropsychiatric approach is exhortative, directive, and repressive.[4, 11, 21, 22]

Neuropsychiatric treatment has many advantages. If effective, the treatment period is relatively short, often a matter of weeks or less. Thirty to fifty patients may be treated during an office day, and each neuropsychiatrist may carry an active case load of several hundred patients at any given time. Neuropsychiatry requires no training beyond the current three-year psychiatric residency program. Furthermore, most people can bear the cost of brief psychiatric treatment.

Some neuropsychiatric methods have achieved general acceptance, such as the use of electroconvulsive therapy for elderly depressed patients without brain damage. Other methods, like the once popular use of insulin coma therapy for schizophrenic patients, have been discarded as useless. Unfortunately, even the apparently successful neuropsychiatric techniques have some serious drawbacks. Few reliable statistics exist on the recurrence of illness in patients treated symptomatically. If a patient "successfully treated" with electro-shock suffers another depressive episode subsequently, should its resolution with another course of electro-shock be recorded as another "success"? Freud, himself, used hypnosis, only to find that either the original symptoms recurred, or that after a short period of apparent health, the patient developed other symptoms.[3] Accepting symptoms as synonymous with illness is as naive as treating a patient's cough with cough suppressants, without resolving the cause of the cough. A symptom is the consequence of an unsuccessful defense mechanism. Removing the symptom often leaves the patient defenseless against his previous conflicts, once the neuropsychiatrist's magic is no longer operative. Deconditioning a woman to a funeral phobia, for example, will help her very little to cope with her fears, anger and depression regarding separation, loss and death, which factors very likely caused the phobia. Nor will hypnotizing a patient out of an hysterically paralyzed arm aid, in the long run, his dealing with his guilt over hostility and destructiveness. He has not learned anything about himself, nor has be learned anything that would significantly improve his relationships with other people or make him a more mature child, worker, friend, neighbor, spouse, or parent. Finally, the dehumanizing effect of deconditioning and behavior therapy in general, which is not unlike brainwashing, resembles the electronic control of robots. One wishes that the ringing of a bell connoted the awakening of a thought or feeling, not the salivating of a beast.

One thing in neuropsychiatry's favor, however, is its pursuit of newer and better methods, drugs, and somatic procedures. Unfortunately, its unwillingness to recognize unconscious conflicts and emotional interaction precludes current neuropsychiatry's being a potent force for successful, durable brief psychotherapy.

The prospect of depending upon the other conceptual approach, psychoanalysis, to supply effective brief psychotherapy is even less encouraging. Except for those affiliated with teaching units and low-cost clinics, psychoanalysts are not even interested in brief psychotherapy. The community and its mental health problems are remote to the psychoanalyst. Most of his patients have already been screened by the referring doctors, who, well aware of the cost of psychoanalysis in time and money, send those patients who can afford both. Of these patients, only those poorly motivated or those with insufficient ego strengths are refused. Since the rest meet the psychoanalyst's requirements, modification of treatment is unnecessary. If not all the patient's conflicts are examined, if the transference neurosis is not resolved, the analyst does not feel that he has permanently helped the patient. A rapid transference cure or a flight into health constitutes psychoanalytic failure. The psychoanalyst scorns brief psychotherapy as a stopgap measure.

One can hardly blame the psychoanalyst for his attitude. Residency, personal training analysis, post-graduate analytic course work, and control cases, all requirements to become a psychoanalyst, may have taken ten years or more of his most productive years. The work so permeates his character that it becomes, not merely a learned skill, but a way of life. It is asking almost too much of the analyst to treat his final achievement as a starting point into a vast unknown.

Yet, when Freud postulated his theories, he stated specifically that psychoanalysis was a research tool. Although psychoanalysis had potent therapeutic application, Freud foresaw that some day it would be superseded by more efficient methods. Theoretical papers abound in analytic journals, but papers on technique are scarce. Even more exceptional are attempts by psychoanalysts to experiment with technique; those who dare are mistrusted by their peers. Reich,[19] Ferenczi,[6, 7] Alexander,[2] Fromm-Reichman,[9] and Rosen[20] all suffered abuse for innovations contrary to orthodox tradition. Ironically many adherents of Freud, a giant of invention and daring, are stodgy and unimaginative. Modern research in analytic technique seeks mainly the perfection of *The Method*, not a search for other effective techniques utilizing psychoanalytic theory.

The very nature of the current analytic method, which requires of the patient not only a good ego, but also enormous amounts of time and money, prevents its widespread use in a country in which the average family income is under $5,000.[13, 17] Even if the government were to subsidize psychoanalytic treatment, with a case load for each analyst of eight or nine patients every two or three years, the nation would require a million psychoanalysts to fulfill its needs!

While neuropsychiatrists and psychoanalysts share the burden of treating patients, the task of teaching medical students has fallen largely to the analysts. More and more major medical school departments of psychiatry are being chaired and staffed by analysts and analytically oriented psychiatrists. One would expect, therefore, excellent analytic training for the students. Such is not the case. Students are glutted with analytic theory, but rarely profit from it. Curricula restrictions in most schools prevent students from engaging patients in the long-term psychotherapy which they had been taught. Student psychotherapy means brief psychotherapy. So a totally incongruous condition exists where students, inculcated with long-term analytic therapy, perform brief psychotherapy under preceptors who neither believe in it nor practice it themselves. What ensues is usually therapy *ad infinitum*, the patient being treated by successive students, each of whom performs standard analytic therapy for a short period of time. Most of the treatment time is spent helping the patient to adjust to the loss of his previous student therapist. Rarely does any student feel that he has helped his patient. Psychotherapy remains an enigma to him. Worse yet, the most common student reactions to his subsequent feelings of disappointment, frustration, and failure are avoidance, withdrawal, and derision. For the want of therapeutic successes that effective brief psychotherapy could provide, crops of potential therapists become anti-therapists.

Psychoanalysts have not realized their potential in teaching medical students. Psychoanalysis is rightfully the basic science of psychiatry. Just as anatomy, biochemistry, pathology, physiology and pharmacology are the foundations of medical education, but are in no way a substitute for clinical method, so psychoanalytic theory of human development, conflict, and defenses should serve as the base from which student psychotherapy evolves. The crucial step is that between the psychoanalyst's basic knowledge and his teaching students the practical use of that knowledge. Psychoanalysis-in-miniature is no solution; it serves neither student nor patient. Psychoanalysis as a technical skill should be reserved for psychiatric residents and students of psychoanalytic institutes. Analysts would scoff at a surgery department that expected its medical students to perform the manual procedures of a gastrectomy, for example. Teaching medical students psychoanalytic technique is no less preposterous.

Pressed with community needs and responsible for teaching psychiatry to senior medical students, the Staunton Clinic Staff* has been experimenting with methods of brief outpatient psycho-

---

* Department of Psychiatry, University of Pittsburgh, School of Medicine.

therapy, using psychoanalytic theory. Encouraged by Michael Balint, of London's Tavistock Clinic, each of us has tested his own methods in private practice as well as in the supervision of students. What follows in this book is offered not as a definitive solution, but as a forthright attempt "to alloy the pure gold of analysis with the copper of direct suggestion."[8] Although over ten years' experience with this method testifies to its effectiveness, it will be vulnerable to attack by both analysts and neuropsychiatrists. Any criticism that spurs others to find better methods would be invaluable. After all, what once sailed so proudly over the dunes of the Carolina coast lies now, an awkward curio of flimsy wood, wire, and cloth, gathering dust in a Washington museum, undisturbed by the sonic booms of jets overhead. I welcome obsolescence. Whoever would help those emotionally ill, take up the challenge.

REFERENCES

1. Aldrich, C.: Brief psychotherapy: a reappraisal of some theoretical assumptions. *Amer. J. Psychiatry*, 125:37, 1968.
2. Alexander, F., and French, T.: *Psychoanalytic Therapy: Principles and Application*. New York, The Ronald Press Co., 1946.
3. Breuer, J., and Freud, S.: *Studies on Hysteria*. New York, Basic Books, 1957.
4. Cobb, S.: *Foundations of Neuropsychiatry*. Baltimore, Williams and Wilkins, 1958.
5. Facts about mental illness. Nat. Assoc. for Ment. Health, Inc. booklet, 1968.
6. Ferenczi, S.: Stages in the development of the sense of reality. In *Sex in Psychoanalysis*. New York, Basic Books, pp. 213-239, 1950.
7. Ferenczi, S.: *Thalassa: A Theory of Genitality*. New York, Psychoanalytic Quart., Inc., 1938.
8. Freud, S.: Turning in the ways of psychoanalytic therapy. In *Collected Papers*. London, Hogarth Press, 2:402, 1958.
9. Fromm-Reichman, F.: *Intensive Psychotherapy*. Chicago, University of Chicago Press, 1950.
10. Funkenstein, D.: The problem of increasing the number of psychiatrists. *Amer. J. Psychiat.*, 121:852-855, 1965.
11. Haley, J.: Control in brief psychotherapy. *Arch. Gen. Psychiat.*, 4:139-153, 1961.
12. Hawkins, D.: The gap between the psychiatrist and other physicians: causes and solutions. *Psychosom. Med.*, 24:94-95, 1962.
13. Hollingshead, A., and Redlich, F.: *Social Class and Mental Illness: A Community Study*. New York, Wiley, 1958.
14. Lewin, K.: A brief psychotherapy method. *Penna. Med. J.*, 68:43-48, 1965.
15. Lewin, K.: Understanding neurotic patients. *Medical Times*, 94:392-396, 1966.

10

16. Lewin, K.: Unpublished data. Staunton Clinic, Dept. of Psychiat., U. of Pittsburgh School of Med.
17. Maciver, J., and Redlich, F.: Patterns of psychiatric practice. *Amer. J. Psychiat.*, 115:692, 1959.
18. Psychiatric manpower bulletin. Amer. Psychiat. Assoc. Commiss. on Manpower, Number 6, March, 1965.
19. Reich, W.: *Character Analysis*. New York, Orgone Inst. Press, pp. 1-248, 1945.
20. Rosen, J.: *Direct Psychoanalytic Psychotherapy*. Chicago, University of Chicago Press, 1950.
21. Wolberg, L.: *Hypnoanalysis*. New York, Grune and Stratton, 1945.
22. Wolpe, J.: *Psychotherapy by Reciprocal Inhibition*. Stanford, Stanford University Press, 1958.
23. Zilborg, G.: *A History of Medical Psychology*. New York, Norton and Co., pp. 21-26; 521, 1941.

Chapter II

THEORY

THE intention of this book is pragmatic. Yet to understand any therapeutic method requires comprehension of its particular theoretical framework. Put briefly, the framework is psychoanalytic, but not entirely orthodox in its perspective. Hopefully, the reader will recognize that its apparent simplicity is merely the absence of jargon.

CONFLICT AND DEFENSE

The core of life is the mother-child relationship. Every child, girl and boy, yearns for a physical union—some analysts would say reunion—with its mother. This desire for union extends from a very early wish to be fed, held and stroked to a later wish for primacy and for sexual union with her. Naturally in our culture these later wishes remain unfulfilled, no matter how pretty, smart, strong, aggressive, or loving the child may be. Life then can be seen as a continuum of frustration. The kinds of defenses that each child uses in growing up to protect himself from the pain of frustration and the unpleasant feelings attendant to it (jealousy, envy, greed, resentment, anger, hostility, fear, shame, and guilt) constitute the eventual character of his adult self. The mature adult is expected to be a civilized social animal; the infant is neither civilized nor social. So while the growing child molds his life around his frustrations, he must also adapt himself to a demanding society. Inherently selfish, self-centered, and acquisitive, he is required by society to give and to share, to work, and to postpone pleasure. Driven by his impulses, thwarted by reality, and shackled by societal taboos, the child is incessantly conflicted throughout life. With it all, the child must follow his instinct for self-preservation. His defenses are reactions to his own feelings about himself and to his environment, reactions that enable him to master conflicts and to reduce anxiety. These defense mecha-

11

nisms are products of the unconscious* mind. (The common defense mechanisms are repression, regression, reaction formation, undoing, isolation, reversal, turning against the self, projection, introjection, displacement, and sublimation. For a fuller description, see Anna Freud's *The Ego and the Mechanism of Defence*.[10]

Regardless whether parents are good or bad as parents, they have very little conscious control over what kinds of defenses their child will choose. No one knows how to enhance a child's selection of healthy defenses. Healthy defenses are those that allow the individual to fulfill, as far as is realistically possible, whatever life goals he has chosen, to abide within the sanctions of the society in which he has chosen to live, and to maintain satisfying relationships with other people. Most provident seems to be the child born to emotionally and physically healthy parents, who want him, are satisfied with his sex, love him and one another, and show their love. Yet, even here, there exists no guarantee that this child will choose healthy defenses against his inevitable frustrations.

Compounding the child's tribulations are potential catastrophes, normal circumstances of life which jeopardize the child's relationship with his mother: weaning, toilet training, the birth of siblings, injury, illness, and death in the family. That so many people stumble into adulthood as healthy as they are is remarkable. To blame or to credit the *actions* of parents is senseless; the *reactions* of the child determine the outcome. For example, the reaction of one child to discipline in the form of spanking might be passive obedience and submissiveness, while the reaction of another child might be defiance, rebelliousness, and vengefulness. True, "good parents" recognize potential conflictual situations and perhaps can modify them, but they cannot eliminate them. For example, following the birth of a sibling, a previously contented child might refuse his mother's bedtime ritual of rocking, reading, and singing, and turn to his father instead. Enlightened parents would recognize that the source of their child's be-

---

* The concept of the Unconscious is taken for granted and will not be discussed further here.

havior was not his father's improved voice, but the child's resentment of his mother for bringing home a new baby. Alerted to the problem, they would encourage the child to voice his anger, envy, and jealousy without recrimination. They might also allow the child certain prerogatives for being the elder. But no matter what they do, they cannot eliminate the child's feelings of loss, desolation, resentment, and anger. Since the child wants every bit of his mother, even the lion's share would be insufficient. Although the problem might seem to be resolved at the time, it could still crop up again when the child grows up, marries, and has his first child, a rival for his wife's attention. Worse yet, if parents did try to shield their child from conflict in childhood, upon stress in adulthood he would probably wilt like a hothouse flower suddenly exposed to heat and drought in the garden. The fate of most "only children" hardly merits, as a mental health measure, the avoidance of subsequent children to prevent sibling rivalry.

Inadvertently, parents have been led to believe, through child-rearing books written by psychiatrists and other experts, that there is a correct way to raise children in order to insure that they reach adulthood mature, healthy, and happy.[6, 20, 28] So, if a child does not turn out as intended, the parents (and society) assume that he was not raised properly. In other words our current generation holds parents directly accountable for their children's personalities, as well as their actions. Somehow everyone has lost sight of the responsibility of the child in his reaction to his parents, in his compliance with or rebellion against the methods with which they attempted to raise him. This short-sightedness has even permeated the interpretation of our laws, where a man can now seek to defend himself against charges of murder because of a history of a deprived childhood.

INTROJECTION

The single most important, but oddly the least well understood, mechanism by which the child defends and strengthens himself is introjection, the process of incorporation of another person, usually a parent, into the child's self, the assimilation of another's personality.[22] Although there is considerable disagreement about the time of its occurrence,[24] very likely introjection takes place within the first year of life, perhaps within the first three months, and *can recur at any time afterward.* That is, a previous introject can be extruded and replaced by another. The process seems to take place easier in very early childhood. Aging makes the process more difficult. Introjection seems related psychologically to the process of eating, a figurative ingestion of mother, to begin with. This is not to be confused with "identification," whereby a child models himself after the admirable qualities of his parents, but an actual ingestion of a total facet of the personality of that parent. *That which is ingested not only molds the personality structure of the developing child, but also serves as the rudiments of its conscience.* Introjection is not static. The process of introjection and rejection can continue through adulthood. More confusing still, there is a duality of that which can be ingested, "good mother" vs. "bad mother," food which nourishes the spirit vs. poison which must be either disgorged or endured with suffering. How it is that one child takes as part of himself a loving, tender, accepting mother, while another child incorporates a cold, disapproving, rejecting aspect of that same mother, a totally exasperated parent, remains a mystery. The choice of introject does not necessarily follow the real, objective attitude of that mother. Position in the family occasionally dictates the choice; if the role of good introjected mother-good child has already been filled by a sibling, the child might well become the bad introjected mother-bad child. Most often, the child introjects that view of his mother that he feels he deserves. If there are aspects of himself of which he feels deeply ashamed or guilty, he is more likely to introject a disapproving, punitive mother.*

---

* I am almost convinced that the final nature of that introject depends upon the child's resolution of his feelings consequent to his discovery that his mother has had intercourse with his father. Anger at the mother upon this discovery often gives the final sadistic twist to the child's introjection of her and ultimately leaves him with self-hatred and a self-punitive conscience. It is ironic that in the final analysis, a well-intentioned, mature, psychologically aware, and loving mother, has no more assurance that *her* child will forgive her marital sexual activity than a mother less well endowed. *It is the child's reaction that determines the outcome and it is impossible for parents to insure a healthy out-*

If this brief discussion of introjection has a mystical, spiritual, or metaphysical quality, it is no wonder. No doubt it is the same process which primitive societies call inhabitation by evil spirits, that can be dispelled only by ritual, magic, and sorcery. Were it only so easy to expel introjects in our culture. Archimedes said of the lever, "Give me a place to stand and I will move the world." It could as easily be said, "Find a way to rid people of undesirable introjects and you cure mental illness."

The abnormal persistence of thumbsucking and the need for love-and-security-blankets by a child indicate incomplete introjection. These are externalizations of introjects, remnants earning the jeers of those more adept at incorporation, who already have their introjects inside, safely out of everyone's sight. "Giving-up" a love-and-security-blanket is not giving it up at all. It means permanently installing it inside.

The presence of a good introject sustains us in time of privation. A good introject constantly replenishes our capacity to give love, to think well of ourselves and of others, and to have an optimistic view of life. It allows us to be alone without the oppression of loneliness. Conversely, the child who does not incorporate, or who ejects that which he previously incorporated without replacement, very likely is schizophrenic, and his loneliness is a terrifying void, regardless of life circumstances. While the child with a good introject is happy within the limits of his actual life situation, experiencing the pleasures of living, the child with a bad introject is in constant psychic pain, suffering in the midst of plenty.

HELPLESSNESS AND OMNIPOTENCE IN PHANTASY

All infants begin life in a state of complete helplessness and passivity. They can do nothing for themselves. Gradually they realize how dependent and helpless they actually are, that their destinies are directed entirely by adults. This realization brings

---

come, *regardless of their methods of child-rearing.* If the child's reaction is forgiveness and acceptance, the final introject and ensuing conscience is benevolent; if the reaction is non-forgiveness and non-acceptance, the final introject and ensuing conscience is malevolent, sadistic, unforgiving, and vengeful.

See Chapter 7 Dreams, pp. 142-162 and Immaculate Conception, pp. 147, 148.

with it insecurity, fear, and shame. In order to compensate for their passive helplessness, children rely on fairy tales and games, daydreams and phantasies. In their minds, they become all powerful, not helpless, but omnipotent. Their imagination becomes their greatest weapon, and their wishes, the vehicle for its use. All sorts of forbidden, wild, and even violent acts are committed within the confines of a child's vivid imagination. Often to a child the boundary between phantasy and reality blurs. Consequently, the child often holds himself accountable for whatever occurs in his mind, as though it actually happened. Subsequently repressed, these wishes persist in his unconscious to cause problems later on.

IDENTIFICATION AND EGO IDEAL

Much later the child begins to identify with those qualities of his elders that he admires. Shame is the chief spur that forces him to keep pace psychologically with his biological growth. He begins to visualize himself as an adult, largely through play and daydream. He overcomes his deficiencies in phantasy and forms an ego ideal—his holy grail—a goal for which he may spend his life trying to reach. Shame is a special form of unease arising from awareness that one has fallen short of his ego ideal. Shame refuels the child's zeal for the attainment of that ideal. The child with a good introject forms an ego ideal that seems almost attainable within the limitations of his actual self. Shame spurs him on. The child with a bad introject forms an ego ideal which is so far beyond the limitations of his actual self that he may hopelessly give up the quest, especially during adolescence, and "drop out." The child with the good introject will proceed to maturity; the child with the bad introject will remain a child, unable to delay gratification or to establish long term life goals. One child grows up, the other only grows older.

As a child's development progresses, he conceptualizes his own body image, which may or may not conform to the actual form of his body. Body image is largely dependent upon the nature of his introject, but it can be influenced by his other defense mechanism, as well as actual life situations, such as injury, illness, or surgery. One's "self" is a summation of body image and psychic identity.

SEXUALITY AND FEMALE HOMOSEXUALITY

The cephalo-caudad development of the child's nervous system is accompanied by corresponding heightened sensory perceptions, starting with the oral and peri-oral areas and progressing to the perineal areas. These roughly correspond to the stages of psycho-sexual development, oral, anal, phallic, and genital. In the male child, there follows smoothly a sequence involving his mother, first as a provider of food and comfort, and later as a source of sexual stimulation. His sexual desires for his mother bring him into conflict with his father as a rival. The resolution of this "oedipal conflict" leads normally to the boy's renouncing his wish for his mother, identifying with his father, and later marrying a woman with some characteristics of his mother. There are many other possible resolutions to this conflict, but eventual marriage and subsequent parenthood is the only solution consonant with the preservation of the race. (As the population explosion reduces the pressure for the birth of children, our conception of the normal resolution of the oedipal conflict may undergo transition.)

The female child follows an almost identical path. She, too, initially finds her mother a source of food and comfort. She, too, finds her mother an exciting source of genital sexual stimulation. A little girl finds it just as arousing as does her male counterpart to have her mother stroke her genitals when she is cleaned during diaper changing, or at a later age when she is washed between the legs during a tub bath. She, too, tries to rub her body against her mother's, mightily enjoys her hugs and kisses, and relishes those delicious moments in her mother's bed. Eventually, her sexual desires for her mother also bring her into conflict with her father as a rival. But even before that confrontation the little girl comes to the realization that married couples are composed of one of each sex. A four-year-old boy, if asked whom he will marry, will likely reply, "My mommy." A four-year-old girl rarely makes that reply; she knows better. *That does not necessarily mean that she wishes to marry her father.* She would like to marry her mother and have a baby with her mother, but she knows that she cannot, because they are both girls. As a lover for her mother, she is disqualified not by inferior size, knowledge, or strength as a boy feels in his rivalry with his father, but by her sex. She develops an intense envy and jealously of her father and his penis, the one obvious thing that he has that she has not, the one thing that enables her father to share the marriage bed with her mother. Later in childhood comes the knowledge that the penis impregnates mother. Her jealousy is magnified, and causes her to wish for a penis of her own. The penis is only the means to an end; it is not an end in itself, although in adulthood it might appear otherwise. The original aim is to win mother sexually. A girl's wish for a penis frequently stimulates phantasies that she had had a penis at one time, but that it had been taken from her by either parent. Secondary elaboration of phantasies based on this theme are numerous. Relatively few girls are able to use the defense mechanism of displacement that goes with sublimation to turn their sexual desires from their mothers to their fathers, and eventually to marry a man with qualities similar to their fathers. *The vast majority of girls do not sublimate that wish. They continue to hunger sexually for their mothers, repress the wish from consciousness, and go through life with the identical motions of those girls who sublimated their sexual desires.* The continuance of their original sexual aim for mother makes them dissatisfied subsequently with their own roles as wife and mother and wrecks their marriages. Most commonly they regress, feeling rejected by mother, to a narcissistic position, bestowing the greatest share of their love on themselves. Some of these women devote hours to preening before the mirror with elaborate make-up and hair styles, not to please their husbands, but themselves. Usually, masturbation is distasteful to them so they circumvent it by utilizing intercourse as a masturbatory equivalent. The aim is auto-erotic, rather than shared love, and the man is used only because he happens to be attached to the other end of the penis. He provides sexual gratification without the onus of actual masturbation. But the act is truly narcissistic; the husband is only a foil. Very few of these women become overt homosexuals. Not a few become promiscuous, searching for the right sexual partner, but always being disappointed ultimately, for it never is mother. This ultimate dissatisfaction with anyone except mother is the chief cause for frigidity in women.

The real basis for complaint of many feminists, who protest that our society is a "man's world," is their resentment about their father's primacy with mother. Ironically, their fathers, very likely married to women who have yearned for *their* mothers, are just as dissatisfied with *their* lot. Nevertheless, consumed with jealousy for their fathers, they use the *real* inequities of our society (prejudicial employment, inadequate salaries, and limited opportunities) as straw men on which to vent their spleen. Of all the hardship women undergo, undoubtedly the most difficult one is the resolution of their oedipal conflict, where a double displacement must take place, from mother to father to eligible suitor. Not everyone can use displacement as a defense, but at least males have only to use a single displacement in order to marry a girl just like the one that their fathers married.

It would seem obvious that the male in our society actually requires artificial bolstering in order to help him compete with the overwhelming importance of mothers to their progeny. Unless the father has a dominant role in the family, unless he is a very special fellow in some way, his sons cannot resolve their oedipal conflict in a healthy fashion, nor can his daughters avoid a permanent homosexual attachment to his wife. In order to give his children at least a chance to construct healthy defenses against their sexual desires for their mother, a good father must be at first an adequate "foster mother," helping to feed, bathe, dress, cuddle his youngsters, and later an admirable male figure, with whom his sons can identify, and to whom his daughters can displace their sexual desires from their mothers. Both parents should make their union appear so strong that the child is discouraged very early from pursuing either of them as sexual love objects.

Probably the most difficult interpretation for a female patient to accept is that involving her sexual desire for her mother. Our society has fairly well accepted the normalcy of an oedipal conflict in the male. The barber-shop quartet from the turn of the century, "I Want a Girl Just Like the Girl that Married Dear Old Dad," was popular long before Freud's oedipal theory. But suggest that a girl has an identical sexual desire for her mother! Most psychiatrists inadvertently avoid the wrath that would follow such an abhorrent and repugnant interpretation, by misinterpreting their women patients' homosexual impulses toward their mothers. When patients direct sexual feelings toward their doctors, the usual interpretation is "father love," the equivalent of the male's oedipal conflict, or a distortion of dependency wishes. Most male psychiatrists are reluctant to see themselves cast in a woman's role sexually. If a woman's declaration of love, correctly interpreted, casts him as a woman, a psychiatrist's male pride might be injured and his own sexual identification shaken. He finds it less painful to deceive himself and to bolster his middle-aged sagging male image by interpreting such declarations of love as heterosexual. This denial of homosexual transference is one of the most common causes of incomplete and unsuccessful analysis.

SHAME, GUILT, AND PSYCHIC MASOCHISM[2, 26, 27]

For the child with a good introject, shame and guilt serve constructive purposes. Shame, by producing anxiety when the child has not measured up to his ego ideal, spurs him to useful action. Guilt, by producing anxiety when the child has hurt others, encourages him to do better by them in the future (the constructive results of shame and guilt are the basis for the Moral Code of Western Civilization). On the other hand, for the child with a bad introject, shame and guilt serve no constructive purpose and become instead weapons for self-punishment and torture. Shame nags him with the humiliation of his debasement from his ego ideal and guilt flogs him for his wrong-doing. Neither shame nor guilt improve his actions in the future; they merely convince him that he is hopelessly ineffectual and bad. In essence, the child with a bad introject treats himself as an exasperated parent would, expressing complete and final dissatisfaction with the errant child. Both shame and guilt encourage him to be enraged with himself, to hurt and to punish himself. The person with a bad introject receives pleasure from this self-inflicted mental suffering. Through suffering he obtains partial relief from his feelings of guilt; that sense of relief from guilt constitutes his pleasure. More often than not, he had been unconscious of his guilt feelings and the conflict that had produced the guilt, both earlier victims of repression. He appeases his conscience, "You needn't trouble me any more, for I am paying for my crimes, whatever they are." This is the essence of what Bergler called "psychic masochism,"[2] the major component of every neurotic illness. By meting out his own punishment, the psychic masochist controls just how much he suffers. However, the conscience that metes out that punishment is the by-product of a bad introject. Remember that the very young child's introject is the anlage of his conscience. That kind of conscience does not require a forbidden *act* for punishment; it punishes just as severely for a forbidden thought or wish. Nor does that conscience *prevent* forbidden action. On the contrary, it entices the person to act and then punishes him harshly and excessively afterward. The original feeling of guilt may have been induced by merely a thought, a wish, or a feeling. But the perverted conscience compounds the guilt by inducing forbidden action which requires further punishment and produces more loss of self-esteem.

Commonly, the psychic masochist tortures himself by creating doubts and fears where none need exist. He worries unnecessarily about trivia or situations over which he has no personal control, merely for the sake of worrying. He contrives to keep himself from sleeping. Through his speech and action, he brings about more self-punishment by "inadvertently" provoking other people to retaliate against him. Not infrequently he becomes the black sheep of his family, antagonizing his relations, driving away his friends, and insuring his ultimate failure in every endeavor—academic, financial, social, and marital. Finally, left alone in the rubble of his life, he complains bitterly that no one likes him or wants to help him, and that the world is cruel.

The ways in which masochistic people collect their quota of injustices are familiar, but the underlying self-punishment is not always apparent. The student who nips his career in the bud by not studying, the young single girl who allows herself to become pregnant by avoiding contraception, the woman who marries a a known alcoholic or a gambler, the fellow who gets himself fired by being insubordinate, and the man with severe peripheral vascular disease who continues to smoke after being warned of the serious consequences are all instances of masochistic behavior patterns. These people all risk ruining their lives, not by sudden suicide but by slow torture. They make themselves lifelong victims.[25]

When ill, whether emotionally or physically, masochistic patients resist recovery. Since their punitive conscience insists that they suffer, masochistic patients are *unconsciously compelled* to thwart the doctor's every effort to help. Although they consciously seek succor, they unconsciously discourage the doctor from helping. They try to provoke him by constantly complaining about symptoms, by not following suggestions, by not taking medications as prescribed (forgetting to take them, taking them more frequently than prescribed, or taking them at improper times), by not keeping appointments, by coming late, by detaining the doctor with irrelevant conversation, or by telephoning him unnecessarily after office hours. If they do take a medication as prescribed, it rarely gives them symptomatic relief, and instead almost invariably produces distressing side effects that are often worse than the original symptoms. If they do seemingly follow the doctor's advice, they do it in such an exaggerated way that it often leads to serious consequences. All in all they give the doctor no encouragement and subtly make him feel inept and bungling for not being able to effect a cure.

CHARACTER DEFENSES AND SYMPTOMS

The defenses that each child uses in growing up to protect himself from frustration and conflict and from the unpleasant feelings attendant to them shape the character of his adult self. The clusters or constellations of these defenses and conflicts are limited in number, like standard plots of stories, and are as easily recognized. Unfortunately, they have been categorized by psychiatrists, *as though each in itself were an entity*, rather than various points on a spectrum of defenses against problems common to all mankind. So psychiatric texts mention obsessional character, hysterical character, paranoid character, etc. None of these character defenses is indicative of illness per se. We all have to be "something," that is, we all have recognizable defenses against common problems.

The chief defenses of the obsessional character, for example, are reaction-formation, isolation, displacement, and ritualistic undoing. These defenses are especially useful against sadistic impulses, conflicts of aggression, obedience, and rebellion. When used constructively, these defenses produce a person who is punctual, neat, and orderly. Not only his person is orderly, but his thoughts and actions are characterized by order and organization. He is also persistent and dogged at his tasks, showing a stubborn tenaciousness, a willingness to see things through to their completion, and the strength to stand firm alone when those all about him are wrong. *The Autobiography of Benjamin Franklin*[9] provides a fine character study of an obsessional man, one of the outstanding personalities of his time. "Obsessional" is not a pejorative term. While certain character traits may be pleasant or unpleasant to others, they are neither "good" nor "bad." Rather, it depends upon how these traits are expressed and under what circumstances, whether they are appropriate, and whether the individual uses them constructively or destructively, that makes them healthy or unhealthy.

What differentiates the healthy character and his sick counterpart is the crux of understanding all emotional illness. *What causes a character trait to deteriorate into symptomatic illness is the perversion of characterological defenses for the purpose of self-punishment and self-destruction. Undoubtedly, the motive force for this perversion of characterological defenses is psychic masochism, the by-product of a bad introject.* (Obsessional character + psychic masochism = obsessional neurosis.) An obsessional neurosis is one in which the individual suffers from compulsions (the need to perform non-goal directed and unnecessary ritualistic acts over and over) or obsessions (frightening and repugnant thoughts), often accompanied by magical thinking, self-doubting and indecisiveness of thought and action. The characterological defenses of reaction formation, isolation, displacement, and ritualistic undoing are used, not to relieve anxiety or to resolve conflict, but to increase anxiety, to prolong conflict and thereby to provide mental punishment. The defenses are not at fault. They are not weak, necessarily. The fault lies with the motive, the purpose to which the defenses are directed, the goal of self-punishment instead of self-fulfillment. Freud's "Rat Man"[12] and "Wolf Man"[13] were the victims of psychic masochism. They were victims of a sadistic conscience. Benjamin Franklin escaped. *The need for self-punishment separates the emotionally ill from the emotionally well.*

Akin to fear, guilt restricts both a person's field of action and action, itself. It prevents achievement and attainment. Since the guilt-ridden person *must* not succeed, he *cannot* succeed. Unless his psychic masochism is overcome, he can no more succeed with his psychotherapy than he could with his life before. Were it not for psychic masochism he very likely could have made a spontaneous resolution of his problems without anyone's help.

REPETITION COMPULSION AND CONDITIONING

The appearance of symptoms of emotional illness almost always follows conflictual situations in the patient's current life that in some way unconsciously remind him of similar conflicts from his past. What Freud called "repetition compulsion" is indistinguishable from Pavlovian "conditioning," that is, a repetition of previous reactions to a given conflict, a stereotyped pattern of response to a certain stimulus. However, in contrast to the simple stimulus—simple response of the bell—salivation of animal experimentation, human stimulus—response is very complex. This confusing complexity probably accounts for Freudians and Pavlovians being at each other's throats. Actually, there seems very little basic difference between stimulus 1 (appearance of new baby)→response 1 (jealousy, envy, resentment) and the conditioned salivation of an animal to the ringing of a bell. Both follow rules of repetition, reinforcement and extinction. In fact were it not for extinction or deconditioning, there could be no such thing as "resolution" of a transference neurosis. To whit: a patient enters treatment with a complex self-punitive reaction to a conflict that is a re-enactment of a childhood conflict. Because of the repetition compulsion, or conditioning, the patient behaves toward the psychiatrist as he had toward those people related to this conflict in his past. The constellation of feelings by a patient toward his doctor, based upon his past experiences rather than on the actual current relationship, is called a transference neurosis. However, the psychiatrist does not react to the patient's provocations as had the people in the past. Their reactions had reinforced the patient's conditioned response. The psychiatrist's lack of reaction extinguishes the previously conditioned response. Unfortunately, resolving a transference neurosis, an extremely complicated relationship, is not a dependable deconditioning procedure.

SUMMATION

I have presented the theoretical framework on which this method of brief psychotherapy is based. I do not claim to be a theoretician. As the bibliography will attest, very little of the theoretical framework is original. The emphasis on psychic masochism as a determinent of illness is noteworthy, as is the importance of introjection. Somewhat unusual is the postulate that women rarely resolve their oedipal conflicts by sublimated displacement. That postulate, if true, has enormous social implications. Also open to criticism may be my objection to categorizing and diagnosing symptom complexes as though they were entities. And finally my attempt to unify Freudian and Pavlovian theory will probably reap abuse for me from both sides. So be it. Whether one agrees or disagrees with my theoretical construct, my therapy is based upon it. Since the results of the therapy are good, the theory merits some consideration. All I ask of the reader is an open mind.

REFERENCES

1. Abraham, K.: Character formation on the genital level of libido development; a short study of the development of the libido, viewed in the light of mental disorders. In *Selected Papers*. London, Hogarth, pp. 407-501, 1927.
2. Bergler, E.: *The Basic Neurosis, Oral Regression and Psychic Masochism.* New York, Grune and Stratton, 1949.
3. Brunswick, R.: The preoedipal phase of the libido. In, Fliess, R. (ed.). *The Psychoanalytic Reader.* New York, International Universities Press, pp. 261-84, 1948.
4. Deutsch, H.: *The Psychology of Women.* New York, Grune and Stratton, 1944.
5. Erikson, E.: The problem of ego identity. *J. Amer. Psychoanal. Assn.*, 4:56-121, 1956.
6. Erikson, E.: *Childhood and Society.* New York, Norton, 1950.
7. Federn, P.: *Ego Psychology and the Psychoses.* New York, Basic Books, 1952.
8. Fenichel, O.: *Psychoanalytic Theory of Neurosis.* New York, 1945.
9. Franklin, B.: *The Autobiography of Benjamin Franklin.* New York, Modern Library, 1944.

10. Freud, A.: *The Ego and the Mechanisms of Defence.* New York, International Universities Press, 1946.
11. Freud, A.: *Normality and Pathology in Childhood: Assessments of Development.* New York, International Universities Press, 1965.
12. Freud, S.: Notes upon a case of obsessional neurosis. *Standard Edition.* London, The Hogarth Press and the Inst. of Psychoanalysis, 10:155-319, 1958.
13. Freud, S.: From the history of an infantile neurosis. *Standard Edition,* 17:3-122, 1958.
14. Freud, S.: Mourning and melancholia. *Standard Edition,* 14:239-260, 1958.
15. Freud, S.: The ego and the id. *Standard Edition,* 19:3-69, 1958.
16. Freud, S.: Analysis terminable and interminable. *Standard Edition,* 23:209-255, 1958.
17. Freud, S.: Three essays in the theory of sexuality. *Standard Edition,* 7:123-243, 1958.
18. Freud, S.: Papers on technique. *Standard Edition,* 12:85-172, 1958.
19. Freud, S.: Inhibitions, symptoms, and anxiety. *Standard Edition,* 20:77-179, 1958.
20. Ginott, H.: *Between Parent and Child.* New York, Macmillan, 1965.
21. Gitelson, M.: On ego distortion. *Int. J. Psychoanalysis,* 39:245-257, 1958.
22. Jacobson, E.: *The Self and the Object World.* New York, International Universities Press, 1964.
23. Jones, E.: The concept of a normal mind. In *Papers on Psychoanalysis.* London, Balliere, Tindall, and Cox, pp. 201-216, 1948.
24. Klein, M.: *New Directions in Psychoanalysis.* New York, Basic Books, 1956.
25. Lewin, B.: *The Psychoanalysis of Elation.* New York, W. W. Norton and Co., Inc., 1950.
26. Menninger, W.: *Man Against Himself.* New York, Harcourt, Brace and Co., 1941.
27. Piers, G., and Singer, M.: *Shame and Guilt.* Springfield, Ill., Thomas, 1953.
28. Spock, B.: *Baby and Child Care.* New York, Pocket Books, 1957.
29. Tausk, V.: On the origin of the influencing machine in schizophrenia. *Psychoanal. Quart.,* 2:519-556, 1933.
30. Tinbergen, N.: *The Study of Instinct.* Oxford, Clarendon Press, 1951.
31. Waelder, R.: *Basic Theory of Psychoanalysis.* New York, International Universities Press, 1960.
32. Whitehorn, J.: A working concept of maturity of personality. *Amer. J. Psychiatry,* 119:196-202, 1962.

Chapter III

TECHNIQUE

THIS method of brief psychotherapy is paradoxical. While the theory on which the treatment is based is psychoanalytic and rather orthodox, the technique itself is the antithesis of psychoanalysis. In fact, this technique violates almost every tenet of psychoanalytic method. The psychoanalyst must be passive, allowing the patient to do nearly all the talking. In this form of brief therapy, the doctor must be active and aggressive. The psychoanalyst is non-directive; the therapist is vigorously goal-directed. The psychoanalyst is permissive and excessively tactful; the therapist is confrontative and frank. The psychoanalyst allows the development of positive transference without interference; the therapist often provokes negative transference. The psychoanalyst, as far as within his power, conceals his personality from the patient to avoid contaminating the transference; the therapist often not only utilizes his personality, but may even emphasize his own reactions for effect. The psychoanalyst avoids interpretations until transference resistance has been removed; the therapist makes interpretations even before real transference has developed. The psychoanalyst relies mainly on the past as the source for insight; the therapist, while using the past, depends on the present encounter for insights. The psychoanalyst removes resistance through positive transference; the therapist undercuts resistance, often without positive transference, and even occasionally with negative transference. In the patient's conflicts between the various parts of his personality, the psychoanalyst maintains strict neutrality; the therapist strongly and openly sides with the patient's ego.

How can one reconcile a psychoanalytic theory and a nonpsychoanalytic technique? Freud found some justification for it in his "Recommendations to Physicians Practicing Psychoanalysis."

"In practice . . . there is nothing to be said against a psychother-

27

apist combining a certain amount of analysis with some suggestive influence in order to achieve a perceptible result in a shorter time. . . . But one has a right to insist that he himself should be in no doubt about what he is doing and should know that his method is not that of true psychoanalysis."[3] To Freud's last injunction, I aver emphatically that this method of brief psychotherapy is not in any way psychoanalysis or a substitute for it. To his first injunction, I will do my best to prove that I know what I am doing.

METHOD

Freud cautioned ("On Beginning the Treatment"),

"Even in the later stages of analysis one must be careful not to give a patient the solution or the translation of a wish until he is already so close to it that he has only one short step more to make in order to get hold of the explanation for himself. In former years, I often had occasion to find that the premature communication of a solution brought the treatment to an untimely end, on account not only of the resistances which it thus suddenly awakened but also the relief which the solution brought."[4]

Freud's warning contains two clues for successful brief therapy methods. First, it claims that the communication of a solution can bring relief to a patient. While an early termination is disastrous for the process of psychoanalysis, it is anything but untimely in brief psychotherapy. Second, it states that the communication of a solution awakens resistances. Resistance, of course, signifies a restrengthening, a re-grouping of ego defenses. If by some means a patient can be stimulated to utilize his defenses so that they are no longer self-defeating, he can experience true ego growth. Therefore if done properly, brief psychotherapy can provide more than symptomatic relief and restoration of function.

COUNTER MASOCHISM

The human body tends to maintain its health equilibrium. Many of the vital organs preserve the body economy by extruding or combatting noxious agents (as in infection), by conserving scarce ingredients (as in dehydration), by altering metabolic process (as in starvation), or by working in other ways to preserve the status quo. Wound healing is one example of the body's tendency to maintain health. Unless some process is superimposed upon it, a wound heals spontaneously. If a wound is continually disturbed, however, by infection or by tearing, spontaneous healing can be prolonged or prevented. While the process of wound healing is exceedingly complex and not entirely understood, for all *practical* purposes the simple expedient of protecting the wound from trauma and infection is enough to allow most wounds to heal themselves. It is not necessary to understand *completely* the process of spontaneous wound healing in order to facilitate it.

Likewise, emotional equilibrium is maintained by certain body processes. Normal mourning is one such process, in which with time a person works through grief without medical intervention. "Time is a great healer" is the lay aphorism for spontaneous emotional recovery. Statistical evidence indicates that a certain percentage of patients with emotional illnesses do recover without any apparent treatment. Unfortunately, most patients do not completely recover from neurotic disorders on their own. Rather than seek the nature of spontaneous recovery in order to promote that process, it seems more expedient to pinpoint the factors impeding spontaneous recovery and then to remove or counteract them in order to facilitate recovery. The common impediments to recovery and maturation in every type of emotional illness, regardless of diagnosis are a regressive infantile expectation of gratification and a complex of anger turned inward on the self. The latter complex represents a combination of displacement of anger from an object of dependency or love, punishment of an introjected person, and attempted prevention or alleviation of feelings of guilt. Whatever the source of the anger turned inward against the self, the need to suffer is paramount, in other words, *psychic masochism*. To counter the patient's masochism is the goal of therapy.

Ideally, the core of the patient's masochism, his bad introject, should be exposed and replaced, along with his sadistic conscience. This is not always possible, whether by brief or lengthy psychotherapy. At the very least, the patient must be confronted with his masochism. From the initial interview on, the therapist must show the patient that the symptoms from which he seeks succor are the consequence of his masochism. At all psychosexual levels, whether the conflicts are oral, anal, phallic or genital, whether a patient feels anger in frustration, or guilt in success, it is his ensuing masochistic self-torture that causes most of his suffering. The importance of conflict is that it fuels the anger turned inward on the self. Dealt with most superficially, if anger could be channelled constructively elsewhere without additional guilt, even if the conflict which fuels it were to continue, the patient would experience some relief. If the conflict were resolved, the source of the anger would disappear. Most people are unaware of their infantile expectations, of their masochism, and even of those thoughts and wishes which arouse guilt. By his being made aware of these causes of his illness, a patient can be truly relieved of his fears that he suffers from a mysterious, baffling disease over which he has no control. He learns that he is largely the instigator of his fate, not the helpless victim of circumstance. That alone is assuring. Even without resolving his conflicts, if he is forewarned of his masochism, he can consciously guard against his own self-destructiveness by examining his motives before acting. Should the therapist succeed in exposing and replacing the patient's bad introject and its co-existing sadistic conscience, the patient will experience real ego growth and maturation, certainly far more than merely symptomatic relief.

ACTIVITY OF THE THERAPIST: CONFRONTATION

Since the therapy is goal-directed toward the exposure and replacement of the patient's bad introject and sadistic conscience, the therapist cannot remain passive, as in the model of classical long-term psychotherapy. Malan sagely observed that the more passive a therapist behaves, the more lengthy the treatment becomes, and the more it resembles psychoanalysis.[11] In brief therapy, the therapist must be active. The material of the interview must be channelled, portions accentuated, other portions virtually ignored. There is a wide latitude for the therapist's range of responses to the patient's offering of material. At times, he may simply acknowledge the patient's affect ("you must have been angry"), and make observations meant to stimulate the patient's further self-examination ("you seem to have rather mixed feelings toward your mother"). Or, he may confront the patient with repressed thoughts, wishes, and impulses ("you were frightened that you might harm your brother in a fit of jealousy"), and interpret the patient's current life situation in relation to his distant past ("your concern that the boss might fire you resembles your childhood worry that your father would throw you out of the house").

Although the therapist's range of responses is great, the direction of his responsiveness is aimed ultimately at the exposure of the patient's masochism. The first step is to confront the patient with the self-destructiveness of his behavior, with his need to hurt and to punish himself in order to satisfy his vindictive, sadistic conscience. Nothing works instantly; this confrontation may require repetition with further evidence during subsequent visits. However, once the patient recognizes the pattern of his repeated self-destructive behavior and accepts his role as perpetrator as well as victim, he should be asked what he could have possibly done to merit such punishment. Usually, the patient will deny all knowledge of bad conduct, or will respond with a few instances of behavior that he later regretted. The source for neurotic guilt rarely lies in past actions. Almost invariably, the origin of neurotic guilt resides in forbidden thoughts, feelings, and wishes, in conflicts with family, and in family interaction while the patient was growing up.

CONFLICTS OF GUILT

Psychoanalytic research over the past sixty-five years has provided insights into those conflictual situations associated with guilt that are common to all mankind:

"AMAE"*

Being forced to share mother's attention with any other member of the family arouses the most intense feelings of envy, jeal-

---

* "Amae" is a Japanese word which I use because there is no single English word equivalent to it. *Amae* is the noun form of *"Amaeru,"* an intransitive verb meaning "to depend and presume upon another's benevolence." *Amaeru* has a distinct feeling of sweetness and is generally used to describe a child's attitude or behavior toward his parents, especially his mother. Balint would call this infantile desire "passive object love" or "primary love." In any case, it is an infantile, selfish insistence upon mother's undivided attention and love.[17]

ousy, greed, competitiveness, aggressiveness and especially anger, both at the competitors and at mother for giving affection to them. The birth of a sibling evokes anger at the intruder, craving for revenge at mother, and frenzy upon the later realization of father's role in impregnation, implying *his* primacy with mother. The yearning for mother's sole attention inevitably fosters wishes for the removal, the extinction, and the annihilation of everyone else. To wish death on those we are supposed to love yields the most reprehensible guilt of all. Yet no one is free of those wishes. We already know that the child would prefer to believe in the omnipotence of his phantasies and wishes, rather than face the insecurity and humiliation of his actual helplessness in life situations. If illness, death, or other catastrophes occur within the family, the child is convinced that he is to blame for having wished harm. This is especially damaging to a child, since it appears to him incontrovertible evidence that his anger is deadly. Also physical acts of violence, such as his hurting a playmate seriously, may terrify a child into believing that he cannot control the deadliness of his anger. By far, aggression and hostility toward loved ones are the most important sources of guilt. Not only does a person experience guilt over his anger, but he fears being rejected if he were to express even a fragment of that anger openly toward the person upon whom he depends. To others he appears passive, acquiescent, and agreeable; underneath he seethes resentfully.

Weaning produces guilt both over the child's dependent and devouring wishes and over his anger at being refused by his mother. While this conflict occurs at too young an age for the patient's conscious recall, its residue is evident in the patient's overly dependent attitudes to his parents, employer, spouse, and his physician.

Toilet-training (and enuresis) arouses shame and guilt over being "dirty," and, it's equivalent in our society, "bad." (In the female, the genitals are included with the organs of excretion in cloacal phantasies.) There is also guilt over the response of anger at being forced against one's will. The feeling of "being dirty" frequently results in the development of the reactive character trait of fastidiousness or compulsive cleanliness. The reaction to being coerced is often stubbornness and passive resistance. Anality is a major component of sadism.

Sexual curiosity and activity bring guilt over what is forbidden by parents and society. It includes masturbation, sexual investigation, and sex play with others. Much sexual guilt is really related to the narcissistic, oral, and anal conflicts intertwined with it.

ASSUMPTIONS

The therapist can safely assume that if there were potentially conflictual situations in the patient's past, he very likely experienced conflict and guilt, whether he remembers it or not, or even actively denies it. For example, a healthy adult, if questioned about his past reactions to the birth of a sibling, will ordinarily acknowledge his initial negative feelings. He will usually recall his feelings of desolation and anger at the intruder's usurpation of his mother's attention, followed by his gradual development of acceptance, tenderness, and affection for his mother and his sibling. On the other hand, the guilt-ridden patient, having squelched those painful memories from consciousness, will usually deny ever having had envy or jealousy. He will protest that he always loved the baby. Like denying hunger, thirst, or the need for sleep, such denial is contrary to human response.

The patient must be shown that his past was not as he would like to remember it. Inevitably, he must be brought to see that he has preferred suffering and self-punishment, so that he might continue to ignore his childish feelings of guilt and the conflicts that produced them. In brief therapy, the doctor must maintain more than healthy skepticism. Many times, the therapist must be openly incredulous.

Knowledge of psychodynamics does not, of course, insure exact knowledge of any particular patient, since individuals are neither simple nor stereotyped. But if care is taken with the initial interview, the patient's manner and his recitation of his symptoms and life history should accurately pinpoint which conflicts torment him, and which defenses shield him. For the therapist to maintain total ignorance of his patient until he learns details only from prolonged therapy is not only enormously wasteful of time, but a slur on psychoanalytic theory. Of what use is a theory if it has no predictability in practice? The purist who refuses to make any assumptions from his previous experiences with patients may feel that he is being true to Freudian tradition. He is not. Freud had to avoid making any assumptions, because until his pioneering there was no scientific pool of knowledge about the unconscious, conflicts, defenses, and life patterns, from which to draw valid assumptions. Must each of us prove with every patient that whatever Freud discovered and what each of us has verified in his own experience is correct? A truly excellent psychoanalyst, Edward Glover, was willing to make assumptions when he wrote of the value of inexact interpretations. He predicted that an interpretation was incomplete, for example, if a patient's sadism was interpreted without its anal component. He had to make the *assumption* that the anal component would be revealed eventually by his prior knowledge of sadism, even though the material from this particular patient had not yet disclosed it.

As an analogy, imagine the medical model of a patient consulting a doctor with fever, dyspnea, cough, chest pain, rales in his lung, and diminished breath sounds. After x-ray, sputum and blood cultures, but before the identification and sensitivity testing of a specific pathogen, is not the doctor justified in beginning antibiotic therapy at once? Is not the doctor justified in having made a diagnosis of pneumonitis, even though his treatment may so alter the course of the illness subsequently that there never is consolidation of the lung? Or should he wait until his patient resolves his own illness by lysis, crisis, or death, and then say with more certainty, perhaps with even autopsy proof, that indeed it had been pneumonia? Upon the insertion of the penicillin syringe needle, should psychiatrists criticize the doctor for committing a symbolic homosexual assault on his willingly passive victim? That kind of criticism may be analytically correct, but it is totally irrelevant. The framework of analytic counter-transference is not applicable in that medical model. As physicians, we should have enough confidence in whatever we have proved to ourselves to be true and in what had been proved to us by past teachers, to apply it therapeutically. Our knowledge of guilt, the common conflicts that produce it, the defenses that conceal it, and the behavior that reveals it, enables us to confront each patient with his own guilt, in spite of his denial and protests.

NEGATIVE TRANSFERENCE

Freud warned that confronting a patient with any translation of his symptoms would "arouse the most violent opposition in him."[4] He was absolutely correct. Almost any activity on the therapist's part will provoke negative feelings from the patient. Contrary to the analytic method of fostering positive transference, however, this method of brief therapy depends precisely on the development of initial negative transference. After all, people get sick from unpleasant feelings—envy, jealousy, greed, and anger—and those will surface immediately, if given a chance. The exposure of the patient's negative feelings toward him enables the therapist to confront the patient with his masochistic response to anger. When I first began experimenting with negative transference, I attempted to stimulate the patient's anger by making comments directed at some aspect of his personality about which there was shame or guilt. ("You seem rather greedy of your mother's attention.") Or I might confront him with a characterological defense ("You would have me believe that every word I say is gospel, but you really hold me in contempt as you do most men," or "You pretend to be super-sweet to disguise how nasty you really feel"). I have since learned that barbs are unnecessary. The therapist's activity and confrontative manner alone are enough to stimulate negative feelings in the first hour.

Almost invariably, patients react to any confrontation with anger, evident to the therapist *only in the manner in which the patient defends against expressing it openly to the doctor.* This is the characteristic masochistic maneuver of turning anger inward upon the self. The patient may flush, fall silent, cry, fumble with fingers, clench his fist, or show suppressed rage in some other fashion. At that point, the therapist confronts the patient, not merely with his anger, but with the patient's reluctance to express the anger openly out of fear of antagonizing the therapist, the figure upon whom the patient depends for help in his illness. He is asked, if he has so much conflict about his expression of anger at his doctor, a relatively unimportant stranger in his life, how much worse are his conflicts about his family and loved ones? The patient's experience in the interview becomes a replica of his current and long past conflicts that are attended by guilt, for which his symptoms are self-punishment.

EGO VERSUS CONSCIENCE

Continuing to focus on the patient's masochism in subsequent interviews, the therapist emphasizes the sadistic nature of the patient's conscience and tries to create a schism between the patient and his conscience. The doctor helps the patient to see what he wants to do and what his conscience forces him to do. Most important, he contrasts the patient's sadistic conscience with the ideal healthy conscience. A healthy conscience is a guide for considerate behavior to others; it reminds and admonishes for transgression, with the expectation of better behavior in the future; it keeps a person from temptation and trouble, and inhibits destructive action. The therapist demonstrates with the patient's own behavior that his sadistic conscience does not guide, but only punishes; instead of reminding and admonishing, it cruelly, viciously, and vindictively torments and tortures far beyond what the transgression warrants; instead of preventing forbidden action, it entices him into further misconduct. Any hope for the successful pursuit of therapy lies in the patient's eventual recognition of his conscience as the *common enemy* against which the therapist is his ego's strong ally.

Ironically, when a therapist is confrontative during the initial interview, patients unconsciously respond masochistically at first. In part, they see the therapist as a potential super-sadistic conscience, who will hurt them more than their own conscience. Whatever anxiety their healthy self experiences in the initial interview is more than countered by the masochistic gratification of their conscience. One must be careful not to feed that aspect of the patient's personality.

It is generally assumed in classical psychotherapy that confrontations and painful interpretations should be delayed until the patient likes and trusts his doctor enough to accept them. However, in this method confrontations are made before the patient can develop a positive transference, so that he need not feel guilt about his anger toward the doctor for his directness. While this confrontative method is similar in impact to Rosen's "direct analysis,"[12] it does not immediately utilize interpretations of specific conflicts or details of those conflicts. The initial confrontations are confined to the patient's need for self-punishment and his masochistic response to anger; it is not "wild analysis."[6]

In American culture, criticism of a person is considered tantamount to disapproval or dislike, a fact utterly amazing to Europeans. Confrontations in brief therapy must be made in such a way that the patient sees them as helpful though painful. The doctor should emerge as a strong figure of assistance who is not afraid of, or repelled by, those traits of the patient about which he comments. The therapist represents both ego and healthy conscience.

The doctor's attitudes should reflect certain principles. Foremost is the concept that he regards all the patient's feelings as human and accepts them, no matter how odious they seem to the patient. To help the patient distinguish an ego-alien thought, wish or feeling from the dangerous enactment of it is crucial. The former is acceptable, no matter how irrational, infantile, or antisocial; the latter must be controlled within the boundaries of the patient's ego—ideal. The therapist should be prepared to accept mild enactment of anger. Naturally, he must defend himself against more severe forms, but without retaliation and with interpretation. If the patient's depression, anxiety, or anger threatfens to overwhelm him, drugs can be used, both tranquilizers and anti-depressants. But they are an adjunct, not a substitute, for psychotherapy.

DRUGS

A. Anti-depressants

The two most effective anti-depressants at the time of this writing are Imipramine and Amitriptyline. Which drug one chooses depends upon the side actions one prefers. Both produce dryness of the mouth and some hypotension. Imipramine often causes vasomotor imbalance and light-headedness with postural hypotension. Amitriptyline tends to sedate and over a period of time frequently effects weight gain. Dosage requirements are similar (average dose 25 mg., t.i.d., maximally effective in 2-6 weeks).

B. Tranquilizers

Since as little interference with normal functioning as possible is desired, large doses of major tranquilizers are contraindicated. Thioridazine 25 mg. or Trifluoperazine 2 mg. can be used as needed up to three times daily for anxiety, but I prefer no tranquilization during the day, if it can be avoided.

The use of single-dose-combination tranquilizer and anti-depressant medication is not encouraged. Modification of dosage of both components is very often necessary and cannot be done with the fixed-ratio drugs. Minor tranquilizers can be dispensed with altogether.

Contrary to the fears of some critics of brief psychotherapy, very few patients become sicker. Regression and dependency are conspicuously absent, in marked contrast to longer-term therapy. While for the first week or two they may have a temporary increase in symptoms, the patients seem uniformly to have an ego-syntonic response to the treatment. Patients rarely require hospitalization, and many previously immobilized have resumed functioning. This will be discussed in more detail in a later chapter.

Positive Transference and Avoidance of Negative Transference

The classical position of psychoanalysis is to encourage the development of a positive transference and to nurture it without interpretation until it has become a resistance. Therapy cannot be brief if a positive transference is to be established. That process, itself, takes a long time. Only after the establishment of strong positive transference do most therapists attack the negative transference which always co-exists in neurotic ambivalent relationships. Brief therapy requires the exposure of negative feelings at once in the initial interview. Truthfully, most therapists avoid negative feelings. Many times therapists even deceive themselves into seeing positive transference when patients merely try to please them, to manipulate them by winning approval, in order to avoid rejection. The wish to be loved and the act of giving love are poles apart. The former is infantile, passive, and taking; the latter is active, mature, and giving of one's self. To confuse the former with the latter, an all too common error in therapy, leaves the doctor in a fool's paradise, where he and his patient will stay indefinitely. There is often unconscious collusion between the doctor and patient to avoid negative feelings by excessive use of "tact," which is really a kind of pussyfooting around unpleasant topics. Anger is unpleasant. The droll definition of a psychiatrist is: a Jewish doctor who can't stand the sight of blood (especially his own). There is actual physical danger to the doctor's person by exposure to negative transference. More commonly, the dangers are subtler. Repeated exposure to negative transference can reduce the therapist's feelings of self-esteem as much as continued positive transference can inflate it. Moreover, there is an economic danger. No doctor wants to make a reputation that might antagonize patients and jeopardize future referrals from other physicians. If brief therapy is successful, the rapid turnover of cases requires numbers of referrals far in excess of those necessary to maintain a full schedule for a psychiatrist practicing long-term therapy.

NON-VERBAL CUES AND TRANSFERENCE[9]

Classical long-term therapy allows the practice of Freud's dictum, "The doctor should be opaque to his patients and, like a mirror, should show them nothing but what is shown to him."[3] In brief therapy, this rule must be broken. As soon as a therapist becomes active, he reveals a great deal about his own personality. I maintain, however, that even the image of the silent "opaque analyst" is an illusion. In any form of psychotherapy, brief or lengthy, the psychiatrist does not speak to the patient about himself, his personal life, or his feelings. This encourages the patient to construct an image of his doctor, a person he does not really know, based largely on the patient's own experiences and conflicts with other people in his past life. But in the construction of that image the patient also uses those tiny bits of the reality of the therapist that are inadvertently revealed to him. Although the patient may obtain certain information from biographical data in professional publications or from gossip by social acquaintances, his most convenient sources are the non-verbal cues afforded by the therapist and his office.

While patients are alert for these cues, most psychiatrists are not. Their training does not prepare them to be. The classical method of supervision of a psychiatric resident is based upon the preceptor's examination of the verbal exchange between patient and resident. Unless non-verbal cues are self-evident to the resident, they are never discussed in supervision, and the budding therapist might never discover their significance in his technique of therapy. Psychotherapeutic technique cannot be standardized from one therapist to another, regardless of training analysis. Technique is a function of the personality of each therapist; each works in his own inimitable fashion. Certain transferences are more likely to occur toward certain therapists, because of their personalities. Recent studies in communication, linguistics, kinesics, and paralanguage suggest that non-verbal cues are among the clues that patients use to determine what the therapist is really like.

The form and manner of the referral actually begin the patient's image-construction of his therapist. Those patients, referred by doctors who praise and express confidence in the therapist, are more likely to form a positive transference than are patients referred half-heartedly by doctors who are ambivalent toward psychotherapy. In addition, the presentation of psychiatry through the mass media of television, radio, and newspapers, as well as the theater and the cinema, influences the patient to have certain expectations of the therapist, depending upon which particular caricature of a psychiatrist he has chanced to see: the cold intellectual, the buffoon, the seducer, the lovable old codger, the saintly healer, or some other stereotype. Since none of these distortions is caused by the therapist himself, they will not be examined further here.

The therapist does create certain images of himself even prior to his first meeting with the patient. The doctor's name, aside from his reputation and prestige, is probably the first potential factor in distorting the transference. My own name is a ready example. Most patients assume that I am Jewish (which is correct), and because of the K (instead of C) in Karl, almost all of them assume that I am German (which is incorrect). Therefore, references to Jews and Germans, especially in dreams, have special significance. Secondary distortions become apparent: those to whom I represent a phallic threat may see me as a Nazi U-boat commander; those to whom I seem protective and nurturing may see me as a German shepherd dog; for those who see me as a stern superego, I may appear as a German police dog; and for those who find me pedantic, a Heidelberg professor may be my role. Since I am bald, one patient humorously dubbed me "Herr (hair) Professor." Although the K in my name is misleading, it is a nonverbal cue.

The location that the therapist has chosen for his office is another cue. If it is a medical building, it can connote respectability, but it also may imply cold, clinical detachment. A setting in an apartment building or private dwelling may arouse suspicion of seduction or quackery, but also may suggest privacy, warmth, and personal attention. The character of the building may reflect the qualities of the therapist: modern, dingy, disreputable, fancy, high-class, austere, or homey. The office itself affords a multitude of clues regarding the doctor's personality. (Does not the well-known photograph of Freud's office conjure up certain images of the man?) The size of the rooms and the brightness of the lighting may indicate expansiveness, coziness, distancing, warmth, seductiveness, or gloom. The furniture indicates not only the doctor's taste, but also whether or not he cares for the patient's comfort. Paintings, and other works of art or decoration, have a potentially great influence on the beginnings of transference. A warm mother-child drawing may induce expectations of nurturing. The sophisticated patient may view an abstract expressionist painting as a poorly concealed ink-blot test meant to stimulate associations, which attitude often results in resentment and subsequent resistance. The magazines on the waiting room table usually indicate what the therapist reads and what he expects his patients to read. *Life, Ladies' Home Journal,* and *Reader's Digest* make quite a different constellation from *Harper's, The Atlantic Month-*

ly, and *The New Yorker,* or *Holiday, Fortune,* and *Réalités,* at levels of sophistication, intelligence, income, and social position. The presence of current magazine issues suggests that the doctor is considerate of his patients; lack of current issues implies indifference, contempt (the old ones are good enough), carelessness, or perhaps that the doctor is a slow reader!

The seating arrangement of the office indicates the kind of relationship the patient can anticipate with the therapist. Whereas most patients strive for equality with the therapist (who, theoretically at least, wishes them to feel equal to himself), most doctors reduce the patient to a subordinate position by placing the patient on the other side of a desk in a vis-à-vis interview. True, this arrangement conserves office space and provides physical and emotional protection for the doctor, but it also creates a barrier between patient and doctor—a distinct separation of "thou" from "I." If the doctor's chair is a different kind from the patient's, this separation is further emphasized.

The comforts which are provided for the patient also reflect the doctor's attitude. A large, functional ashtray, placed conveniently, invites smoking; a small, ornate one, inconveniently located warns, "Smoke if you must, but I do not really want you to." The presence of a box of facial tissues indicates that crying is allowed and anticipated; if none is provided, the assumption may well be, "Cry, if you can't hold it back, but expect no sympathy from me." A cigarette lighter that always works makes the therapist seem dependable, or even omnipotent, and a faulty one may indicate the opposite. However, a lighter that occasionally does not light can also mean, "The doctor is only human, too," relieving some of the shame of the patient's shortcomings. If the doctor seems to do everything right, the patient (1) has an ego-ideal he cannot hope to emulate and thus feels shame, and (2) feels little justification for hostile feelings that may arise in the transference, so that he experiences increasing guilt, too. Perhaps we can be consoled that some of our awkwardness may be therapeutic to the patient. It is easier for the patient to say to his doctor, "Your damn lighter doesn't work," than, "I hate you," or, "You're a fool." Once he realizes that nothing terrible has happened from his criticism of the therapist's lighter, the patient may feel encouraged to express previously suppressed hostility to the therapist himself.

Many times, the therapist believes that he is encouraging the patient to express anger at him, yet non-verbal cues reveal the therapist's unconscious desire to avoid that anger. For example, charging a patient for a missed appointment is very likely to incur his wrath. Many therapists will avoid this situation by rationalizing a loop-hole for the patient, such as, "If 24-hour notice is given, there will be no charge," or, "Everyone needs a vacation at times." Another way to avoid the patient's anger is to be so nice to the patient that he feels too guilty to express anger. This "niceness" includes helping the patient with his wraps, opening the doors, giving more than the contracted 50 minutes, altering appointments to suit the patient's convenience, etc. To the patient, what the doctor does is much more convincing than what he says.

There are numerous other non-verbal cues out of which the patient can make what he will. If the doctor arranges a regular appointment time, it not only stamps him as being orderly but it may also give the patient an added feeling of security. Otherwise, at each visit the patient may wonder not only when his next appointment will be, but also whether the doctor really intends to see him ever again. An office with the entrance and the exit separate from each other allows the patient to avoid meeting other people in the reception room and thus to retain his anonymity. It connotes privacy and individual treatment. On the other hand, it also might confirm the patient's fantasy that it is shameful to consult a psychiatrist, since the doctor insures that no patient is seen by any other patient, implying that he shares the patient's fantasy. If the therapist prescribes medications, it may be accepted as evidence of his willingness to feed, nurture, and comfort. It might also indicate that the doctor does not approve of the patient's emotions and is trying to dampen them down and to tranquilize them—evidence that he, too, is afraid of the patient's feelings. The patient is expected to be on time for appointments. If the doctor is repeatedly tardy, he confronts the patient with a double standard. On the other hand, if interviews begin and end on the exact minute, the doctor appears compulsive and demanding.

The fee and the doctor's method of billing have repercussions in the transference. The amount of the fee, especially compared with that of other psychiatrists, will be significant to the patient in assessing not only how much the doctor values himself, but also how the doctor appraises the patient's worth, aside from financial considerations. A low fee, then, could be viewed as a sign of kindness, or as pity, or contempt; a high fee might signify greed or self-importance, but also respect for the patient. The patient's being permitted to run up a bill suggests the doctor's laxity, carelessness, indifference to money, personal attachment to the patient, or indulgence. It also may mean that the doctor wants the patient to owe him something, so that the patient dare not express negative feelings toward him. The doctor who laughs at his patient's jokes before analyzing them and their purpose reveals not only that he has a sense of humor, but also that the patient can move him emotionally. The doctor who does not laugh is stolid, immutable, and, perhaps, a prig. It is possible for the doctor to influence the patient by the amount and kind of attention and response that he shows the patient with his eyes, facial expressions, gestures, and head movements, murmuring, and grunts. Even the doctor's handwriting may influence the patient's attitude toward him. One of my patients, an amateur handwriting analyst, made certain observations about my script on an insurance form which suddenly changed her impression of me and markedly altered the transference.

Some therapists take notes; some do not. The patient usually finds it remarkable that the doctor recalls so many minute details without notes, and may attribute this to an amazing memory or to a personal interest. If the doctor takes notes, how assiduously he does so reflects whether his major interest is in the note-taking or in what the patient is saying or doing. Moreover, the patient can tell what the doctor thinks is so important by observing what things are said that result in sudden, brief but avid, note-taking. If the doctor so wishes, he can reduce the intensity of the transference at any given moment in an interview by becoming immersed in note-taking. The doctor's staring out the window, picking lint off clothing, cleaning his nails, fiddling with his pipe, or doodling on his note pad will also have a marked effect on the transference.

Many attributes of the therapist, such as age, appearance, manner of walking, and sitting in a chair, are so obviously likely to distort the transference that they will merely be mentioned here. It is apparent, for example, that a handsome male therapist would probably stimulate erotic fantasies in a woman, whereas an older, gentle female therapist would be more commonly viewed as a kindly maternal figure.

I have not suggested that these non-verbal cues be manipulated artificially in order to attempt to control the transference. I personally feel that any acting on the doctor's part is a sham, a dishonesty, which is contrary to the very basis of analytic therapy. Rather, the doctor should be aware of the importance of non-verbal cues and whether they tend to conceal or to reveal his own personality, so that he may anticipate and deal with the patient's responses. Otherwise, certain resistances will develop without the doctor's knowing their source. While he searches fruitlessly for the cause in the patient's past, the answer may lie, neglected, within the confines of the doctor's office.

OMNIPOTENCE AND HUMILITY

Not every therapist can do, and not every therapist wants to do, brief therapy. It demands activity, aggressiveness, responsiveness without personal involvement, frankness, skepticism, and sincerity. Most difficult of all, it requires a combination of audacity and certainty on one hand, and humility on the other. From the standpoint of knowledge, the therapist is well fortified. He draws on the knowledge of two generations of research in the fields of psychology and analytic psychiatry along with his own personal experiences in clinical practice and life. He can have such confidence, for example, that if certain feelings are aroused in him during an interview, he can be fairly sure that the patient is actively responsible in some way. It is unlikely that any patient will be able to tell him something that he has never heard before about emotions, conflicts, defenses, or life patterns.

As powerful as the therapist seems in his omniscience, in the

46

outcome of the therapy he is absolutely impotent. The therapist
has no control over the results of treatment; the motive power is
entirely the patient's. Even in psychoanalysis, Freud wrote, "The
analyst cannot determine beforehand exactly what results he will
effect. He sets in motion a process. . . ."[5] Brief therapy is no different. This method of brief therapy aims to replace a faulty introject. Against the enormity of the importance of that introject,
which he hopes to displace, the doctor is of no more consequence
to the patient than a bucket of water against the ocean. Only the
most unrealistic conceit would, with any expectation of success,
pit a relationship of 50 minutes several times a month for a few
months against possibly a whole lifetime of a relationship in
which the patient had been cared for, fed, clothed, cuddled,
sung to, protected, encouraged, and loved. While the doctor possesses a vast store of knowledge, in reality he is just a hired man,
paid to do a job. The statistical evidence of critics, friendly as well
as otherwise, even casts doubts whether he merits that pay.[2] Besides, psychiatry is only one approach to human problems and
must hold its place along with economic, political, philosophical,
and religious approaches. We have answers, but they are not necessarily solutions. The witch doctor in Africa has an easier therapeutic role. Armed with an aura of might through magic, he frightens the introject out of an extremely suggestible patient, who believes implicitly in a procedure backed by centuries of tradition.
We have no might, no magic; our patients are ambivalent, stubborn, and unbelieving; and no one yet really knows the exact
process by which a faulty introject can be replaced. We can only
try our best, and demand the best, both of patients and of ourselves.

REFERENCES

1. Balint, M.: *Primary Love, and Psychoanalytic Technique.* London, Hogarth
    Press, 1952.
2. Eysenck, H.: *Uses and Abuses of Psychology.* Melbourne, London, Baltimore,
    Penguin Press, p 198, 1953.
3. Freud, S.: Papers on technique. *Standard Edition,* 12:118.
4. *Ibid.,* pp. 140-141.
5. *Ibid.,* p. 130.
6. Freud, S.: Wild psychoanalysis. *Standard Edition,* 11:221.

7. Glover, E.: The therapeutic effect of inexact interpretation: a contribution to the theory of suggestion. *Int. J. Psychoanalysis,* 12:397, 1931.
8. Hale, E.: *Silent Language.* Garden City, N. Y., Doubleday and Co., Inc., 1959.
9. Lewin, K.: Nonverbal cues and transference. *Arch. Gen. Psychiatry,* 12:391-394, 1965.
10. Lewin, K.: *Penna. Med. J.,* op. cit.
11. Malan, D.: *A Study of Brief Psychotherapy.* Philadelphia, Tavistock Publications, 1963.
12. Rosen, J.: *Direct Psychoanalytic Psychotherapy.* op. cit.
13. Ruesch, J.: Observer and observed. In Grinker, R. (ed.). *Toward Unified Theory of Human Behavior.* New York, Basic Books, Inc., 1956.
14. Ruesch, J., and Bateson, G.: *Communications: Social Matrix of Psychiatry.* New York, W. W. Norton and Co., Inc., 1951.
15. Ruesch, J., and Kees, W.: *Nonverbal Communication.* Berkeley, Calif. University of California Press, 1956.
16. Sapier, E.: *Culture, Language and Personality.* Berkeley and Los Angeles, University of California Press, 1958.
17. Takeo Doi, L.: Amae: a key concept for understanding Japanese personality structure. In Smith, R., and Beardsley, R. (eds.): *Japanese Culture: Its Development and Characteristics.* Aldine, pp. 132-139, 1962.
18. Weiss, E.: In Alexander, F., and French, T., op. cit., pp. 50-54.

Chapter IV

INITIAL INTERVIEW

THERAPY begins with the initial interview, the most significant one of the entire treatment. Not only is there a fresh presentation of symptom complex, defenses, and life patterns, but the tone of the whole doctor-patient relationship is established and the style of the treatment is settled, sometimes irrevocably. Moreover, one need only to re-examine the initial interview of completed cases to discover that hints of almost every important truth yielded by subsequent therapy were contained in that first brief encounter. While subsequent sessions are fifty minutes, the initial interview is about ninety minutes as a single visit.

There should be no interview devoted exclusively to evaluation. The only valid excuse for an "evaluation interview" is to help another physician to understand his patient better, so that he can continue the patient's care more effectively himself. In actual practice, that is hardly ever the referring doctor's aim. He wants the psychiatrist to make a diagnosis and to ascertain the advisability of continued psychotherapy by that consultant or by another psychiatrist. This practice squanders time, money, and energy, especially for the patient. Worse still, if the person who evaluates him is not the person who treats him, the patient is subjected unnecessarily to feelings of rejection which will intrude upon his future treatment. Inevitably, the question will continue to nag at the back of the patient's mind, "What was *my failing* that the first doctor did not want to continue to see me?" It lends credence to his original low opinion of himself, which had been based on the frustration of his infantile desires toward his mother. In subsequent therapy with the next doctor, he acts like an adopted child, longing for the mother who abandoned him. Sometimes, more harm than good is done by clinic "evaluation programs." Except for unusual circumstances, patients should not be seen in consultation unless the doctor has time available to continue the treatment of that patient, should he require it. Otherwise, one risks breaking one of the most traditional axioms of patient care: "At least, do no harm." Most people feel rejected enough without a psychiatrist adding his unwarranted expulsion from his appointment book. That does not mean that a psychiatrist must continue to see in therapy every patient referred to him. Some patients are not suitable for psychotherapy. Many do not really want therapy in the first place; they had been *sent* by their doctor or by their family or by their employer, a fact the psychiatrist learns only after the patient has begun the initial interview. Other patients may not have goals amenable to psychotherapy. The most common reason why a psychiatrist refuses to see a patient after the initial interview, but sends him to another psychiatrist instead, is counter-transference. The patient had provoked some unconscious disagreeable feeling within the doctor who rationalized his re-referral. If the doctor is consciously aware of the source of his reluctance to treat a patient, he owes it to the patient to admit it as his own weakness and not burden the patient with feelings of worthlessness. Every patient referred elsewhere deserves an *honest* explanation.

RECOGNIZING DEFENSES

The manner of the patient's referral for the initial appointment offers the doctor some clues, not only to the patient's defenses, but to his method of inter-acting. If the appointment was made by someone other than the patient, the doctor should suspect that the patient is passively dependent, denies it, and uses other people for his gratification. If, in making the appointment himself, the patient has difficulty finding a time suitable for him, of course he can be suspected of ambivalence about the treatment, but also of considerable narcissism.

If a patient is seen, even for a single interview, it should be a therapeutic experience. Sometimes it is not enough to offer the patient a mirror in which to see himself; often he must be encouraged to open his eyes and be shown where to look. Very few patients are knowledgeable and mature enough to do all the work themselves. The others can use only those same self-defeating defenses that drove them to the doctor originally. Therefore, if treatment is to be successful and brief, the doctor must aid, not only in the focus and direction of the therapy, but in awakening the patient to his self-defeating mechanisms.

Freud felt, "What the material is with which one starts the treatment is on the whole a matter of indifference—whether it is the patient's life-history or the history of his illness or his recollections of childhood."[3] Meandering works well in psychoanalysis. But, in brief therapy, the patient is asked immediately and specifically what brought him to see the psychiatrist. A reply, "Doctor —————— sent me" bodes ill for the treatment. It implies an externalization of anxiety. Assuming, however, that most patients are aware of some inner turmoil, their description of it will quickly reveal their characterological defenses against impulses by the symptoms that they have developed. For example, if a woman has developed a fear of hives when in her mother's presence, one can assume that she has aggressive, sadistic impulses with phallic tinges toward her mother, which she deals with by denial, isolation, and projection.[8] The chronology of symptoms is often useful in connecting the onset of symptoms with a particular event or an anniversary of an event. The chief complaint usually exposes the patient's masochism immediately. It may also hint at identification with another member of the family with similar complaints.

Working at peak efficiency, the therapist must, within the first few minutes of the interview, appraise not only the nature of the patient's illness, but much of his underlying personality structure and his characteristic defenses, as well. Observation of the patient's general appearance, dress, speech, manner, and affect is crucial. Knowledge of semantics, kinesics, and linguistics, the essentials of character analysis, is indispensable. An initial impression of a "baby face" or childlike voice may be the only clue necessary to recognize an infantile personality. The patient who uses a euphemism for death, such as "passing away" or "being no more," reveals strong fears of loss and separation. A clenched fist on the lap discloses poorly repressed anger. Fluttering eyelashes and histrionic manner unmask an hysterical character. Evasiveness gives away the paranoid, reasonableness the obsessive, psychomotor retardation the depressive.

There is no time for a second or third hearing of material so that its direction may become apparent to the therapist. Sometimes he must rely on educated guesses, based not only on the slim evidence from the interview, but on his previous experiences with other patients with similar problems. The young lady who calls the doctor, "Sir," will probably be competitive, with a strong masculine protest, setting the therapist up only to degrade him in the end. "Not really," in response to a question, almost invariably means an unconsciously affirmative answer. The "damsel in distress" usually turns out to be an angry, nasty, destructive person who trades on apparent helplessness. The man who asks permission to use the ashtray by his chair will likely turn out to be passively aggressive, and so forth.

Furthermore, if there were situations in the patient's past which could have been conflictual, it is likely that they were. If a patient has siblings, for example, there will have been sibling rivalry whether or not the patient has stated so, or even is aware of it. No matter what the family constellation, the therapist can assume that there was conflict over wanting sole possession of the patient's mother's love. When the therapist acquires skill through practice, his evaluation has begun long before the patient's entire revelation of the content of his life history, which follows the chief complaint. In fact, the content of the history should be mostly confirmatory, revealing the why and the how of the illness.[6]

CONFRONTATION

Although the therapist may respond to the patient's offering of material by acknowledging his affect, by stimulating his further self-examination, or by interpretation, the first real therapeutic effort should be made to confront the patient with his masochism, his self-defeating, self-destructive actions. *No interpretations or confrontations should be made in the initial interview, except those which are tied directly to guilt and self-punishment.* The symptoms themselves should be translated as mechanisms meant to harass or to torture the patient. Compulsions, phobias, insomnia, fear, conversion reaction, anxiety, depression, angry outbursts, anorexia and worry should all be explained as components of self-punishment, products of a guilty conscience. The patient should be shown how each symptom hurts him in some way, by mental anguish, by destroying his feeling of well-being, or by provoking others to hurt him or to leave him. Whenever the therapist confronts the patient with a characterological defense, the same procedure should be followed. For example, if the patient has a sneer on his face, and expresses contempt for the treatment, the doctor might face him, not only with his need to hide fears of inadequacy or depression behind disdain, but with his use of the type of facial and vocal expression calculated to drive people away so that he can suffer from loneliness. Similarly, the patient who presents himself as a poor candidate for treatment by his description of the severity and the long duration of symptoms, and of ineffectual treatment in the past should be confronted with his attempts to discourage the doctor from treating him, so that he can remain a victim of his cruel conscience. History of accidents, such as those resulting in physical injury or unwanted pregnancies, should be vigorously examined to determine the patient's active participation and contribution to the incident, once again from the standpoint of self-punishment. "Accidental" pregnancy almost always is found to be the result of unused contraception; it should be incontestably equated with "Russian roulette," a purposeful attempt to hurt one's self, using Chance to deny one's own responsibility for the act.

Confrontations of masochism should be made incisively, directly, and with the confidence of certainty. No matter what other factors are involved in the patient's symptoms, conflicts, and defenses, the therapist can be absolutely sure of the element of self-punishment. The patient's very illness that necessitated his being in the doctor's office is in itself incontrovertible proof of the presence of some self-punitive drive, even in acute situational reactions, and in identity or family crises. It is the need for self-punishment that prevents most patients from bumbling into a spontaneous resolution of their problems without anyone's help. There is no need for hesitancy, doubt, timidity, or obscurity. The doctor's confrontation must be firm, direct, and insistent: "Look what you are doing to yourself! See how you hurt and torment yourself!" This is the one time in therapy for forcefulness. There can be no wavering. Either the patient is willing to examine his role in hurting himself or there can be no therapy. The two most dependable criteria for successful prognosis, using this method are the ability of the therapist to understand quickly the patient's conflicts, and the patient's acceptance of this initial confrontation. By acceptance I do not mean an intellectual understanding. I mean an emotional reaction. Even if the confrontation produces a negative emotional response, the prognosis is good. If the therapist detects no reaction, or if the patient merely intellectualizes, the prognosis is bleak. No other variable, such as age, sex, education, social standing, diagnosis, or chronicity or severity of illness seems relevant in determining the outcome.

Following the patient's acceptance of his use of self-punishment will come his inevitable question, "Why? What have I done?" The search for the answer to that question will probably constitute the bulk of the rest of the treatment. Inexorably, the focus of the therapy has been set at the initial interview to search for the origin of the patient's masochism and, if possible, to counter it. The goal may vary from patient to patient, from symptomatic relief all the way to extirpation of his punitive conscience and his bad introject. The goal should not be too broad or ambiguous ("I want to be happy"), but rather limited to those results possible in attacking the problem of masochism. Until the goal of therapy is agreed upon by both parties, no commitment should be made by either party for any further visits beyond the next succeeding one. Unless there is assent on a common goal, therapy will be aimless, and except for the therapist's active interventions, indistinguishable in form from long-term analytic therapy. Once the goal is set, the doctor can offer his rules for the treatment, which the patient must be willing to accept or the therapy cannot proceed. There is no contract for treatment unless there is agreement between patient and doctor on the goals and rules of treatment.

RULES OF THE TREATMENT

The rules of treatment are simple: the patient is to come at his appointed time and to pay the doctor's fee. The patient will be charged for missed appointments regardless of the reason. If a patient is late for an appointment, his time will not be lengthened beyond its normal expiration. For his part, the doctor will tell the patient his vacation plans as soon as he makes arrangements, himself. Aside from his knowledge that he has done his job as well as he can, the doctor's only other allowable gratification is his fee. Therefore, the doctor's fee cannot become a battleground without counter-transference problems ruinous to the treatment. The appointment time and the fee must not be manipulated. If they are, the doctor will retaliate even without meaning to, and the patient will feel obligation and guilt. (Frequently, doctors unconsciously encourage this kind of obligation to ward off expressions of negative transference.) The doctor should not be placed in the role of arbiter, to determine whether a missed appointment is excusable and reasonable, or not. The inflexibility of the fee arrangement affords the doctor equanimity in the absence of other rules. This should be explained along with the rules of treatment. The patient is told that he owes the doctor *nothing* else beside the fee, not even consideration, kindness, cooperation, trust, friendliness, assistance, loyalty, compliance, nor even eventual recovery. The only rules are to come at the appointed time and to pay the fee. In time, the patient will learn that money is the least expensive commodity in the interpersonal relationship of patient and doctor, and he will be satisfied and relieved that his fee is his only obligation.

Unfortunately, it is necessary to charge physicians and their families for the treatment. My personal policy is not to charge members of the health professions for the initial interview. Not charging for the treatment beyond that leads to unsurmountable transference—counter-transference problems.

After explaining his rigid but simple rules, the doctor adds that he could help the patient *best* if he told the doctor whatever comes into his mind during the interviews, whatever thoughts and feelings that come to his awareness, even though they might seem trivial, irrelevant, foolish, immaterial, embarrassing, or upsetting, or even personally directed at the doctor. Also, the doctor expresses interest in hearing any phantasies or daydreams and dreams that the patient remembers. However, these are not part of the *rules;* they will only allow the doctor to do a better job. To incorporate those standard analytic cautions into the rules is ridiculous. It is unrealistic to expect unexpurgated talk; the patient cannot and will not comply to such rules. He would break the rules and feel shame and guilt at his continual breach of contract, often without the therapist's knowledge. Worse still, to require the patient to say everything tempts him into a regressive, passive, oral-anal-sadistic, obstinate resistance, which would be difficult to overcome and which would unnecessarily prolong the treatment. Removing the standard analytic cautions from the rules avoids such costly diversions.

The therapist cannot give the patient any idea of how long the treatment will take, nor whether it will ultimately be successful. He can encourage the patient to the extent of telling him that he has helped patients with similar problems in the past. But he must also warn the patient that his sadistic conscience, their common enemy, is capable of throwing all sorts of roadblocks in their path, and that their enemy is wily and devious. As hard as they both try, they must expect that the patient's sadistic conscience will try to avoid extinction by all kinds of interference. For that reason, the doctor cannot accurately predict the outcome, aside from reviewing the patient's previous successes in life, evidence of ego strengths.

EXPRESSION OF ANGER

American child-rearing inadvertently encourages children to make their parents suffer, by performing badly or by suffering themselves. Therefore, it is essential that the patient be told and shown that his illness, his masochistic suffering, does not move the therapist. The patient's insomnia, anorexia, pain, fear, anxiety and depression do not in any way affect the doctor's sleep, appetite, mood, or well-being. Most masochistic patients try to express anger toward their doctors by "suffering," implying that the doctor's ineptitude is the cause. This attempt must be countered immediately by the doctor's assurance that only the patient suffers in this; the doctor is not perturbed. Instead, the patient must be encouraged to express his anger, whatever the cause, directly and openly toward the doctor. Usually, this anger is the consequence of the doctor's confrontative technique. In order to ensure his own physical safety, the doctor should restrict the patient's expression of anger to verbal assaults. Physical attack on the therapist is indicative of inadequate ego control; the patient is not suitable for this form of treatment as an outpatient. Should the doctor's furnishings be damaged (broken ashtrays, burned carpet, torn chairs) the patient should be charged with their replacement. Otherwise there should be *no* retaliation against the patient regardless of what he says to the therapist, nor how abusive his language. If he has made errors of omission or commission, the doctor should simply acknowledge the mistakes with which the patient confronts *him*. Any retaliation will lead to a very destructive sado-masochistic relationship. In encouraging a patient to express his anger, one must be careful that the patient does not merely do the doctor's bidding in a compliant intellectual exercise. What is required is emotional release without retaliation, not merely the mouthing of vulgar language. Also, one must differentiate the expression of real anger with what Bergler called "pseudo-anger," provocative gestures meant to antagonize the doctor, just as the patient had characteristically done to others in the past. The doctor must not defend himself with excuses, but he should confront the patient with any distortions from reality. The doctor should emerge as a strong, helpful figure, who is not afraid of or repelled by the characteristics of the patient of which he is critical, and who can "take it" as well as "dish it out." Most important, the doctor should be observed as a human being capable of error, but willing to acknowledge and to correct errors, without self-recrimination or loss of self-esteem. In essence he is the *model of a healthy conscience.*

ABDICATION OF CONTROL

Even though the patient had been controlled by his punitive conscience, the therapist, in his role of healthy conscience, should not attempt to control the patient in any way. Even the usual analytic rule that important life choices be delayed for the duration of treatment should be waived. Actually, ruling against making significant decisions in itself would constitute directing the patient. Instead, the patient should be cautioned that his decisions might be affected by his current emotional state, and that he should be especially vigilant against his punitive conscience. Whatever decisions he chooses to make will be his own responsibility. The therapist has no control over the patient's destiny. He should be told specifically that should *he* really *choose* to hurt himself, no power on earth could prevent it. The therapist can in no way be his protector. This avoids much acting-out of the kind patient's use to demonstrate their wish for dependency, their need to be controlled, and their wish to control others. By abdicating his position of power, authority, and control, the doctor removes most of the patient's indirect expressions of anger and rebellion that would delay the treatment. There can be no power struggle, once it is established that the doctor is merely expert hired help. The patient must assume responsibility both for his actions, and for the progress of the therapy. He is expected to continue functioning, regardless of his illness, and to be treated as an outpatient. Under no circumstances during the treatment should the patient be hospitalized against his will, not even after attempted suicide. (The only possible exception might be an acute psychotic episode with grossly disordered judgement.) The doctor should try to uncover the reasons for the attempt, especially any possible breakdown in his communication or relationship with the patient. These should be discussed openly. Otherwise, the doctor should not in any way alter his attitude or behavior, dealing with the attempt only as another self-destructive device of a punitive conscience. The actual treatment of the suicide attempt should be left to others (emergency room pumping of stomachs, etc.). Actually, suicidal attempts are very rare during brief therapy. But the patient must understand that the doctor means business in his firm stand that if the patient decides to hurt himself, the doctor cannot stop him and will not be intimidated by the attempt.

Whatever success accrues from the treatment is also on the patient's account alone. If a patient feels that the doctor derives any pleasure from his recovery, he may very likely withhold it. As a corollary, it is most unwise to select a patient for brief psychotherapy with the intention of including the patient in a list of successful cases for presentation. Such an investment in a case assures almost certain failure. For the method to succeed, the doctor must be absolutely impartial, having no other axe to grind except to aid his patient against his punitive conscience. The doctor should eschew any expressions of gratitude from the patient, even upon his recovery. There is a fine distinction, but an essential one, between being pleased for the patient, and merely being pleased. Just as a schoolchild deserves credit for a good report card, but the parent has no right to be proud of it, so the patient's recovery is to his credit alone.

NOTE-TAKING

Since brief therapy is focused and goal-directed, the patient and therapist must maintain the thread of thought and feeling from the previous hour. The condensation and abbreviation of material makes it essential to have accurate records. The usual analytic technique of "evenly-suspended attention" is not adequate. After repeated hearing of material in different settings of time, place, and characters, an analyst will eventually understand the meaning of a patient's message. In brief therapy, there is usually no chance for second or third hearing of material. If the therapist does not receive the message the first time, it will be irrevocably lost, unless it is preserved until it becomes understandable. Some form of note-taking is necessary during the hour. The vagaries of the doctor's memory and his unconscious resistances being what they are, attempts at delayed note-taking by recall are totally unreliable. Tape recording, while it preserves an interview accurately in word and tone is not feasible. The review of a previous interview on tape requires a full fifty minute re-hearing. Therefore taping is impractical, except for future research purposes. Yet, for the therapist to become immersed in note-taking during the hour distracts him from the task at hand, to understand the patient's communication and to interact with him. A compromise, not entirely accurate, but the most satisfactory, is to jot down the conversation in condensed form, expandable in the therapist's mind, a kind of individualistic shorthand. The doctor's statements are recorded, as well as the patient's. The doctor should allow a few minutes between patients to review both the completed hour and the previous hour of the next patient. Summing up his notes can be accomplished within five minutes time. It will fix the previous hour in his mind and remind him of the unfinished work of the next. Very likely, in reviewing the notes, he will discover new meanings that were not obvious when he was engaged with the patient. He might also discover that he must modify some statements of his own.

Writing on analytic technique Freud opined, ". . . as soon as any one deliberately concentrates his attention to a certain degree, he begins to select from the material before him; one point will be fixed in his mind with particular clearness and some other will be correspondingly disregarded, and in making this selection he will be following his expectations or inclinations. This, however, is precisely what must be done."[4] Thanks to Freud's care, analysis was conducted open-mindedly. His very open-mindedness allowed him to reach conclusions solid enough for us to use as a base for assumptions in brief therapy. Freud also ruled against note-taking because of distraction of the doctor's attention, unfavorable patient reaction, and the skewed selection of material detrimental to analytic method. Unfortunately, this gave refuge to many insecure therapists, who, hesitating to let their work be scrutinized by peers, let alone by hostile critics, keep only the sketchiest notes of treatment. Without accurate records of therapy, learning is impossible. The fact that scientific method is thrown out the window is the least calamity. There is no way for an individual therapist to assess his own treatment method without accurate records. How can he improve his own work if he does not really know what he has been doing all along? What he may believe he is doing and what he actually does may be two far different things. Anyone who has precepted the therapy of another person will attest to that. Even personal analysis does not give any therapist the right to believe that every moment of his working life he is consciously aware of all of his motives and that he automatically and eternally acts in a mature fashion. We owe it to ourselves and to our patients to criticize our therapy. Without precise records of our own utterances as well as the patients, we cannot even review our therapy, let alone correct and improve it. Performing brief therapy, making incisive confrontations, and recording one's own words expose the therapist's personality to his patient and to whomever the record might be shown. Brief therapy is not psychoanalysis. Since real transference is not the tool of brief therapy, there is no cause to fear contaminating it. The only reason to conceal one's own personality is shame. If we are expected to accept patient's shortcomings, should we not accept our own?

With that preface, it is time to present a typical initial interview in brief therapy. The comments in italics are my asides to the reader and are not part of the interview.

INITIAL INTERVIEW

Case Illustration: Mr. S.F., a 34-year-old supermarket manager, called my answering service for an evening appointment. When told that I had no evening hours, he called my home, since he had no telephone where I might return his call. We spoke very briefly and arranged a late afternoon appointment, after I had suggested he might call other psychiatrists who might have evening hours. "Dr. G. spoke so highly of you, I would rather see you, even if it's inconvenient."

He came on time and greeted me cordially. He was a solid, massive man, obviously once even more solid, now going to paunch. His dark suit and white shirt starkly set off his florid skin. A pale red glow suffused the purplish blotch of his face. The skin of all his exposed surfaces was thickened, rough, coarse and colored like his face. In short, he appeared at a glance to be suffering from a chronic skin eruption, erythematous, maculo-papular, diffuse, confluent, excoriated and crusted. His deep set, bright, dark eyes and turned down jowls bore the expression of long suffering. I asked the patient what brought him to see me.

Patient: "Dr. G. sent me." *An externalization of illness and a bad prognostic sign when a patient is "sent" instead of coming of his own accord* (With a sound of pride) "I'm difficult."

Doctor: "You sound rather proud of being difficult."

Patient: "I have this neuro-dermatitis all over. I've had it for the past year and a half." (He pulls up his sleeve and trouser leg to reveal more of the same eruption. I lean forward and with my fingers touch the lesions and gently slide over them, a definite contact.) *Before there is any chance for transference to develop further, I show him that I am neither afraid nor re-*

pelled by his illness, nor by the feelings that have brought it about.

Patient: "I had eczema as a young child. It went away. I flunked my Naval Academy exam at 18 when it flared up, but it cleared up a couple of months later and never came back until now. But this is different—it's a neuro-dermatitis and looks different. It came on gradually and I couldn't attribute it to anything. There's pressure on my job—retailing—I've been manager of a supermarket. I've got a better job now with another chain as supervisor.

"I've been dabbling in law school evenings, but I don't know what to do. I need money. I work and my wife is a school teacher.

"I'm basically nervous, get tensed up, get red from head to toe. Dr. G. said I'm ready to explode."

Doctor: " 'Explode.' That sounds like anger."

Patient: "I might as well level with you. For the past 8-9 months I've been writing checks without money in the bank to cover it. Next day I come in and make it good to the person. All it does is embarrass myself. I haven't done it in two months. Only small amounts, like if I want a drink or go out to dinner or make a small purchase. It's like floating a loan."

Doctor: "It must damage your reputation." *The first implication of his self-punishment. He believes he is confessing a crime; I suggested that the "crime" is in itself punishment.*

Patient: "I get angry with the checks and worry about it. But it drives my wife crazy." *This suggests that his actions are meant partly to distress his wife.*

Doctor: "How do you express your anger directly?"

Patient: "Not at all, at work. I control it there. A good boss doesn't express anger at his employees. There's no justification for it. Of course I get home and yell and shout at my wife."

Doctor: "You have a peculiar value system. You live with your wife, but it's more important for you to control your temper with your employees." *He already had suggested acting out anger at his wife before, about the checks. She is the scapegoat, but for more than the employees.*

Patient: "I've been married two years. This is my second marriage, her first. My wife is 33. I'd known her a year, met her through mutual friends. It was a pleasant courtship.

"My Mom committed suicide, four years ago in August."

He was speaking of his wife, when thoughts of his mother's suicide intruded. There is a connection between the two; very likely his wife is the scapegoat for his mother.

"I was an only child and very close to my mother. My uncle's a priest. He footed the bill for my education, a fancy prep school on Long Island. I didn't speak to him for 9 years. He was my mother's brother; I felt he didn't do enough for Mom."

Doctor: "He hadn't done enough for you?" *A comment on his dependency and expectation for gratification.*

Patient: "I never knew my father. My mother never married. My mother wouldn't tell me the details. She said she would when I was 21, but she never did. I resented not having a father. My mother was a nurse. She went with a fellow for about five years. He suicided—left her $15,000.

"My mother had a drinking problem. Also she had a problem taking pain pills and sleeping pills. I had to see that she was in condition to go to work. I remember once she fell, from the pills and alcohol, bumped her head, got a lump the size of a rock. She had to take care of her parents. And my grandmother had only one leg, an invalid. My mother was a long-suffering person."

Doctor: "And you've been raised diligently in her image. Her suffering sounds like that of a professional martyr." *Confronting him simultaneously with his self-punishment and his imitation of his mother—the bad introject?*

Patient: "That's an appropriate description. Her entire life was a mess of her own making. There's a bizarre twist about the suicide. I was in Pittsburgh and she called me to tell me what she was going to do. She'd told the same thing for 15 years, so I ignored it. She did it the next day with pills. There was an elderly woman staying with her at the time, but I guess she didn't know what was going on or couldn't stop it.

"I wanted to be able to give love to someone, so I got married."

Doctor: " 'Love'?"

Patient: "Thinking of the other person first, before yourself." *A pretty good definition, but hardly appropriate here.*

Doctor: "Your wife 'first'? With the checks? And the yelling and shouting?"

Patient: (Abashed) "No. You're right. It's not true. It's not love, even by my own definition. We are compatible. We both like the theater and reading. We'd like a fine home. She's encouraging my further education. I want to go to law school. *We have no time to pursue this at the moment. What are his motives?* I went to my uncle for a loan to take 15 credits of night school courses. My uncle said I'd gotten money too easily all my life, now I should work for it.

"I got married the first time at 23. Mother didn't want me to marry. I knew the girl only 3-4 months. I was just being rebellious."

Doctor: "Why didn't you do something constructive, if you wanted to rebel, instead of getting yourself in a *mess?*" *His words of his mother were, "Her entire life was a mess of her own making." I am making two comments here, one, that he acts self-destructively, and two, he imitates his mother.*

Patient: "I only lived with her a couple of months, separated, and was divorced all within 12 months. Incompatibility. Actually we were sick of each other. Our sex life had only been fair. I had a couple of girls on the side, all married. The main one had had an illegitimiate child before."

Doctor: "That sounds familiar."

Patient: (Muses) "Yeah, but every guy who's married and has kids is sleeping with a mother." *Without my saying it, he has seen the incestuous meaning and is trying to refute it.*

Doctor: "Your whole life seems to have revolved around your mother."

Patient: "You might say that. When I was married and my mother objected, excuse the expression, it was like being be-between shit and the fan." *I presumed his mother was the fan.*

Doctor: " 'Excuse'? 'Shit'?"

Patient: "Well, I shouldn't talk that way to you. Educated people shouldn't resort to that kind of language. Dr. G. says with my potential I should be more than a grocery store supervisor. I taught high school, but I cuffed a kid and got suspended." *This is his first open expression of anger in physical violence. Ironically, he was punished severely for it. At the next hour it will be taken up.* "I was a guard on the football team at prep school—actually, I was captain of the team. I'd wanted to be a back, but I was too slow and heavy. Then four years in the Navy. I'd enlisted to get a congressional appointment at the Naval Academy. When I flunked the physical with my eczema, I was stuck in the Navy, the Korean War. I was on the Underwater Demolition Team for two years."

Doctor: "That's a volunteer outfit, isn't it?"

Patient: "Yes."

Doctor: "That's awfully dangerous. Were you trying to kill yourself?"

Patient: "I got a shrapnel wound in the head."

Doctor: "You got a medal?" *Meaning a Purple Heart.*

Patient: "Yeah—I got the Navy Cross."

Doctor: "That's for heroism."

Patient: "When I was wounded, I pulled in a buddy from the water."

Doctor: "That *was* heroic."

Patient: "He was hurt worse than me. I was just saving my own neck."

Doctor: "Isn't it interesting you can't accept a sincere compliment, only criticism?"

Patient: "That's the way I am. You know when you asked was I trying to kill myself, after my mother died, I thought at that time of taking pills and committing suicide. The next day. But then I forgot about it."

Doctor: "You had decided on slow torture instead. The working of a guilty conscience."

Patient: "I knew she'd threatened. But she'd threatened for 15 years. I know it's not really my fault; she'd have done it anyhow."

Doctor: "Maybe your conscience is punishing you for wishing her harm. Kids get mad at their parents even at little things, like restriction of TV, or no candy, or early bedtime." *The first really tentative statement—notice the word "Maybe."*

Patient: "Why would I wish her harm? I never had any reason to be angry with her."

Doctor: "No reason to be angry with her! Illegitimately pregnant, no father for you, chronic alcoholic and drug user, left you guilt ridden with her suicide, and you have no reason to be angry?!" *Nothing tentative about that.*

Patient: "All that rings true. I must have been angry about not having a father. I was ashamed. I used a cover-up story, 'My dad was killed in the war.' And I do remember my resentment of her drinking, and the pills. I've never thought of it—

pushed it from my mind. I didn't go to the funeral. My uncle took care of everything. I was afraid of facing people. I felt it was my fault." *We'll go into his reactions to her death and more of his ambivalence next time.*

Doctor: "So you took on the mantle of guilt, not for the suicide, but for wishing her harm." *This is a mistake—the comment is undoubtedly correct, but I have little more evidence than my original assumption.* "You've taken on where your mother left off—a chronic sufferer. You've learned from a master how to suffer."

Patient: "I've never looked at myself the way you're looking at me. I can see you're right. Even my wife tells me I feel sorry for myself.

"Good old Sam? Would you believe everybody tells me their troubles? And I listen to them all. I'm just good natured and easy going."

Doctor: "That's a big fraud, an act! You're really afraid of all that anger inside you! You're afraid all the shit will well up. 'Good natured and easy going,' that's a lot of shit!" *This fecal conversation is quite intentional. First, it counters the defense he tried to use that "educated people shouldn't resort to that kind of language." Second, it unmasks his characterological defenses of denial, reaction-formation, and undoing. Third, it tells him that I consider anger and its verbal expression here, safe. And fourth, I connect anger with its anal component in a rather vivid fashion.*

Patient: "I'm a black belt Judo and Karate expert, why do I back away from arguments in a bar?"

Doctor: "I don't know. Maybe you're afraid of what you might do, that the anger will get out of hand. Like right now."

Patient: "Could I kill someone?"

Doctor: "Well, could you?"

Patient: (Looking down at his hands, in a half whisper) "I have. On a demolition job in North Korea, I garrotted their patrol sentry—with piano wire. Not even my wife knows about it. I came in behind him with the wire. He never heard me. The only sound that came from him was a soft sort of gurgling. Sweat was pouring out on my head, I began to tremble, then shooting began. I forgot everything and ran."

Doctor: "I can see looking at you and hearing you that you're afraid of your anger." *Another mistake. Even though he paused, he should have been encouraged to discuss his feelings about anger, killing, and death. In retrospect, I was probably not a little concerned about my own neck. I neglected his anxiety for my own.* "I know that you're afraid of expressing anger at me. Several times I've angered you today and you've held it in without any expression at all. You have to express your anger at me verbally. If there's physical violence, we'll have to terminate the treatment."

Patient: "That makes sense. I don't blame you. Do you think I can control my anger?"

Doctor: "Except in war, you have so far. *I forgot his cuffing the school kid.* If I thought you wouldn't control your anger, would I consider continuing seeing you?"

Patient: "That's reassuring. Would you be willing to work with me?"

Doctor: "What do you think, that I'm repelled by all this shit? Remember, I touched your dermatitis. Neither your anger, nor the way your skin shows it bothers me." *I have connected his skin eruption with repressed rage.*

Patient: "I consider my skin repulsive. I'd like to crawl out of it. I can't figure what started the dermatitis."

Doctor: "Doesn't it strike you that the dermatitis started shortly after your mother's death and your subsequent marriage? Might they not be related?"

Patient: "I wanted to be married. I had so much love to give. I missed married life." *Is he referring to his mother?*

Doctor: "Is that so? Then how do you account waiting for ten years between marriages, having so much love to give a wife?"

Patient: "You're right. That doesn't make sense. And you've already showed me I don't really love. I get it, all right. I was looking for someone to take my mother's place. I guess I did want a substitute for her. I'd lived with Mom all that time. I didn't have anyone else. Now I don't have anyone but my wife. My uncle won't help me." *Watch his dependency.*

"My wife has been very understanding of my illness. She had psychiatric treatment at one time. She said I should tell you everything. I've tried to cooperate."

Doctor: "I realize you have. It's that sadistic conscience of yours that stands in our way. It wants you to suffer."

Patient: "Funny you should say that. My mother always said to me, 'Let your conscience be your guide.'"

Doctor: "Sure, a healthy conscience guides you, admonishes you, so you can do better next time. Yours doesn't guide, it just punishes for mistakes—it even encourages mistakes so it can hurt you. Is that your mother's idea of a conscience?"

Patient: "Until today I never saw things this way. I'd never even considered it. You make it so clear I can't avoid it. You don't let me escape it. Bam, bam, bam!—nailed right into place." *I missed the allusions here: coffin? rape? crucifixion?* "Why I have reasons to be mad at mother. I can't ignore it, or pretend it doesn't exist. I need more than to control my conscience. I've got to change it. I've been kidding myself—all this potential—I'm just a flop. Good supermarket manager. I could be a good garbage collector, too. Dr. G. saw right through me. He said I needed somebody tough with me, somebody who wouldn't let me get away with anything. He sure thinks a lot of you. Are you willing to help me? I can see I need help about my conscience."

Doctor: "Right from the start you warned me that you're a tough case. You tried to discourage me from helping you. But what about the captain of the football team? The Navy Cross hero?

"I'm willing to see you for a couple of visits and we'll see, both of us, whether we should continue. Your goal seems reasonable to me. I know that your conscience will be a stubborn enemy. 'I'm difficult.' And me against your mother's influence is like a drop of water against the ocean."

Patient: "I'm willing if you are."

Doctor: "OK. My rules are simple. Just to come at your appointed time and to pay the fee. I charge $30 for a 50 minute visit. Today's visit is one and half times as long, so it will be commensurate, $45."

Patient: "That's OK with me. Whatever time you say, I'll make that time." *A far cry from his original insistence on an evening appointment.*

(We agree on a time.)

Doctor: "I can help you best if you say whatever thoughts and feelings come to your mind, even if they seem irrelevant, immaterial, foolish, embarrassing, upsetting, or if they're about me, even very personally, just as they come, without censoring or editing. I'd also be interested in your dreams and day-dreams."

Patient: "I go to sleep with a daydream that relaxes me. I'm in a cave holding off a horde of attacking North Koreans. That's it."

Doctor: "Have you any ideas what that might mean?"

Patient: "No. It just relaxes me."

Doctor: "What *your* ideas are is what is important. The only thing that strikes me at the moment is that they're North Ko-reans—yellow—cowardice—perhaps you're fighting off your fears. Maybe you can think more about the daydream and the other things we've talked about today." *We are out of time and cannot adequately pursue the significance of the day-dream. However, I wanted to do something with it, in order to maintain his interest in remembering dreams and daydreams, and to demonstrate simply the associative process.*

Patient: "OK. I want to pay you today with my wife's check. After this I'll be caught up with my own." *I may have been in error accepting this.*

Doctor: "I may want to give you medicine."

Patient: "Dr. G. gave me Librium. It had no effect, so I didn't take it."

Doctor: "That's good medicine. But it's a .22. To fight your conscience we need a .515 Magnum." *I support the doctor's treatment, but again warn the patient about the strength of our adversary, and in the language of his ego-syntonic heroics and daydreams.*

Patient: "I'd prefer no medicine."

Doctor: "OK. We'll give it a try without and see how it goes. You've been very depressed for a long time." *This tells him I'm not like his conscience: I do not want him to suffer.*

Patient: "It had never been expressed in specific words in my own mind. Now that you've said it, I realize it's been true. But it's funny. Somehow I feel like a huge load has been taken off, just knowing what the problem is and where we're going."

He offers his hand, and we shake firmly. *And come out fighting?*

AIM OF TREATMENT

This initial interview describes the essence of this method of brief psychotherapy. Insight is not the goal. Intellectual understanding alone is worth very little. What is afforded the patient is a therapeutic experience, an intense interaction with a person who wants to help him. Psychiatrists are accustomed to a passive therapy lasting many months, perhaps several years. But "brief psychotherapy" is brief only to the psychiatrist. Except for those sophisticated in the ways of psychoanalysis, most people have never had even a single personal, intensive, interrelated interview with a doctor. To these patients, even a half dozen such sessions seem a providential windfall, rather than the unsatisfying, incomplete experience the psychiatrist might anticipate. Using the confrontative techniques, the interview experience becomes an awakening, an intense stimulation of mind and spirit, and hopefully a corrective emotional experience. The interaction should be an unforgettable episode of tremendous impact, should the patient continue the pursuit alone, like the wedding guest confronted with a tale of guilt and penance in Coleridge's *The Rime of the Ancient Mariner,*

> "He went like one that hath been stunned,
> And is of sense forlorn:
> A sadder and a wiser man,
> He rose the morrow morn."

In the single initial interview mentioned above, the therapist focussed attention on the patient's masochism, his need to punish himself. He identified the patient's conscience as his enemy, the source of his self-destructive behavior, and began isolating the patient's conscience from his healthy self. He also laid the groundwork in searching for the bad introject that spawned the patient's sadistic conscience. But the interview went far beyond the stated and intended goal of treatment. It allowed the patient to see the gulf between his self-image and his aspirations, a threat to his self-esteem, as a by-product of the inhibitory effect of his conscience that prevents his achieving. Moreover it began clarifying the patient's identity. Whether subsequent therapy succeeds or not, it will be an ambitious undertaking far exceeding the symptomatic relief of his neuro-dermatitis. It will afford him the opportunity of being a better person than he was before his illness. If he never attains that objective, at least he will have a chance to accept himself as he really is.

No matter that he is a self-admitted sociopath. Actually, it is of no great importance at the moment whether his feats of daring and bravery are real or phantasied. While the history of his never having made a lasting meaningful relationship with anyone does not augur well for the treatment relationship, at least someone has encountered him honestly, and without fear, rancor, repugnance, or promises.

In stark contrast with this active, confrontative initial interview stands one conducted in a more traditional manner. The patient is a 37-year-old truck driver, swarthy, muscular, and tough-looking. However, he slumps dejectedly into the chair, his shoulders drooping, and he pours out his mournful complaints, as though this interview is his last resort.

Patient: "I don't know if you can do me any good. For the past year and a half I've got prostatitis. I have this terrible burning when I urinate. The burning is the worst. Then there's this pain, kind of a heavy feeling inside. Sometimes I urinate every fifteen minutes, I can't get any rest. Nothing seems to do any good. The doctors say it's not cancerous. I don't know, when you got something like this so long, there's something wrong. I think it must be cancer. The doctors examined me and tested my urine. They say it's prostatitis, but I still think it's cancer." *Were this brief, confrontative therapy, now would be the time to compare his attitude with that of the legendary old maid who is afraid there's a man under her bed. His conscience wants him to have cancer; his conscience feels he deserves to have cancer.*

Doctor: "What makes you feel that it's cancer?"

Patient: "Like I told you, it goes on and on and doesn't get better. I go from doctor to doctor. Maybe I ought to go to Cleveland Clinic or Johns Hopkins. All I get is pills (he pulls out two pill boxes from his jacket and slaps them into the ashtray), bills, and the doctor sticks his finger up my ass. Week after week the same thing. If this keeps up, I'm afraid I won't be able to go to work. I'm so depressed. I don't get any sleep. And to tell you the truth, I'm not the man I once was."

Doctor: "What do you mean?"

Patient: "I mean with the wife. I can't have intercourse more than once or twice a week. I can't seem to get hard. The men at work do it every night with their wives and most of the guys have girl friends on the side besides. And I'm not allowed certain foods—no pepper, no spices, no drinking. What the hell's the point of living? I'm doing everything they tell me, but nothing helps." *There are a number of confrontations that could be made, for example, his resignation to having rectal massage by a doctor every week as being an affront to his manliness, or his measure of manliness being the number of times he has intercourse, or his anger at the doctors.*

Doctor: "I wonder if you could tell me about yourself and your life."

Patient: "Well, I was my father's favorite. He had a dream about Salvador and that's what he named me. He expected big things from me." *The doctor should find out the significance of the name.* "Somehow I always disappointed him. I dropped out of school—I had to finish my high school diploma in the army. I became a truck driver. I really can't do much. I have no skills. I can't even drive a nail into the wall." *He should be confronted with the unlikeliness of the really favored son's being a failure. And did the father's naming him Salvador mean that he was not supposed to engage in sex?*

"My father was a jack-of-all trades. He could do everything: lay masonry, fix wiring, a little plumbing, carpentering. Me? I can't even put a nail into a wall! I have a brother, four years younger than me, and he turned out just like my father. He's altogether different from me. He finished school, got married, he's happy, got a good job, nothing bothers him. And he's handy, he can do everything like my father. Huh! I can't even put a nail into the wall." *One would almost imagine he is asking for some comment by his repetition.*

"My mother was a nice woman, a good mother. She died in 1954, and my father in 1958. I sure miss them. Doctor, do you believe in God?"

Doctor: "Do you?"

Patient: "I don't know. I worry, though, that I'll go to hell and burn. That idea frightens me."

Doctor: "Why should you go to hell?"

Patient: "Doctor, the Ten Commandments. I broke one. I committed adultery with a couple women before I was married. The other thing, I use birth control and I'm Catholic." *If ever a statement cried for examination of conscience and guilt, these do. And a connection could be made to his guilt and go-*

ing to hell with his current symptom: burning. This is not to say that the burning is a conversion reaction—only an emotional meaningful connection between his need for punishment and his illness. Of course the crimes he is confessing are not the ones that are troubling his conscience. I would suspect his anger at the birth of his brother, especially considering that he constantly compares himself to other men, his father, and brother. His guilt probably relates to death wishes toward his mother, father and brother.

"I'd give anything to get rid of this prostatitis. I'd give away my car, my house—that's all I've got. Sometimes I think I'll go to Johns Hopkins and have them cut it out. The doctors here say that surgery is not indicated in my condition. But they don't do me any good. I'll just have to go to Johns Hopkins and have them cut it out." *He seems quite willing to be mutilated, if not castrated.* "I don't know how my family can tolerate this with me not working and being home all the time, sick."

Doctor: "How are things at home? Tell me about your marriage."

Patient: "My wife is doing her best, she's trying to make the best of it. We've been married since 1959." *Not until his father's death did he marry.* "We have two nice girls, five and two. My wife was in a mental hospital after the birth of our last child. I think that's what made her sick. She hasn't been right since. She doesn't have any energy to do anything, but she tries to take care of me the best she can." *Once again he presents an opportunity for the doctor to inquire about his guilt in contributing to his wife's illness by impregnating her, a sadistic-phallic phantasy. He "can't drive a nail into the wall."*

Doctor: "You'd like to be taken care of?" *Instead of confronting him with guilt, the therapist chooses to confront him with his dependency. The order should be reversed.*

Patient: "Yeah, when you're sick everybody would like to be taken care of. I thought of staying home from work. If I did I'd go nuts after a week at home with nothing to do."

Doctor: "Being sick is a good excuse not to work. But you must be upset that nothing helps you." *Secondary gain is overestimated as a cause of illness. That kind of confrontation has little therapeutic value.*

Patient: (Defensively) "Well, I go to doctors. They don't do anything for me, except give me pills and stick their finger up my ass. That's all I've gotten for a year and a half." *He has taken the doctor's comment as an attack and is retaliating.* "But I still got all this burning. It's driving me nuts. Can't anybody do anything to help me? You think it feels good to have to live next to a bathroom all day?" *The rest of the session contains a repetitious description of his symptoms.*

Doctor: "Let's continue talking about this next time."

Do you believe that this patient will keep a second appointment? Why should he?

REFERENCES

1. Bergler, E.: *The Basic Neurosis.* op. cit.
2. Birdwhistell, R.: *Introduction to Kinesics.* Louisville, University of Louisville, 1952.
3. Freud, S.: Papers on technique. *Standard Edition,* op. cit.
4. *Ibid.,* p. 112.
5. Hayakawa, S.: *Language in Action.* New York, Harcourt, Brace and Co., 1941.
6. Lewin, K.: A brief psychotherapy method. *Penn. Med. J.,* op. cit.
7. Lewin, K.: Understanding neurotic patients. *Medical Times,* op. cit.
8. Shoemaker, R.: A search for affective determinants of chronic urticaria. *Psychosomatics,* 4:125-132, 1963.

Chapter V

INITIAL INTERVIEWS

The bulk of this chapter will be devoted to other examples of initial interviews. Although emphasis will be placed on methodology, the contents of the first three interviews support my hypothesis of the strong primary homosexual attachment of girls for their mothers. In these three instances, the patients appear on the surface to have made mature marital adjustments, but very little probing exposes their unresolved infantile conflict of wanting mother and being unable to have her. Naturally, this conflict would be even more obvious in those patients who are sexually frigid, promiscuous or overtly homosexual. If the therapist is aware of the ubiquitousness of the conflict, he can readily recognize it. If he is ignorant of the conflict, it will be overlooked.

> *Case Illustration:* Mrs. B.K., the 32-year-old wife of an insurance agent and mother of two children, aged 6 and 4, was referred by her gynecologist, whom she had consulted for routine examination. She had voiced fears of cancer to him in such a way that he had suggested psychiatric evaluation, "at least one visit."
>
> Mrs. K. was an attractive woman, who gave the immediate impression of intelligence, quick wit, and competence. She spoke spontaneously and so rapidly that it was difficult to keep up with the meaning of her remarks, let alone to record and respond to them. My impression was first, that she had so much on her mind that she feared not having time to get it all out in one visit, second, that she wanted to get her money's worth, and third and most important, that her rapid speech was a characterological defense to control other people, to overwhelm them, to prevent their reply. (In a later interview when she spoke of her remorse at uttering words that may have hurt others with her sharp tongue, I replied that "sharp tongue" was not at all accurate; "avalanche" was, a complete enveloping.)

74

Doctor: "Could you tell me what brought you to see me?"

Patient: "I tend to worry and be fearful of a lot of things, and it seems to be spreading. Mainly those worries bearing on physical health. The first I recall having such fears was when I read articles on cancer—I can't remember exactly when—but it was sometime between my graduating from college and teaching. Prior to that time I never gave concern to my health. I had been a straight A student, summa cum laude. I may have had a drive to perfection, but I had never been morbid. I suddenly became introspective, whereas before things had never touched me and I was unaware of the world.

"I married at the end of my junior year of college. We lived with my parents for two years. Actually, marriage changed my life very little." *Directly and indirectly, temporally and by association, she has implicated the onset of her illness with leaving home.*

Doctor: "So your illness began between graduating college and leaving home."

Patient: "It started with a pain under my arm, a drawing, pulling sensation. The doctor felt it was an emotional reaction from starting to teach. He told me to soak in the tub three times daily. I had taught from September to June without being depressed or morbid. We moved that May, 1960, a month before the semester was over. After that, during that summer, I began having complaints, especially a pulling in the left groin. Again the doctor felt I was just worked up, nothing organic. During that summer, I had a traumatic experience with warts on my feet while I was a counselor at camp. My cousin was the doctor; he didn't help, and caused me pain. I worried it would become cancerous. Finally, my husband took me to a dermatologist who cleared it up.

"We'd been married five years and I got pregnant. After six months I quit teaching. After the delivery, I became aware of pain in the groin again. An orthopedist gave me three cortisone shots, which I stopped because I feared some harmful side-effects. I went to another orthopedist who told me I had no business there and the symptoms disappeared.

I was OK until a lump appeared on the bottom of my foot. The dermatologist gave me two x-ray treatments and I became fearful of cancer.

"Now for the past two years I walk around with a million

and one fears. I'm nervous about x-rays and cancer. My beautician's son had hepatitis. Now I'm afraid of injection, seafood, and even utensils."

Doctor: "You're afraid of being contaminated from something bad on the outside?"

Patient: "Now I'm conscious of the silverware in restaurants. I inspect every piece carefully. It's very embarrassing."

Doctor: "Surely you don't expect to see a hepatitis virus with your naked eye. There must be some other purpose—to embarrass yourself or to upset yourself in some way. This is mental torture."

Patient: "I don't even like to visit a friend in the hospital, for fear I'll catch something. A friend of mine had blood clots of the leg that went to her lung. Now I worry about clots. I never forget these things. I realize I'm becoming neurotic, depressed, and morbid. I assume I'm afraid of death! Or afraid to suffer! I have no religious beliefs, heaven or hell. Maybe it's an overeagerness for life."

Doctor: "Two things seem apparent to me now. First, you have some need to torment yourself with all these unrealistic fears. Your whole purpose is to cause yourself anguish. I detect the workings of a guilty conscience. Second, whatever bad thoughts and feelings you have that make you feel guilty, you try to deny and blame on forces outside yourself, like x-rays and viruses."

Patient: "You did make me feel foolish about looking for viruses on the silverware when I know very well it would require an electron microscope. You may be right about punishing myself. But what for?"

Doctor: "I don't know. Tell me about yourself and your family. That's usually the source."

Patient: "My parents are opposite types. My husband feels I get these feelings from my father. He's afraid of a million things. He approaches life with caution. He can't stand risk or change. He checks the doors, the stove, the furnace several times every night. I couldn't have a bike; it was too dangerous. For the same reason, I couldn't have a sled. Partly, he couldn't afford things, but mostly it was safer where he could see me. He wouldn't go to a swimming pool; maybe in his youth he got athlete's foot? He's afraid to drive, but he's a travelling salesman! He has to use the bus, with that heavy suitcase. We've tried to get him to change jobs, but he won't. He's 66 and the work is too hard for him. His main virtue: he's a loving father. He works, watches TV, and goes to bed. Life is a struggle for him, just to pay the phone bill, a traumatic event each month. He tried to be good to me. To this day I feel my father doesn't know what he had in my mother. While I'm critical of him, it's never been openly." *An excellent description of an obsessional character of whom the patient is probably imitative. She feels her mother has been cheated, but she imitates the person her mother has chosen as a mate.*

Doctor: "Why did your mother pick him?"

Patient: "My mother's mother died when she was 16. Her father remarried a year later, a woman with two children. They were poor, living in an overcrowded house with rats. My father was a kind man and it provided her with an escape."

Doctor: "You're saying that hers was a marriage of convenience, not love."

Patient: "My mother told me as much. That's how I know all this; I was her confidante."

Doctor: "Do you think it wise for a mother to tell her daughter this? What kind of phantasies might this stimulate in a child to come between her parents?"

Patient: "You're right. I was absolutely the worst one to be her confidante about my father. Intellectually, it seemed all right. But emotionally it tore me apart. Even though I agreed with her complaints about my father, he was my father; there's loyalty involved. It hurt me. I couldn't stand to hear her complaints. It was painful. She's an extraordinary person. Even my girl friends' mothers were envious and jealous of her and our relationship. She's perfect except for a few qualities—no—mistakes: marrying my father. She should have left him or made a life of her own, grown in another direction. You're right, she shouldn't have confided in me. I guess the children came first in my father's life, too—I have a sister, 38. They weren't a well-matched couple. I've given my mother a lot of pleasure, but she's missed something in life. I grew up the example in the family, respectful, good, I tried hard, made all A's. My mother said it was even a pleasure arguing with me. I talked things over reasonably, never screamed or got hysterical. My mother is sensitive, intelligent, compassionate, kind. She appreciates culture and the finer things in life (all of this said with obvious adoration). We're close, she's my good friend (tears)—" (She blocks)

Doctor: "Could you tell me about the feelings that just overcame you?"

Patient: (Very defensive) "I didn't want you to get the wrong idea, as though there's something the matter, something peculiar about our relationship."

Doctor: "*I* said nothing at all. Apparently that thought just occurred to you and frightened you in some way."

Patient: "I do love her deeply. I admire her. I think of her so dearly. My mother-in-law complained that she could never get close to me because I was so emotionally attached to my mother. As though there were something abnormal about it."

Doctor: "Do you feel that it's unusual for little boys to have crushes on their mothers?"

Patient: "Of course not. We studied that in our psych courses —that's the oedipal conflict, isn't it?"

Doctor: "Then why should it be any different for little girls to be hot for their mothers, to desire them sexually?" *Notice the intentional use of the rather low common phrase "hot for," an emotional jolt to avoid intellectualization.*

Patient: (Affronted, indignant) "That's an awful thing to say. It's one thing to be 'over-attached' to my mother. But to imply I want her to be my lover! I never read anything like that in my books. You must have this theory yourself, to treat it so natural.

Doctor: "Your reaction shows that I am close to the mark. Otherwise you would have shed my comment like water off a duck. Apparently, you have a great deal of guilt about what I consider normal feelings to your mother. And you seem also to feel guilty about resenting your father's mere presence as your rival. Apparently, your conscience tortures you for that with all these seemingly senseless fears—that's your punishment —a life of suffering."

Patient: "I can't agree with this physical business. You seem to be fitting me into a niche, a pat answer: 'you love your mother and want to get rid of your father.' But this idea of punishment, that's a new approach that makes sense. But for what?" *Notice her confirmation. I only said she resented her father's presence, whereas she distorted my comment into "want to get rid of."*

Doctor: "Are you willing to pursue the reasons for your conscience punishing you? Perhaps *I'm* all wet." *Continuing the illusion of water and the duck.* "But, what if I'm right? You owe it to yourself to find out, instead of remaining the victim of your punitive conscience with these fears of cancer, hepatitis, and the rest."

(She agrees tentatively to continue to pursue that problem at least for another visit or two and for the remainder of the time we discuss the fees, rules of treatment, and schedule the next appointment.)

Notice that the confrontations in this interview about guilt and self-punishment were extended to include the conflicts that may have triggered the guilt, namely the patient's greedy insistence on her mother's undivided love, her incestuous desire for her mother, and her wish to remove her father versus her negative feelings about greed, incest, and homosexuality, and her loyalty to her father. Ordinarily, confrontations in this initial hour are not so sweeping. But the patient seemed to be almost aware of the conflicts herself. As a patient once commented to me, confronting a patient with his conflicts is like telling a child the facts of life. You tell him what he needs to know, as well as what he wants to know, but only after assessing how much he already knows, so that he can understand and assimilate whatever you tell him. In this case, I felt the patient was ready for what I said, even though she protested and vehemently denied it. Subsequent events proved me correct. The progress of this patient will be followed later.

The next initial interview is with a patient quite different from the first. She is not as articulate nor knowledgeable about her interpersonal relationships, nor is she as intelligent, educated, and sophisticated. Her symptoms are depressive, not phobic, and are almost incapacitating. In fact, the referring doctor and the family were contemplating hospitalization at the time of her first visit. In addition, she had had unsuccessful psychotherapy for the present illness several months prior to her referral. On the surface, even her feelings to her mother seemed quite dissimilar to the first patient's, but their conflicts are very much alike.

Case Illustration: Mrs. D.C., a 42-year-old housewife and mother of three, was referred by her family physician, who encountered me on the street one day. He related that he was about to hospitalize a woman, whose family he had treated for forty years. She had been emotionally ill for about a year, and although she had been treated by a psychiatrist and had received numerous anti-depressant and tranquilizing drugs, her condition had gradually worsened to a point where she had ceased functioning as a wife and mother. He asked whether I would assess her potential for outpatient care. She was now on a small dose of a long-action phenothiazine because of vague paranoid ideation. Later that day, he called from his office and personally put the patient on the phone to make an appointment with me.

Mrs. C. was a taut-faced, tight-lipped, slowed, bent woman with pale blonde hair and empty blue eyes. She gave the appearance of a stiff, aged, Nordic crone from a Gothic tale. Her clenched teeth and contracted jaw muscles disclosed that her grim visage was attributable at least in part to the extra-pyramidal tract effect of phenothiazine drug. She spoke spontaneously, but with little animation.

Doctor: "Could you tell me what was bothering you that you decided to see me?"

Patient: "I've had depressed spells. I cry a lot. I have no get up and go, no pep, I do a bare minimum of work. It started eleven months ago when I found out that my husband had an affair with another woman. I just haven't been the same."

Doctor: "Do you feel that you have aged in appearance?"

Patient: "Oh yes, doctor. I'm only 42 and I look 46 or 48." *This made me wonder about her grasp on reality and her self-image. She looked well into her sixties.* "My husband actually never had the affair. He hadn't bothered me sexually for months." *Notice her negative attitude about intercourse with her husband: bothered me.* "I guess truthfully I haven't been receptive for years. I kept count of his rubbers. One day one was missing when he was out of the city on business; the next day it was back. I confronted him with it and he admitted that he was going to use it, but didn't. Ever since, I've gone to pieces." (She continues, almost whining.)

"I've never been a happy person our whole married life. My husband accused me of just wanting him to bring the money home. The way I've treated him he has a right to think that. I guess I'm jealous. I didn't want him, but I don't want anyone else to. I cried and became apathetic. I've been a terrible mother. We have three sons, 20, 17, 8. The last was a plain accident. He's been a trial to me. He's constantly on the go, and I've waited on him hand and foot, even though it's no good for him."

Doctor: "It sounds as though you feel guilty toward him for not having wanted him and are trying to make up for it by being overly attentive."

Patient: "I've come to realize that. It's not good for either of us."

Doctor: "Perhaps you've been guilty about your marriage, your whole role in life. You certainly don't sound enthusiastic about your marriage."

Patient: "You're right and I never admitted it to myself. I realize it's my fault; I did everything but drive him to another woman. We have no life together and never did. Don't even have any interests in common. Over the years, my husband has gotten tired. We don't go out. We've lost contact with any friends we had. We're just stay-at-homes. My husband started to college after our marriage and I worked. Our first child was born while he was still a freshman. We lived on very little. Now he's a physicist, the head of a department (at a large Pittsburgh industrial plant).

"I'm too big a coward to suicide. I saw Dr. X. last spring. He felt that I was over-reacting to my husband's infidelity, that it was a very ordinary thing. I saw the doctor for a couple of months, but I didn't feel he had any sympathy for me. I guess it was a personality clash.

"Now my husband tries to make me happy. He tries to take me out and pay attention to me, but it doesn't do any good. He says he'll do anything to help me get well."

Doctor: "How did you happen to marry him."

Patient: "I was 20 years old, a student nurse. One night I was with some of my classmates and met him at a bar. He'd just gotten out of the army. In a few months, I was married to him. Of course I had to drop out of nurses' training, because I was married, and I had only six months to go. I never did finish."

Doctor: "That was very self-destructive, nipping your career in the bud. You could have waited or kept the marriage secret."

Patient: "That isn't half of it. Two months after we married he quit his job and decided he was going to school. I was angry, but didn't show it. I was afraid of him. He made all the decisions."

Doctor: "So you were resentful and seethed underneath."

Patient: "I guess that's what I do when I'm mad at him. He's Catholic. I turned for him. We practiced the rhythm system. My pregnancy got him angry and when I lost my job he walked out on me."

Doctor: "What do you mean?"

Patient: "I worked in a scrap and lumber office. One day I blew my stack at the boss and he fired me. It was over something trivial."

Doctor: "For a girl who doesn't express anger, that was unusual. Maybe you just wanted to lose your job, more self-punishment."

Patient: "I can see it, not only about that job, but even about nursing. I could have had a career, been independent. Anyhow my husband came back and said I had to work. I became a family helper and did practical nursing. My second child wasn't planned, either. We had both stopped going to church, so it wasn't for religious reasons that we hadn't used contraception."

Doctor: "You've made it clear that none of your children were really planned or wanted. They seem to be your cross to bear—you didn't avoid pregnancy and you haven't enjoyed any of them. Somehow they seem to be your punishment."

Patient: "I'm lonely. It would have been nice to have a girl. Maybe she'd have been company for me. I was raised by housekeepers. My father was a railroad man. He got tuberculosis when I was 10 months old. We lived with an aunt. It was during the depression and my uncle lost his job. My mother went to work as a stenographer. My grandmother had taken care of me until I was five. Then she got sick, lost her mind and was institutionalized when I was five. She set fire to the mattress. I came home to find fire engines there. My grandfather had been dead before I was born—they had been divorced long before.

"My father died when I was thirteen of a hemorrhage. He didn't live with us after I got spots on my lung when I was little. He stayed with his parents. He would have had more time for me than my mother. It wasn't just that my mother worked. Lots of nights she didn't even come home for dinner. She'd stay downtown with her girlfriends, maybe shop or go to a movie. She hardly ever came home. We've never been close."

Doctor: "You sound resentful."

Patient: "Talking about it now, I guess I did feel resentful. My mother always saw to it that I got whatever I wanted—clothes, toys. I never did without. In fact, I guess she spoiled me with material things, making up for not being with me."

Doctor: "Just as you do with your youngest boy."

Patient: "She lives in the city now, a happy well-adjusted person, helpful to other people."

Doctor: "You must feel guilty for being angry with her."

Patient: "She remarried when I was 18. He's 15 years older than her and a strict religious fanatic. He's always been good to me, though."

Doctor: "She remarried when you were 18 years old and two years later you were married, rather suddenly."

Patient: (Sullen) "I was resentful when she married. Pushing me aside for him! Just when we finally had a chance to be close. I guess it was partly out of spite. I showed her. She never showed me any affection, never hugged me or kissed me. I cuddled *my* children!"

Doctor: "You seem to have 'showed her' all right! You're the one who's suffered. It would seem your conscience found a way to punish you for your resentment of her."

Patient: "I can see where I've built up the resentment over the years and buried it. I never think about it. You get used to it and I've been away from home a long time." *Notice it is still "home" to her.* "I could never tell her any of this. She'd feel very badly if she knew she was to blame."

Doctor: "It's not what she's done. It's your reaction to your feelings about what she's done—it's your conscience that makes you suffer, ruining your marriage, driving your husband away, instead of trying to make the best of the situation."

Patient: "What can I do?"

Doctor: "What do you have in mind? What is it that you want to accomplish?"

Patient: "I want to get over this illness and be like I was before I looked in my husband's drawer to count the rubbers."

Doctor: "And what about your marriage?"

Patient: "I think if I was well again I could improve that. I know I've been wrong."

Doctor: "All right. There are two things I would suggest. First, we'll modify the medication so you can have more energy. I think your muscles are tight from it. And second, you ought to talk more about your guilt and your anger."

I discussed the rules and the fee and we set up an appointment. I discontinued the long-acting phenothiazine, instituted Imipramine 25 mg t.i.d., cautioning her about the side actions of lightheadedness and dryness, and gave her Thioridazine 25 mg h.s. to begin in 48 hours. (The history from the physician of paranoid ideation made me reluctant to discontinue phenothiazine completely, especially when giving Imipramine.)

Case Illustration: The third initial interview is that of a 22-year-old recently married young girl, a new-comer to this city from New York. She was referred by her freshly acquired family physician to assist him in his treatment of her bronchial asthma. Mrs. O. A. appeared to be a perky smallish youngster of about 14. Her dark straight, short-cropped hair hung carelessly combed over her forehead, meeting the thick dark frames of her outsized glasses. She wore no make-up. A twinkling impish smile played about her eyes and mouth. She had a rather boyish figure hidden under a gray outsized pull-over sweater, that revealed the thinness of her shoulders when she shrugged. And she shrugged, waved her arms, and gesticulated frequently, enthusiastically, outrageously, widening her eyes, and uttering "oh boy" and "gee whiz" appreciatively to my comments. It would be inadequate to call her performance hysterical and exhibitionistic, because it was entirely persuasive and winning. Only a psychiatrist would not have said she was an adorable gamin. This was her obvious characterological defense: the cute, loveable, asexual, little kid.

Doctor: "Could you tell me what brought you to see me?"

Patient: "I have asthma. I'm new to Pittsburgh. My husband's job brought me here. I've been to a psychiatrist before, from January to April this year for the same reason. I was married in August (the interview took place in November). Actually, the psychiatrist encouraged me to marry. I've had allergies most of my life, hay fever since I was eight. I had asthma during my senior year in high school, but for three years it was mild, just a little wheezing. "Then Mother's Day, last year, I had a real attack. I couldn't breathe—I couldn't get any air—they had to take me to the hospital and I got adrenalin."

Doctor: "Do you recall the circumstances that led to the attack?"

Patient: "Not really. My other psychiatrist" *she has already accepted me as her psychiatrist apparently* "found out the problem stemmed from my mother. You see, she played the horses too much. And she'd lose. To cover her losses she'd spend the money meant for household expenses. She'd be at work, so she'd ask me to hide the milk bill from my father. He has a bad temper—if he found out he'd yell at her. He's a construction worker. He bets on horses, too, but not to extremes like my mother. So I'd hide the bills from him."

Doctor: "So you and your mother were in collusion against him."

Patient: "Oh boy, I guess you could say that. We weren't wealthy and I guess she was trying to win money for the family. My mother always handled the money. I resented my father not being a man and handling the situation. He should have taken the money out of her hands. I felt guilty and resentful to my mother for putting me in that situation. I never knew I resented my mother until the psychiatrist brought it out. I didn't like myself for doing it."

Doctor: "Yet apparently you continued doing it; you sacrificed your self-respect for popularity, winning your mother's approval." *I confront her with the other side of her ambivalence, her wish for her mother's love.*

Patient: "I'm an only child. I would have had a brother 9 years older than me but my mother lost him at 7 months. I always wanted a brother or sister." *She denies she wants her mother all to herself.* "I always had cats, dogs, birds, rabbits, even snails. And we always had friends at my house."

"My mother is warm and outgoing. Until I saw the psychiatrist, I never really spoke to her. She never told me anything about sex. My girl friend's mother sat her down and they discussed sex." *That is some of the warmth she covets.*

Doctor: "That was 'really speaking to her?'"

Patient: "She asked me once if I knew about sex. And I said yes. I guess I was embarrassed—and that was the end of that. Except for the betting she was a good mother. She's warm, friendly, and helps people. She has common sense. She had a part time job as a waitress when I was in second or third grade. She was a school crossing guard after third grade for ten years, then a waitress after that.

"My I.Q. is over 130. I skipped eighth grade and graduated at 16, but I didn't have a good average in school. I wasn't pushed, so I didn't develop my mind." *She is encouraging me to push her to think.* "I used to like to read, mostly ballet books or about horseback riding. My dream is to become a professional rider. I have been riding since I was 13. I guess I've been kind of a tomboy.

"My husband went hunting after my birthday. We had a big fight because we didn't go out for my birthday. We'd dated two years and always went out for my birthday. This year nothing. I walked out on him and sat on the stoop. It was just childish and spiteful. I didn't want Fred to come to Pittsburgh. Since I was 12 I'd gone out with another boy, Rich, who dated other girls. I couldn't bring myself to date anybody else. I forced myself to go out with Fred, my husband. I dropped Rich hard. I was told by people who knew him that I hurt him." *Vengeance, rather than love.*

Doctor: "In a triangle someone gets hurt."

Patient: "Ooh gee whiz! That hits home—my parents—that was a triangle. My attacks always come near tests. I can't take the pressure. I dropped out of college my junior year to marry. Statistics terrified me." *She makes her own interpretation about the triangle and apparently connects it with the asthmatic attacks only to deny it and blame it on school pressure, which could hardly be operative since she has dropped out of school.* "I don't know anyone in Pittsburgh. It's lonely. Terrible."

Doctor: "You're homesick."

Patient: "Very. I used to have 70 million friends."

Doctor: "And your mother."

Patient: "I don't feel I'm missing my parents. Fred felt this would be a good start for his career. I think he makes $780.00 a month. I don't even know how much he makes. I leave financial matters in his hands." *Sound familiar?*

Doctor: "You sound like your father."

Patient: "Oh boy, I see that. You know I take after him with my bad temper. I sound just like him."

Doctor: "Your mother married him, and if that's what she wanted, that's what you'll give her. It's her love you want."

Patient: "Ooh gosh, oh boy, did you hit the nail on the head! As a small child I was afraid of the dark. I was allowed to jump in bed with mother if I was afraid of the dark. I'd hop in the middle. I even knew then I was keeping my father away from my mother. Why did I do that? That's not right. I was spoiled as a child and got everything I wanted. It isn't homosexual; it's not perverse like two lesbians. Society says it's wrong. My mother finally got a night light. To me that meant she didn't want me in bed.

"I was always afraid of sex. I wouldn't kiss boys. I was uncomfortable when I began to menstruate. I like kissing Fred. From the beginning I was disappointed in sex. I didn't achieve an orgasm. We haven't had relations much since my last asthma (past several weeks.) I enjoyed it once. We had champagne— I got high—no diaphragm—it was beautiful (she remembers no phantasies on that occasion). I'm depriving him, I know.

"My mother just called me—she calls every Thursday." *Notice her train of association, sex and mother.* "She asked me to promise her to come to her first if we needed money. I wouldn't promise. She got mad. She's afraid we'll ask my in-laws." *Her mother encourages her dependency on her.* "She got cold, her voice changed. When I was growing up, if I was naughty, she'd stop talking to me. That was the cruelest thing. I'd rather be slapped across the face. When I got older, I ignored it."

Doctor: "Do you feel that any of my comments have been like a slap across your face?" *Truthfully I hadn't seen any evidence of repressed anger.*

Patient: "Heck no. You're a great guy; you don't pussyfoot around."

Doctor: "What do you think we can accomplish in the treatment?"

Patient: "After talking to you, I think I want you to help me grow up. I better learn to get along without my mother. My relationship with my allergist in New York I'd known since I was five, he cuddled me, gave me antibiotics and cortisone. My doctor here didn't."

Doctor: "Nor have I."

Patient: "But maybe too much cuddling wasn't good for me."

Doctor: "Maybe we can narrow down our goals next time. Growing up is a pretty broad order." *That broad a goal is an invitation to dependency, regardless of her avowals.*

We discuss the rules, and make another appointment. Notice that many important areas have been untouched. We have not heard anything about her emotions that may have triggered off her asthma, except allusions to her homesickness, dependency and bad temper. We haven't heard anything about her intense feelings about suffocation and death, which one would anticipate in a patient with severe asthma. It would be a mistake to wait for this material in brief psychotherapy, for therapy would then not be brief. Therefore, these areas will have to be explored within the next visit or two.

SPECIAL INITIAL INTERVIEWS— EXTRA-BRIEF THERAPY

What makes the following initial interviews special are the circumstances. Occasionally, for one reason or another, a patient is seen with the understanding, either specified or implied, that it will be for only one or two visits. One such patient, driven to a psychiatrist by her need for a piece of paper with the doctor's signature, rather than for therapy, is the woman who desires a therapeutic abortion. In the Commonwealth of Pennsylvania, a woman may have a therapeutic abortion, extra-legally, not illegally, if she obtains the written statement of two physicians that her continued pregnancy would be seriously injurious to her physical or emotional well-being. Frequently she visits first a gynecologist, who then refers her to two psychiatrists for evaluation. The psychiatrist is doing the patient a disservice if he does not convert that consultation into a therapeutic session, rather than merely carrying out the mechanical task of deciding whether her emotional well-being will be injured or not and writing the gynecologist a letter to that effect. If any single group of patients can be labeled masochistic, the ones who manage to get themselves pregnant against their conscious will are the prototypes. No matter what other neurotic conflicts are being enacted through pregnancy, the need to hurt themselves is paramount. In twenty years, I have seen literally hundreds of women with unwanted pregnancies. In only three instances, all married women, was the cause of pregnancy a failure of the contraceptive method. All of the other pregnancies were the result of *unused* contraception, an equivalent of Russian roulette. Just as Chance is blamed for the suicide's fate if the chamber of his gun happens to have been loaded, so these women delude themselves into believing that their pregnancies were "accidents." Very likely, their unwanted pregnancy will be only one of the first serious episodes in what will become a life-time of self-destructive acts. Since, characteristically, most of these patients are under thirty years of age, the psychiatrist could conceivably spare them that life-time of suffering were he to confront them with their need to punish themselves before they ruin their lives irreparably.

Case Illustration: Miss R.A., a 20-year-old high school graduate, was referred by a gynecologist for evaluation for therapeutic abortion. A very pale, distraught young girl, she barely acknowledged my greeting and slumped into the chair. Her eyelids were puffy, her eyes were bloodshot, and her nose was red and swollen as though she had been crying recently and copiously. Her breathing was rather shallow and jerky, and her thin chest heaved spasmodically from what soon appeared to be vain efforts to control her sobbing.

Doctor: "What brought you to see me?"

Patient: "I don't want to have this baby—I'm going on three months. I can't sleep, I can't eat, I just cry all the time."

Doctor: "Tell me about the circumstances of your getting pregnant."

Patient: "I don't care about the person from whom I'm pregnant. I had too much to drink at a party. Usually, we just dance at those parties. I never have more than one drink."

Doctor: "What made you behave differently this time?"

Patient: (Weeping uncontrollably) "I found out the person I was in love with was getting married to someone else. I used to see him a couple of times a week. Tom is twenty-five—he's nice and understanding, a fiberglass laminator. I hadn't wanted to marry right away. I'm too young. I have a sister who married young and she missed out on life. But that isn't the reason he broke off with me. We argued over stupid things that I started. I was too demanding and bossy. Like I expected him to call me at certain times."

Doctor: "You recognize that you were driving him away.

It sounds like a part of your personality is trying to see to it that you don't get what you want" (at this point she stops crying).

Patient: "I couldn't seem to stop doing it. I knew that I was doing it, I told myself what would happen, but I kept doing it. Then one day he told me that he was marrying the girl he used to go with—that was one week before I got pregnant."

Doctor: "How did you feel when he told you?"

Patient: "I cried. At first I was angry and then I just didn't care any more."

Doctor: "Did you express any anger to him?"

Patient: "No. In fact I even forgot that I was angry until right now. All I thought was—just not caring about anything any more."

Doctor: "You were angry at him and took it out on yourself. He's not suffering from this pregnancy; you are—look at you! You have the kind of conscience that punishes you for angry feelings. And I suspect it was working on you even before, forcing you to drive him away from you in the first place."

Patient: "Looking back on it, it does seem almost deliberate. I got myself drunk, which I never do, went out with a guy I don't even like after the dance, let him park and have intercourse with me, when I never did that before with anybody. And even drunk I knew he wasn't using any protection, but I didn't stop him.

"I thought of killing myself so as not to tell my parents. I always wanted to make my father proud of me. We're very close. He was disappointed in my sisters. My mother and father were divorced and both remarried. I'm living with my father and stepmother. I have two sisters, thirty and twenty-seven, two step-sisters, twenty-six and twenty-five, a step-brother twenty and half-brother, sixteen. My mother lives by herself now. She's very sick with a nervous condition. She can't work— she has pains in the head. I was a baby when they were divorced. I don't know anything about that. I lived with my mother and two sisters until I was six. During that time, I visited my father a lot. He had a big house and had lots of toys for me to play with. It was lots of fun. Whatever I wanted was given to me. I moved in with my father when I was six."

Doctor: "What made you leave then?"

Patient: "I don't know. It was my idea. My father had remarried about two years after the divorce. My mother remarried when I was five. My sisters didn't get along with her husband, but I did."

Doctor: "That sounds like more than a coincidence. You'd been mother's baby and then she remarried and a year later you move out for no reason. Is it possible you were jealous of her new husband and the attention he took from you for your mother?"

Patient: "I don't remember ever feeling jealous."

Doctor: "Have you had any feelings about your having left her?"

Patient: "I do feel guilty about her being sick. Maybe I could have helped her if I stayed. My mother's all alone. She divorced again about ten years ago. They didn't get along and my sisters didn't get along with him."

Doctor: "I don't know whether this is part of the guilt that makes your conscience punish you, but it could be. Your present predicament also followed someone's getting married, hurting you."

Patient: "I think I'm an awfully nervous person." *The adjective she used to describe her mother's illness.* "I get impatient, like when I'm stuck in traffic. I feel like screaming. Maybe it's my spoiledness, getting what I wanted all the time as a child. Sometimes I'm afraid of ending up like my mother."

Doctor: "Your conscience would be pleased with that—it would feel that's your just reward for jilting your mother. You seem to feel disloyal, living a soft life with your father."

Patient: "I was in no hurry to marry. If I found the right guy —I wouldn't settle for just anyone—I planned to marry for security reasons." *From one foster mother to another.*

Doctor: "You mean some day your father will die and you'll need someone else to take care of you?"

Patient: (Flushing) "You know I never considered how babyish and selfish I'm being until I heard you say that. That's exactly what I've been feeling. He's taken care of everything for me. He had to find out anyhow for me to have this pregnancy ended because I'm under twenty-one. He accepted it very well —both my sisters had to get married—but I know I let him down. He expected better of me. But he's paying for everything. I feel guilty about the expense I'm putting him to." *Notice the double meaning of "he's paying for everything."*

Doctor: "You were angry at what I said, but you're afraid of antagonizing me, because you need the letter. I intend to write it regardless of what you say, so go ahead."

Patient: "I came here feeling sorry for myself. Maybe I needed a good spanking. All right, it did hurt, hearing you say it. I sound like a terrible person. But you didn't say anything that isn't true. I guess it's time I grew up. I'm twenty years old, I shouldn't be a baby any more. I have to do it on my own."

Doctor: "I'll write the doctor today. I wonder if you'd mind letting me know how things are with you after you get out of the hospital. You could call or drop me a note."

Patient: "Mind? It's kind of you to care. You've opened my eyes to something I didn't want to see." *She never did express any resentment for the temporary pain I caused her.*

I help her with her coat. Part solemn, part smiling, she strides out the door.

Seven weeks later, I received this note, with a check representing full payment for the consultation:

"Writing to let you know everything is over with and I feel like an entirely different person. It's going to take time to forget the happenings of the long last four months.

"I'll be visiting the doctor soon for my three weeks' checkup. He's been so wonderful to me I can't thank him enough.

"Presently, I'm working as a secretary for an attorney right here in my own community. It's very convenient since there aren't any more traffic jams every day. Sitting around at home every day before going into the hospital was really getting to me. This opportunity came up so I started working two weeks before going into the hospital. My new job is working out very well.

"I want to thank you so much for everything you have done for me. Your comments have not been forgotten or ignored. Many times they come across my mind. That's one reason for the delay in payment of my bill. My dad was more than willing to pay it, as well as all of the others, but I was determined to 'do it on my own' as soon as I was back to work.

"Again, many, many thanks.

Sincerely,
R.A.

The same day I acknowledged her letter with a brief note,

thanking her for writing, congratulating her on her mature way of dealing with the situation, and wishing her well. I added that should she ever wish to see me again she was welcome. She has not communicated with me since.

Another type of patient seen for only a few visits is one who experience has shown is not treatable or who has such a poor prognosis that both patient and doctor are reluctant to expend a great amount of energy on treatment. In this category would fall those brought for treatment against their will, those severely mentally retarded or grossly brain damaged, and those with characterological problems and acting out of sociopathic or anti-social traits (drug addicts and recidivist criminals). One group of patients with whom psychiatrists have not had much success are sociopathic alcoholics. If little can be done with their characterological problems at least they might be helped to be less self-destructive sociopaths.

Case Illustration: Mr. V.Q., a single 24-year-old manufacturer's representative for a packaging company, had his mother make the initial appointment by telephone. "My son is sorely troubled. He stays out all night—I don't know where he goes. He's been expressing thoughts of hopelessness. He's a nice boy; everyone likes him. He couldn't bring himself to call for an appointment. That's part of his problem—he can't call on his customers either. He may do something desperate. The priest cannot help him. I got your name through a woman where I work. You helped a friend of hers."

That the patient has not made his own appointment is already a poor prognostic sign. Not only is he ambivalent about therapy, but apparently the pressure for him to come to a psychiatrist is external. The fact that the call comes from his mother suggests her manipulativeness and his great dependency on her.

Mr. Q. is a tall, muscular, darkly handsome youth, grinning and affable, hardly resembling the picture of abject misery that his mother had painted. He greets me with a hearty, hale-fellow-well-met handpumping and a proper salesmanlike full toothed smile—only this time the product obviously is himself. Because of the mother's note of urgency I had scheduled him for my first open time, which was fifty minutes, rather than the ninety minutes I usually allow for an initial interview.

After the initial greeting and introductions, the patient is asked what brought him to see the doctor.

Patient: "For no reason, I'm dissatisfied. Nothing is going right the past year. I'm very depressed. I find it impossible to assume responsibility. I'm a sales representative for a packaging company and for some reason I don't work. I've got a good job, it's well paying and I like it, but I'm not doing right by it. I'll bet I haven't seen six customers in the past month. I like selling. I don't have any trouble talking to people, they like me, no antipathies but I don't like myself. I just can't get myself to call on customers. I can't explain it. I'm not a tremendous success. All night I stay out drinking beers with a couple of girls." (All this is said with the original smiling affability.)

Doctor: "How come you want to stay away from home?"

Patient: "It's not that. I like my family. My parents are swell people. There are six of us; my brothers are twenty-six, twenty-two, nineteen and twelve. I have a sister seventeen. They couldn't be nicer; we get along fine. Never any trouble there. We're not a bunch of drunken brawling Irishmen." *Already the doctor sees massive denial, both in the content and the manner in which it is communicated. In brief therapy, this must be attacked vigorously and immediately. Otherwise, therapy will be at best lengthy, or more likely, abruptly terminated after one or two visits.*

Doctor: "So, according to your story so far, everything's fine with your family and you're just a lazy slob?"

Patient: "That's it, I guess, I'm just a lazy slob. What do I do, just learn to live with it?"

Doctor: "Something's screwy. There are some inconsistencies that I see already. First, if you really are just a lazy slob, then why should you *care* at all. Second, you tell me how depressed you are, yet outwardly you're all charm and smiles. Obviously, you are hiding something, protecting someone. Since you are willing to call *yourself* a lazy slob you must be shielding your family." *Actually the ambivalent symbiotic relationship with his mother has been tipped off by her phone call.*

Patient: "Why does everyone blame the family? You sound like my psychology books."

Doctor: "You must think I'm pretty stupid then, to try to show me that you don't even have the envies and jealousies of your brothers and sister, that your books have told you are normal in every family."

Patient: (Snatches a piece of Kleenex angrily, crumples it in his hand.) "When I was twelve years old, my brother, he was ten, I broke his elbow with a fork. We were finishing dinner. I'd half eaten my cake and went into the kitchen for some milk. Leo grabbed my piece of cake and ran. I threw my fork at him and it chipped a bone in his elbow. They had to take him to the hospital. Mother insisted that I apologize, but I never did." (Defiantly)

Doctor: "What kind of household do you have, that each child has to protect what is rightfully his? Doesn't your mother establish any rules? No wonder you're brawling Irishmen." *The patient, in response to the doctor's attack on his use of denial, has confessed a small crime to appease him. The doctor ignores his confession and proceeds directly to whom he perceives is the person being shielded.*

Patient: (Plaintively) "Mother has her hands full raising us. My father never could be depended on until six years ago when the priest talked to him." *Remember the mother's comment on the phone: The priest cannot help him.* "It was awful—he drank and gambled and ran around. He did it stupidly—he took this woman to the club—in front of everyone. I saw her—she was terrible looking and no good. He was boozing and gambling too; but nobody ever knew outside the family. My Dad is a great guy—he just suffers from the same sickness as me. I have a great deal of respect for my father. He's very intelligent. He's a druggist. He's been a conscientious worker— never missed a day. Since seeing the priest he's been on the straight and narrow." (Shreds the Kleenex in his hands.)

Doctor: "You try to protect your mother by making your father out to be the villain, but you even have to end up defending him, too."

Patient: (Throwing the Kleenex into ashtray) "I sound like Queen for a Day." (Sheepishly, but still angry.) *He identifies with his father—and the threat of castration by mother by way of the priest.*

Doctor: "Queen for a Day?"

Patient: "You know that television program where a bunch of ladies tell their hard-luck story and the one who evokes the most tears from the audience is Queen for a Day."

Doctor: "Funny you should think of yourself as *Queen,* a girl."

Patient: "That's what occurred to me when I saw myself tearing the Kleenex."

Doctor: "I guess your sister, being the only girl, has it better." *Beginning clarification of his identification conflict.*

Patient: "Sure, her life is entirely different from mine. She and Mom are pretty close. But I'm the favorite, Mom says."

Doctor: "Do you believe that?"

Patient: "Yeah."

Doctor: "Favorites rarely end up in this office. You probably feel you've apple-polished your way at home, the same as you tried here—all smiles while you wanted to punch me in the nose for what I was saying. (He flushes, looks down.) "But hell, if you think you have troubles being mad at me—I could drop dead tomorrow and it wouldn't matter to you, except to find another psychiatrist—but to be mad at your own mother, that causes you trouble."

Patient: "I'd never want to hurt her. She's suffered enough. What she had to put up with my father. He's not an affectionate man."

Doctor: "Did you ever wonder why she married a guy like that? And if you had to choose between hurting her and hurting yourself?"

Patient: "That's easy—myself." (With honest feeling.)

Doctor: "What did your books say about masochism?"

Patient: (Smiles) "OK I'll bring my whips next time, to beat myself.

Doctor: "Some people use whips, some drink and ruin their careers, some marry men who booze, gamble and run around with other women."

Confront with his masochism, his mother's masochism, implying his imitating her.

Patient: "You mean I'm doing all this to myself?"

Doctor: "Because you have a guilty conscience, you're punishing yourself, trying to ruin your life."

Patient: "I know I could have done better at school. I didn't study. Just like now with my job. You think I'm trying to ruin myself? (muses—obviously accepts the idea) Why?"

Doctor: "You have any ideas, beside what we've uncovered so far?"

Patient: "You've got me thinking. *I really had me fooled:* 'Everything's fine.' (Snorts) But how can you be so damn sure! You don't sound like I figure psychiatrists to be from what I've read in school, 'screwy,' 'lazy slob.' I got to hand it to you. Boy, you sure come on strong!"

Doctor: "What have you got to be frightened of? You're taller than me, outweigh me a good twenty pounds, you're half my age—if we got into it you sure could beat the crap out of me." *The patient, finding himself yielding, may be frightened by his passivity. I don't want him to "hand it to me." If not reassured by reality, he might flee in homosexual panic.*

Patient: (Laughs) "See what I mean? Who ever figures a psychiatrist to talk like that—'beat the crap out of me'" (laughs again).

Doctor: "Are you interested in finding out more about why you want to ruin yourself? We're out of time today."

Patient: Sure. You name the time; I'll be here. By the way, what's your fee? You want me to pay now, or after a month?"

Doctor: "Whoa, hold on. We haven't even agreed yet that you're going to be my patient or that I'm going to be your doctor, let alone when you're going to pay me." *By this I let him know that neither of us will be dominated and that it will be a cooperative venture.*

Patient: "I have a confession. I called a psychiatrist before you on the phone. He didn't even ask what my problem was, he just asked, 'Can you afford me?' I just hung up." We discuss the rules of our tenuous relationship and make an appointment six days later.

At his second interview his attitude is quite different. Gone is the salesman's smile and the glib tongue. Instead he is contemplative and serious. He borrows matches, which I request him to return. He reports feeling better this week and calling on his customers regularly.

Patient: "I'm not altogether sure about the treatment, I don't have a lot of faith in it."

Doctor: "Why should you? You don't really know me. And this isn't a religion—not faith—understanding."

Patient: "I'm scared. I find myself thinking just the opposite of what I started saying here when I came here."

Doctor: "You're afraid of being dominated—you seem to want to be passive and be taken care of, and at the same time you fear it as though it means being a girl, like your sister, or a fairy."

Patient: (Hesitantly, shamefully) "At thirteen I was at the seminary, I had homosexual tendencies. There was a classmate I was enamored of. We slept in the same dorm. While he was asleep, I'd touch his genitals. Once he awoke and told the priest. I was thrown out of the seminary. My parents knew why. My mother kept asking me who it was."

Doctor: "That's ironic, when your relationship with *her* is probably related to your behavior."

Patient: "After that I went to our local high school. Sometimes I slept at a friend's and I used to do the same thing with him. He never knew. Three years ago we were drinking and we happened to go to the bar john together. I wanted to play with his penis and he said, 'No.'" *Wait until I'm "asleep" later, jerk.*

"Then two weeks ago at 4:00 a.m. at a supper club, I was drunk and picked up a girl at the bar. After I bought her a few drinks, we went to her room. 'She' turned out to be a female impersonator. I hadn't known. When he took off his clothes, I was turned off."

Doctor: "Apparently that triggered off your having your mother call a psychiatrist, instead of reassuring you. All this seems to be related to the idea that you want to be a girl to please your mother."

At our third interview, two weeks later (the patient had been working his territory diligently in the meantime) the patient walks in resolutely. With a mixture of defiance and pride he announces that he has brought his *own* matches.

Patient: "I don't want to talk about anything. I've decided I'm not coming back. Things are going better and better. I've had success in my business. I even went to the main office in Philadelphia where I got hell for not having been working right."

Doctor: "Did I scare you with what I've told you, that you're running away?"

Patient: "Partly, I guess. But I think it's healthy, too, what I'm doing."

Doctor: "We ought to talk about the healthy part and the fear, too."

Patient: "I can't put it exactly into words. I don't have enough confidence in myself. I don't want to lose my self-respect. I'm afraid of giving in to my dependency. I want to try to be what I want to be, not some reaction to what somebody else wants me to be."

Doctor: "You've been afraid that your mother wants to convert you into a goodie-goodie, just as you felt she used the priest against your father."

Patient: "I always felt my father's spirit was kind of broken after that. She's had the priest talk to me a couple of times. I know now one thing that you said for certain, that I've been vacillating between trying to please my mother and rebelling against her. Now I realize that I've been fooling myself." (He reviews his adolescence, his drinking and 'running around.') "Now I've decided I want to go it alone. It's the manly thing to do. I want to be independent. I'm going to leave the city and get an apartment near our branch office."

I encourage him, congratulate him, and wish him well. I tell him that if he ever wishes to see me, or if he'd like to drop me a line, I'd be happy to hear from him. Two months later I receive a check from him; the envelope bears the address of a small town near Philadelphia. I write to him at that address acknowledging receipt of the check, and asking how things are coming. To this day I have had no reply. Under no circumstance would I contact his mother, even for information.

CRISIS INTERVENTION

Whether it occurs in the course of therapy or whether it is the sole motive for a single consultation, a crisis for which he seeks counsel from a psychiatrist often arises in the life of a patient. A crisis cannot wait for analysis; it must be resolved quickly. Confronted with an emergency, usually the patient asks the doctor directly for solutions or for decisions. It might seem tempting in brief therapy for the doctor to be directive, seemingly resembling the incisiveness of his confrontative technique. But for the doctor to be directive during a crisis would be a grievous error. There is no guarantee that his solution would be the best for the patient. The possible aftermath of his solution might not trouble the doctor, but it might be intolerable for the patient. Worse yet, to *make* a decision for a masochistic patient is courting disaster. If the decision was not wrong in the first place, the patient will see to it that it turns out wrong eventually. And self-destructive or not, a patient will not experience ego growth if decisions are made for him. Having decisions made for him will only foster infantile dependency and helplessness.

The only reasonable way to help a patient quickly with a predicament is to help him to consider his alternatives and to examine the consequences of each. Then he must choose which alternative is best for him. The following situation is illustrative of a current common crisis.

A 22-year-old freckle-faced boy had called me directly for a consultation. Slight of build, wearing large thin-rimmed glasses, he seemed much younger than his stated age. He spoke spontaneously and earnestly in a youthful voice.

Patient: "I called because I have to make a decision about the draft. I'm student teaching now and applying to graduate school in education. I like it very much and I want to continue. I'm just scared. I heard that they're dropping graduate school deferments. This thing about Viet Nam. I'm just plain scared. I don't know what to do."

Doctor: "What choices have you? And what are the pros and cons?"

Patient: "There's expatriation. But that would mean moving away for good. I couldn't leave the country. That would mean not seeing my family or friends. That's out. Then there's burning my draft card or not stepping forward for induction. But that means five years in prison. I can't see that. . . . I'm not a conscientious objector. . . . That leaves medical rejection. That's very unlikely, because I'm pretty sure I'm physically fit. I wonder about mentally. I guess being scared is hardly what the draft board would call a psychiatric disorder. Some of my friends are going to claim to be homosexual or enuretic. I don't think I'd do that. That would be a shameful thing to have on your record. It would be too humiliating. I wouldn't do that, I don't think."

Doctor: "It depends on whether your fear is greater than your shame. Could you tell me exactly what your fear is."

Patient: "I have this mental-block. I keep thinking I'll come home from Viet Nam without an arm or leg. My fear of being shot at is the thought of being mutilated. I've been afraid of being injured that way since I was a teenager, especially since driving a car. When I was seven or eight, I got punched in the eye once or twice and since then I've tried to avoid fights. Most guys are bigger than me, I'm thin and I'm only five-four."

Doctor: "Can you tell me more about yourself and your family?"

Patient: "I'm an only child. My mother couldn't have any more children after me. I think she had a couple of miscarriages. My father is the greatest guy—if I asked for the moon, he'd get it for me. He's liked by everyone. He helps me with my problems, from talking things over to pulling strings for me. He seems pleased with me. We both enjoy sports—football, baseball. He likes shopping with me. We have the same taste in clothes.

"Now my mother—that's the hard one. I'm not as close to her. I don't know how she feels about me. I can't tell what she thinks. I know she wanted more children."

Doctor: "You think she wanted a girl?"

Patient: "Maybe so I wouldn't be so spoiled, being an only child. She feels I am. Before she thought I'd have a nervous breakdown. Now she tells me that the army will be a great experience."

Doctor: "Could she be trying to bolster your ego?"

Patient: "That's what it appears, reassurance that nothing's going to happen to me. I go to my father for advice. She's the disciplinarian. My father doesn't like the role. She gets mad, screams what I've done wrong. My father tries to calm her and sometimes bears the brunt of her anger at me. It could be over something little, like making footprints on the kitchen floor. She yells at me, 'Good for nothing,' and won't talk to me. She yells at everyone; even the newsboy makes her mad. She runs the family, The Boss. My father is good natured. Whatever she says, goes. She's 54, five foot five. My father is 58, five foot seven. But she runs the show. She didn't want me to learn to drive a car. She said it would hurt my grades and get me in trouble. If my father ever disciplined me, he'd give me a slap on the rear. But my mother would hit me in the face."

Doctor: "Are you aware that you're afraid of your mother?"

Patient: "I never thought about it. I just try to avoid trouble at home. It really got worse ten or eleven years ago. She had a hysterectomy and went through menopause. That made her more cranky and irritable."

Doctor: "So you were going through puberty while she was going through menopause. You give me the feeling that your mother doesn't approve of you as a male. What do you think?"

Patient: "She says she's trying to make me into a better person."

Doctor: "This 'better person,' is it a girl, do you suppose?"

Patient: "I don't think I'm effeminate. I'm just not ready to fall in love. I date, but I don't have a girl friend. You're tied down and required to take them out, do this and that for them."

Doctor: "Where do you observe that? at home?"

Patient: "There, too, and my friends. Right now I don't feel the need for a girl. I'm still a virgin. I'll wait until I get married. I could go to a whore house—I don't want to. It can wait till marriage."

Doctor: "I wonder what influence your observations about your parents have had about girls and marriage."

Patient: "Now that we're talking about it, I guess it's true. I'm kind of leery of girls."

Doctor: " 'Leery'? I get the idea that your fear of being mutilated might be connected with your fear of your mother and her trying to make a girl out of you."

Patient: "Wow! That's something to think about! One thing I realize talking today. I put my father on a pedestal. Maybe I wish he'd stand up to my mother. In the back of my mind, what I've been thinking about this fear is that I'm a sissy. I guess it would be all right for a girl to feel this way. Everyone would expect it. Girls aren't supposed to fight. I probably expected you to say I wasn't fit to be in the army and you'd write a letter to the draft board excusing me because I was a coward. I know I won't do any of those nutty things to stay out. I'll sure as hell try to get a deferment from graduate school and from teaching. If that doesn't work, I'll have to go. I know I have no desire to fight in Viet Nam. They should spend all that money in the ghettoes instead. But we don't make the rules.

"You've really given me something to think about my family. Like it's a whole new ball game. You haven't given me any answers, but I guess I'm supposed to find my own. I guess a spoiled kid would want to get taken off the hook."

Not only are alternatives considered, but the conflicts that underlie them are examined as well. In this instance, the boy's fear of his mother and his wish to please her combined to heighten his fear of/wish for mutilation/castration. This is not to be construed to mean that it is mature and healthy to be fearless in the face of being shot, nor is it a panegyric for the army or for war.

Another example of considering alternatives is the dilemma in which a 40-year-old woman found herself. She was being treated for a depressive reaction herself, when the teenage daughter of a "talented" friend was hospitalized for severe, but ill-defined neck pains. After several weeks of hospitalization and numerous fruitless laboratory examinations and procedures, cervical myelography was contemplated. The young girl, feeling hopeless and despondent, called my patient to tell her that she intended to suicide. The girl's mother always felt that her daughter was overly dramatic, so that she would make light of a suicide threat. Telling the mother about the phone call would be useless. In the patient's words to do that and nothing more would be equivalent to her having done nothing at all. If the girl did suicide, the patient could never forgive herself. Her guilt would be unbearable if she stood idly by while the girl killed herself. The only other alternative would be to notify the attending physician, which would probably jeopardize her relationship with her friend, who could not tolerate others meddling in her private affairs.

After her discussing the alternatives, it became apparent that she considered herself the only force standing between the girl's life and death, a distortion of reality. After all, the girl could have warned her doctor, herself. The patient was fighting her own ambivalent feelings of impotence versus omnipotence.

Her use of the adjective "talented" disclosed an envy of her friend similar to her feelings about her "talented" sister, of whom she had spoken previously. Her guilt about the possible suicide was akin to her guilt about repressed death wishes toward her kid sister. The fear of the loss of her friend's affection resembled her fears of losing her mother's love, a catastrophe that her guilt forced her to provoke repeatedly. One of the patient's symptoms had been a fear that everyone disliked her.

She decided to notify the physician, who, she discovered, had just been given the same information by his resident. A psychiatric consultation was arranged for the girl, following which she was immediately discharged from the hospital. Everything ended well and the patient learned a good deal about herself.

Chapter VI

CONTINUED TREATMENT

THE velocity of the initial interview cannot be sustained in subsequent interviews. Even were it desirable, neither patient nor doctor could maintain the pace. Either emotional fatigue or unending intellectualization would ensue. The doctor's confrontations in the initial interview are his most incisive and important ones. They focus attention on particular problems. Thereafter it is the patient's responsibility to supply the motive power. At the beginning of the second interview, if the patient seems hesitant where to begin, instead of giving him carte blanche to talk about *anything*, which is the usual analytic procedure, the doctor asks the patient whether their previous meeting has stimulated any further thoughts, feelings, daydreams or dreams. A negative response bodes ill for continued treatment and should be immediately challenged. Homework is never assigned; it is assumed. The patient must come to the realization that the treatment is not only fifty-minute periods of intense interaction, but twenty-four hours a day, seven days a week besides, on his own. What he learns from the treatment, unless put to use, is worthless. There is no prize for the best informed neurotic. Insight is no substitute for corrective experience. Awareness of one's punitive conscience is useful only if one battles against it. So long as one gets his measure of punishment, his guilt need never surface to consciousness, and the confrontations of the initial hour will go for naught. Besides, although the patient hears the doctor's words, frequently he does not listen to them. And even what he attends he may not really believe. Often, the second hour is one of testing and retreating by the patient. He may even try to modify, deny and undo feelings that he expressed in the first hour. Usually, the second interview is the most therapeutically disheartening one of the entire treatment. The most common patient gambits are (1) "what you said isn't so"; (2) "if it is true, so what?" (3) "the knowledge that you afforded me has made me worse"; (4) "what new magic do you have for me today?" The doctor's responses are simple. (1) "Time alone will tell what is correct, if you honestly pursue the problem with an open mind"; (2) "If you use what you have learned in your daily living and in your interaction with others, you will find changes for the better." (3) "It is entirely possible that you temporarily feel worse from the unpleasant feelings arising from being made aware of that which you have concealed from yourself. You can obtain relief from those feelings by talking about them with me. Some of those unpleasant feelings are related to anger at me for what I have said to you. Instead of expressing the anger at me, you have turned it on yourself. You can begin relieving yourself of it now, if you wish." (4) "There is no magic. From here on, your efforts will largely determine whether or not you achieve your goal."

One of the most difficult ideas for a patient to comprehend is that the doctor's sole interest, aside from the fee, is to perform his job the best he can, regardless of the results. Likewise, the patient finds it difficult to understand that another person can be interested in his welfare without being personally involved and without being affected by the outcome of his efforts. Very early, the patient tries to prove to himself that the doctor does not really believe what he says, that the treatment is a giant hoax, a massive hypocrisy. He may try to bring in material wholly extraneous to the problem, but potentially very enticing from the standpoint of psychodynamics. Primed by television, novels, and motion pictures, the patient commonly tries to introduce a treasury of sex. The therapist must remain adamant and consistent in his focus. Any material not *related* to the initial hour, and especially if not in the areas of dependency and masochism, should be ignored, not pursued. One might argue that this is a narrow-minded approach to therapy, that the therapist will prove only that which he wished to prove initially. From an analytic viewpoint, that complaint is totally justified. But from the standpoint of brief therapy, the therapist is not trying to *prove* anything. He has made a series of assumptions, not to verify a thesis, but to effect a specific result. No doubt there would be merit to pursue any offering from the patient, were the treatment open-ended. But since brief therapy is goal directed, excursions from the main themes of the initial hour must be avoided. The gentleman with neurodermatitis described in the very first interview complained after unsuccessfully attempting numerous diversions during the second interview, "I feel like today's session has been a complete waste of time." I replied in a tone of total agreement, "I couldn't agree with you more. Now maybe during the next week you'll work on what we talked about in our first visit, so we can get somewhere."

No single case merits its unabridged verbatim presentation. However, the highlights of the continuing interviews of the patients already introduced can illustrate the nature of on-going brief therapy.

A week after the initial appointment of Mrs. B. K., the 32-year-old woman with phobias, we had our second visit. In the interim, I had discussed my evaluation with the referring doctor. He informed me that the day following our consultation the patient had called his office for an appointment, then called back immediately to cancel it. I assumed that she wanted to berate him for sending her to me, and then changed her mind.

Patient: "I can't tell you how provocative our conversation was. When I got home, I found it hard to believe that you said what you did. I wrote the whole interview down on paper and discussed it with my husband word for word. My mother, I told that I shouldn't talk about the treatment with anyone."

Doctor: "You were upset for her to know what I said, but not your husband."

Patient: "The next day I felt horrible, I had such anxiety—the highest anxiety and the lowest feeling of depression. All I do is cry. It isn't like me. I never even cried at sad movies. I feel utter frustration with myself. I'm impatient. I want to get things done quickly. I can take getting depressed once a year and be told, "OK, forget it," as the orthopedists did. But now my fears are spreading. I'm becoming a neurotic person—everything is beginning to worry me."

Doctor: "You're overcome with anger at me and don't know how to express it. Your complaining that you are worse is an oblique way of expressing anger at me, as though you're carrying a sandwich-board saying, 'Dr. Lewin is my doctor and look what a mess he's made me.' "

Patient: "Well, don't the results get to you? Doesn't it upset you that I'm sicker?"

Doctor: "For your sake, it's too bad. But for me personally, I couldn't care less. If you can't sleep, I don't stay awake. If you don't eat, my appetite is still good. If I had to depend on my patients' improvement for my well-being, I'd be the puppet for each one's manipulation."

Patient: "Well, we'll wait to talk about that. Two things, though, seem to corroborate what you said about punishment. First, I don't believe in God—but I'm not sure. Dave (her husband) says that I believe in a vindictive God. He reminds me that he's heard me say 'I hope God doesn't punish me.' Until I was married, I believed in God and said my prayers every night. Perhaps I was influenced by my husband. Dave feels that there's no heaven and no hell. He has no fear of death. He just feels it's 'all over.' Once he wanted to make love on Yom Kipper (the Jewish High Holidays). I was horrified; it seemed sacrilegious. He thought my attitude was inconsistent. I never go to the synagogue or even light candles.

"The other thing concerns a general philosophy of mine. I was happy when I graduated from school. I had everything. There were three stars after my name. Summa Cum Laude. I was grateful; I had my parents, a good job waiting for me, and I was married. But I kept thinking, 'The axe will fall.' Things are going well, I expect something terrible to happen. If Dave gets a raise in income, I begin to worry, 'I hope every one will stay well.'

"I have a problem with Dave's mother. She's just not a nice person. It isn't just me. She doesn't get along with anyone. She's hypocritical. She likes to make a good impression on other people, ingratiating and smiling. Then behind their back she'll cut them up unmercifully. She's tactless with me and a braggart besides. She insults me continually, criticizing everything about me, while she brags about me all the time to others, as though she's a loving mother-in-law. There are many times I'd like to say something to her, but can't. We all went to the opera Saturday night—we've always made that a wonderful evening. His mother gave me a grunt, not even a 'hello.' After the opera, I said, 'I'm too tired to go out and eat,' and we went home. I was so angry at her."

Doctor: "So, who suffered from it? Your sadistic conscience saw to it that you did. Well, I suppose if you're going to talk about your anger gingerly, in our culture the mother-in-law is fairest game to start with."

Patient: "I think you've hit upon something, my difficulty with anger. When it's seemingly under control, I feel feminine and nice. But being really angry—animals fight. I guess I ought to scream and get it off my chest. There's only one incident I can recall about anger in my childhood. I was sick, about age 7 or 8, with tonsilitis, I think. My mother was tired. I lost my temper about something, grabbed on to her and followed her to the bathroom, berating her all the while. What exactly I said I don't recall, but it made my mother cry and I felt horrible—sick inside that I'd done that. I had a big mouth and talked back to adults. Once a word is spoken, it can never be taken back. I have a sharp tongue."

Doctor: "If you do, I haven't heard it. That isn't descriptive of what I've heard—a more appropriate word would be 'avalanche.'"

Patient: (Laughs) "That's it—it's the quantity—it just overwhelms people. But at least my thoughts used to be wholesome."

Doctor: "Get rid of your guilty conscience and your mind will be wholesome again."

Patient: "Dave hollers a lot, at the children. It used to upset me. He works under tremendous tension, long hours. He says in life people aren't going to whisper. He's relegated the checkbook to me. It upsets me deciding who should get paid. He didn't have time to take care of it when he tried to, so phone bills weren't paid and checks bounced." *Anger has now shifted from mother-in-law to husband. Remember her complaints about her father, that the phone bill was a traumatic thing each month.*

"My husband comes home at midnight, sits on the sofa reading a magazine and listening to records. He doesn't come to bed. He says that he has to unwind. He doesn't get to bed until after 2 a.m. and he has to be up before 8. Naturally, it's hard for him to get up."

Doctor: "What about your sex life?" *The double meaning,* *"it's hard for him to get up."*

Patient: "We had our babies by appointment. Don't write that down."

Doctor: "I guess you're feeling guilty talking about your husband to me. Ordinarily, it's only your mother you confide in. Talking about him to me gives you pleasure and makes you feel disloyal."

❋ ❋ ❋

On the following visit, the patient appeared openly angry for the first time. Her tone was icy and she fought to maintain her lady-like composure.

Patient: "You've implied that my mother encouraged me to feel that I was the center of her universe, that she led me on. And you've as much as said that I married my husband because I didn't really want a mate.

"You're very condescending, as though looking down on us. I'm sure you make errors. You make assertions. They're not necessarily correct.

"But I'm not going to descend to what you seem to want me to say. I'm not going to tell you 'go to hell' or 'screw you'!"

Doctor: "You just did."

Patient: "I don't want to come back. It's too much pain. It's not that I want to see another doctor. You're arrogant, egotistical, and self-righteous. After I leave here, I hear your voice saying all those things to me."

Doctor: "Apparently what I've said to you hit home, that you carry it with you and hear the words. But you're absolutely correct about my making mistakes. That was a stupid blunder I made at the end of the last hour, and very pompous, too, comparing myself with your mother in your estimation. However, that doesn't erase the correctness of my other comments."

Patient: "You're right. I am angry at my husband. Now I realize it's my current problem. We have a tremendous verbal ability to communicate. But there are shortcomings. Even though he understands me and my needs, he isn't always able to give me what I want, the day-to-day things—his working hours and the *quantity* of our sexual relations, not the quality, he's not a selfish lover. He cares. But he's dead all the time from work. It happens we go from period to period without making love. It bothers me that he doesn't want me more. The whole time I was pregnant with Barbara (the 6 year old), he made no overtures to me. He's not affectionate, nor demonstrative; perhaps I'm overly romantic. I haven't been perfect. Living with my parents wasn't the best way of starting out. Then I got involved so early with all those aches and pains. That's not being a tempting mate. I guess it turns people off. At first, I wasn't womanly or mature and didn't have many sexual needs, but that's changed as I've gotten older. Now he doesn't even come home for dinner. And when he isn't working at night he's either at a political meeting or with his fraternal organization. He says people have to put up with a lot worse than a hard-working husband."

Doctor: "I guess the kind of distraction an attentive husband could provide you to take your mind off your mother, your husband doesn't provide."

Patient: "You keep on bringing this back to my mother."

Doctor: "That's right, the most important person in your life."

Patient: "Over-attachment, I could accept. But this physical business—"

*   *   *

At the following interview, the patient appeared calm and relaxed.

Patient: "I'd asked my husband whether he'd like to come with me. But he didn't think he'd gain more than from what I told him."

Doctor: "Perhaps you wanted him to see me for your own sake."

Patient: "Not that I'm aware of."

Doctor: "Perhaps you were feeling guilty about complaining about him and at the same time you might have been hoping that I'd tell him to give you more attention."

Patient: "I wanted his approval of you. I thought of our argument—no—discussion last time. Our first meeting took away my confidence. You've made some comments about me and my marriage on assumptions. I feel that enough things you hit right on the head. And the worst of my reaction is over. The big solid revelations that were shocking to me aren't shocking any more. I don't think you're a bastard. Your profession requires detachment. I think you sincerely have my interest at heart. You seem anxious that I continue. You must feel you can help me. And last time, your admission of a blunder, you came off the pedestal I put you on. I appreciated that you cared. I'm not as objective about our marriage as a third person would be. I even think that what you said about me and my mother was right; it's just that the terms were shocking.

"Dave agrees with you that I have a punitive conscience. I go into a tizzy of self-recrimination, I feel horrible, if I do something even unintentionally. Last month I was getting out of a tight parking place and I thought, in backing up, that I heard my bumper touch the bumper of the car behind. There was heavy traffic and I couldn't stop to get out and look. So I drove around the block in a pouring rain, but when I got back to the parking place, the other car was gone. Even though I know at most I touched the bumper, I had this awful feeling that I had done something wrong. All month I've been looking for that other car to see if I damaged it. One part of me told me I was being foolish, getting upset for nothing, while another part had me frantic. What I want to do and what I feel I should do.

Doctor: "What you're experiencing is a conflict between yourself and your punitive conscience, that constantly tries to torment you."

Patient: "And my handling anger. I got involved in a tea with a very good friend, as co-hostess at her insistence. She became emotionally ill and left me stuck with the whole mess, so I had to do all the work. I felt so tense and nervous, even after it was over. Now I recognize that it must have been my *anger* at my friend for having gotten me involved. And this whole eleven years with my mother-in-law eating at me, now I see it's all anger that I've bottled up. I couldn't express it, because one was my best friend and the other was my husband's mother.

"Incidentally, I hate to admit it, but you're right about little girls, too. Dave told me to tell you that you were right. The night before last Susie said to him, 'I don't want to kiss you, I want to kiss my Mommie goodnight,' and then she said to *me,* 'After you finish the dishes and your other work, will you come upstairs and make love to me?' You know, I'd forgotten, but it just occurred to me that I slept with my parents until I was 7 or 8. If it got too crowded, my father would get out and go into my bed. I don't recall much except the last time, when I tried to crawl in with her and she hollered at me that I was too old to get in bed with her."

* * *

A week later she came in with a novel, *Michel, Michel.*

Patient: "I've been reading this book about a little boy, whose custody is being contested by Jews and Christians. Whoever befriends him seems to be ill-fortuned and the boy is guilt ridden, feeling it's his fault. I can see how a child could develop those feelings when as an adult he'd know better.

"My symptoms aren't much better, I give in to them."

Doctor: "It's like saying, 'I'm guilty; I accept my punishment.' By acceding to its demands, you're only appeasing your conscience."

Patient: "I thought our conversation would just make the guilt evaporate. Isn't that how it's supposed to work?"

Doctor: "Only on television shows. Stop punishing yourself and you'll experience guilt as a feeling, not just an idea."

Patient: "Aren't other people angry at their husbands?"

Doctor: "Yes, but they don't feel that they deserve cancer because of it."

Patient: "Maybe I was spoiled by all that attention from my mother, being the center of her universe. Maybe I expect too much from my husband as a consequence. I used to think that a good marriage was a physical attraction, a compatibility of background and interests. But the ones I see aren't so great. This idea of giving so much of yourself to your children that they'll be eternally grateful, a bond of obligation—I wouldn't want my kids to feel that I've sacrificed my own life for them. I'm a free agent, and I want them to feel free.

"You know, for me to say that I'm not much better is grossly unfair. My neurotic habits are only an outward show. Basically, I'm not where I was when I came here. I'm very much more optimistic. It's already been useful to know my feelings of anger. Even if I walked out today and didn't come back, I feel that somehow I'd overcome this."

* * *

The course of treatment of Mrs. D. C., the severely depressed woman, who appeared so aged and retarded, followed a different pattern. At her second interview she appeared much brighter, younger and more animated. Her facial muscles were re-laxed, and the grim expression of her mouth had disap-peared along with the tautness of her jaw muscles. She smiled as she told me that she felt much better, that the pills seemed to be giving her more of a push, more energy (this, in spite of being on anti-depressants less than five days). She also noticed that her sleeping habits had improved. Whereas formerly she had gone to bed early because she was tired, slept only fitfully, and was awake, tense, by 5:00 a.m., now she retired at her usual hour, slept restfully, and awoke refreshed. She spent a goodly portion of the hour discussing her symptomatic improve-ment in her day-to-day work patterns. She returned to the de-scription of her feelings of well-being whenever I attempted to bring up the subject of anger at mother.

Patient: "I've always had a quick temper, although the past week I've been more even tempered with my husband. I've especially been quick-tempered with the boys. After I clean a room I don't want things to be disturbed. All my life I've had to do certain things on certain days. I used to wash Monday, iron Tuesday, and clean Thursday and Friday. Somehow all that changed within the past year. I might do my work at any time, or more likely, not at all.

"But one thing has been constant the past year. I've been a good screamer."

Doctor: "You've had a reservoir of anger full from your anger at mother. If you add only a drop, it will spill over."

Patient: "I never realized it until I came here. How could I talk with my mother about it now? I don't want to hurt her feelings by blaming her."

Doctor: "It might be possible to talk with your mother about it without the idea of blame. You might ask her about her feel-ings at the time she had a seriously ill husband and the respon-sibility of a new baby." *Actually my comment was also meant to suggest compassion for her mother and her circumstances, to soften her hatred and blame of her mother, her introject, and of herself. Obviously, the patient is nearing the goal she set, symptomatic relief, and I am trying to insure its longer en-durance. Who knows how long it might last?*

* * *

At the next interview, Mrs. C. appeared even more lively than the previous hour, but apologetic.

Patient: "I couldn't bring myself to talk to my mother. I felt I might blurt out something that would hurt her feelings. I wouldn't want her to feel responsible. Doctor, I do feel so much better." *I've got what I came here for, please don't force me to interact with my mother and chance antagonizing her.*

Doctor: "You 'wouldn't want her to feel responsible!' Apparently you do hold her responsible."

Patient: "I don't know. I had never been aware of hating my mother in the past. I knew I hadn't been especially close to her these past years since I've been married.

"I know that she always did the best—she never felt I was neglected." *The patient couldn't quite get herself to say that her mother had really done the best she could.*

"One thing did come back to me during the past week. In second grade I got scarlet fever. They'd put a quarantine on our house if I stayed there and no one could have left; my mother couldn't have gone to work. So I was sent to Municipal Hospital and no one was allowed to visit me. I wasn't very sick, a mild case, 'scarletina' they called it. I was there for thirty days. I felt awful. I had my birthday there. I remember crying and not even blowing out the candles on my cake the nurses gave me. I felt pushed out. I never felt I was worth anything to them. How do you go about feeling you're worth something? If your family doesn't make you feel that way when you're small?"

Doctor: "I guess as a child you do tend to value yourself only as you think your mother values you. But as a grown-up you ought to be able to assess your worth, yourself. Apparently, your husband feels you're worth something—he tells you he'll do anything to get you well."

Patient: "I realize since talking with you that I've been cold to my children, just like my mother with me. I hope they don't have the same problem as me. I've always thrown tantrums since my marriage, broken dishes, screamed, and slammed doors.

"But the other night I could feel I was improving. Our youngest son broke a tea pot, a very old heirloom, given me by a friend. I surprised myself. I didn't feel angry, and instead I comforted *him*—he felt so bad for having broken it. Before I would have hollered at him. But I just didn't feel any anger.

"And again the past week our middle boy cut school. He'd

never done that before. He's been the easiest of the three to raise. He'd just gone with a boyfriend to another school to see some of his old friends. His father punished him by restricting him to the house for the rest of the week. But all I thought was, 'Gee, that's not so terrible. I played hooky myself once in a while.'"

Something is altering her conscience; compassion had been foreign to her.

"You know I also thought of my father's father. I was his favorite grandchild, although he didn't see me often. He was very kind. I rocked in a rocking chair with him. He was a fat, jolly man. Yes, he was very kind. In fact my father's family, they'd kiss you the first time they met you. My mother's wasn't like that."

Some improvement could be ascribed to the elimination of the long-acting phenothiazine and its extra-pyramidal side-effects. That cannot explain, however, her softening in her attitude toward her sons and her fond reminiscences of past love.

"My husband has been so repentant. He's basically good to me. I'd been upset with him when he got angry after I got pregnant and then lost my job while he'd started to school. I guess many times I've been angry with him. He's 'the boss!' He's always been 'the boss.' Everything has to be his way. When I was working, I bought a new inexpensive dress. But he never approved of charge accounts. He said if I couldn't afford to pay cash then, I had to take it back. I took it back, but resented his attitude. He's always been strong-willed. At first I tried to exert my independence, but I'm a follower, not a leader. He'll ask me to make decisions on small things, but not on big things like major purchases, or disciplining the kids."

Doctor: "Have you remembered any dreams?"

Patient: "I had one but forgot it when I woke up. But I do recall a dream from childhood that I had several times."

I'm at my grandfather's house (paternal). (The house was old fashioned with low windows. I'd sleep with my grandparents—there were two double beds. I don't remember which.) Somehow I rolled out the low window and down the hill, further and further away from the house. I was afraid. (She has no associations to the dream.)

There seemed to be ambivalence in the dream. She voluntarily leaves the warmth and security of her grandparent's house, probably to return to her own cold family, but is afraid. Her immediate spontaneous comment following the dream is probably representative of the dream's intent.

"You know, I'm feeling well again, as well as I did before I got sick. That's what I asked you for when I first came here. I want to stop our visits."

Doctor: "It sounds like you're declaring your independence here, something you tried and failed to do with your husband. You have a good point. You have achieved what you set out to do. I'll go along with your idea with two provisions: first, that you continue your medication with the exact dosage you are now taking, and second, that you call me within the next week or ten days, just to let me know how things are going."

Patient: "You know, I really wanted to tell you, first off today, that I felt I was ready to quit. But I was afraid to say anything about it before. I thought I'd be put down like my husband always puts me down. I'm encouraged a couple of ways. You see that I'm better, too. You don't think I'm so dumb. And you're giving me a chance to try it *my* way."

Actually the treatment has not been terminated. Only the visits have been terminated. Depending on her continued well being, the telephone "visits," which will last only a few minutes, will be spaced further apart until after several months the medication can be gradually reduced and eventually discontinued. She will be encouraged to call for an appointment if she ever feels the need.

THE TELEPHONE

The telephone is an important adjunct in brief psychotherapy, but must not be abused. In an emergency, patients should know that they are no further from the doctor than their telephone. Other than real emergencies, telephone communication should be reserved for specified purposes. Whenever patients are given medication that they have not received before or doses of familiar medication to which they have not been accustomed, they should be told to call within three or four days and immediately, if they have side effects beyond those about which they have been forewarned. This relieves patients of a great deal of anxiety about taking drugs. Patients who are being treated symptomatically should be instructed to report by phone at specified times. In this way, their dependency is diluted while being continued. If a patient has an intercurrent organic illness during therapy, the telephone is an appropriate medium by which the doctor can express interest or concern. It is also a simple instrument to investigate the fate of those patients whose closure of treatment had been indefinite or those who had been seen for a single specific consultation. The mere expression of interest by the doctor usually evokes an enormous therapeutic response in enhancing the patient's self-esteem. The caring, not the calling, brings results, so if the doctor does not *really* care, he should not call. Insincerity is amplified on the telephone.

Mrs. O. A., the young-looking, asthmatic girl, and her husband had a visit from their families for Thanksgiving shortly after her initial interview.

Patient: "Thanksgiving was a mess. My wheezing wasn't bad enough for me to be in bed. But I needed the mothers' help with the turkey. When they came into the kitchen I announced, 'Which end is the head of the turkey'?"

Doctor: "That sounds like a statement of adorable helplessness."

Patient: "I set the relish tray. That's all I could do. And I helped serve. Fred didn't know how to carve the turkey and neither did I. I felt like an idiot, a fool. I told them Thanksgiving was a failure. I'd wanted to do everything myself."

Doctor: "Is that really true, when you made no actual preparation to do anything yourself? Even without the wheezing, you hadn't even read up enough to know how to stuff or to carve the bird. You were just adorably inept."

Patient: "Put in that light, 'adorable' doesn't sound very nice. I guess I was just being the baby of the family, the pet. The next night I really acted like a baby. I thought we'd all go out for dinner, but Fred came home from work and said he was too tired to go out. I got mad, went out into the front hall and sat and sulked. I was ready to cry. The mothers took all the turkey and left-overs out of the refrigerator and set the table without saying a word. I guess the mothers know their children. After dinner, we all had a good time playing poker. I lost 36 cents. But everyone gave me all their pennies."

Doctor: "That fits."

Patient: "After you called me 'adorable,' I began wondering about what kind of work I'd be suited for. Actually, I don't like to work at all, but I'm afraid I'll be forced to. Christmas will kill us; it will be devastating financially.

"I'd thought of being a teacher, but from the sound of things I'd be operating down at their role, growing up in a world of children. It would be better to work with people of my own level. I can't type well. I'm terrible at math. I used an adding machine in my only job before. The truth is I really don't want to work. I'll need desperate circumstances. All I'm fit for is to learn more. I couldn't work with children until I'm an adult equal with my mother."

Doctor: "I notice you're carrying a book with you about ghosts." *I felt we'd gone far enough into her dependency for the moment and the opportunity to approach the subject of death seemed more important. Why had she brought this particular book to the interview?*

Patient: "There's a question in my mind. Are ghosts real or aren't they? I've spoken with people who've had experience with the supernatural. I'm interested in psychic phenomena and ESP. I've read about witchcraft and voodooism. I know that's all in the mind—people who believe in it actually worry themselves to death, it's not some mysterious force working on them."

Doctor: "What about your feelings about death?"

Patient: "No one likes the idea of dying, of not being—unless maybe you're a devout religious fanatic, live the Ten Commandments to the law and accept everything on faith. I don't like the thought of death for myself, my mother, and father. And now I have my husband. I don't want to think about his dying. I want to hide my head in the sand, I suppose. I can't stand even thinking about Viet Nam.

"My mother had a tumor. She had it since I was three years old. But she wouldn't go to a hospital because I refused to stay with my grandmother. She had it operated on in June a year ago. (The month after the Mother's Day on which her asthma began.) If she'd waited three more months she'd have been dead. The tumor was the size of a basketball causing pressure on the intestines—they had to cut out a couple of feet of intestines. I was terrified before the operation. I thought it might be cancer."

Doctor: "You would have felt to blame if she hadn't survived?"

Patient: "Uh-huh. My mother realized that. The time of the operation was 11:00 a.m., Mother told us. She knew it was 7:00 a.m., but she didn't want us to worry. By 11:00 a.m. she was back from surgery. In the back of my mind, it kept going through, 'If she dies, it's my fault.'"

Doctor: "Do you ever remember wishing her harm?"

Patient: "No. I did hate my father's family and resented spending time with them. But even so, if I wished someone dead, I don't believe they'd die. Like voodooism. I could never picture my mother dead. She looks ten years younger than she actually is. She's been a professional dancer and acrobat. I feel about mother like the existence of God—like *always* being. Around thirteen to sixteen years old I'd talk with my girlfriends. None of us could stand the idea of our parents' death. My father has a massive hernia and an ulcer, but he won't go to the doctor. If I sneeze cockeyed I run to the doctor. My mother says, 'Your father and I aren't going to be here forever.'"

Doctor: "Forever? Do you believe in a hereafter?"

Patient: "Yes. Heaven is all around. Your soul goes there. A spiritual picture of a body without any substance. God is there, everywhere all the time. If you're good, you'll go to heaven, harmony, peace, no fighting. Only very bad people go to hell. No one can be in his right mind to kill another human being. It's not really his fault. He shouldn't be punished. The same with suicide.

"Hell-is-very-empty."

Doctor: "Your idea of dying and going to hell is to be left, deserted, abandoned."

Patient: "Being alone. How can anyone accept being alone? Not being? My first attack of asthma, my toenails and fingernails were black, and I thought I was going to die. I prayed, 'God, please, God, don't let me die.' It was an unfair request. When your number's up, it's up. Everyone goes back to the Creator. No one lives forever. The whole topic of death is frightening.

"When I was about seven, I killed one of my birds, a parakeet. He was almost human, flew around free in the house, and talked. I accidentally caught him in the door and broke his neck. I cried. They got me a new bird and after two weeks I didn't think about him again.

"I have gotten mad at my mother. She bugs me to death. I contradict her in front of people. She twists stories. Like she'd brag to people about my art work. I was only an average art student. I didn't like to be bragged about."

Doctor: "She exaggerates? Perhaps she'd given you an exaggerated idea of the importance of your relationship to her."

Patient: "You mean like leading me on? Being more important to her than anyone else?"

(As the patient takes her checkbook out of her purse, a small plastic container for vaginal tampons is exposed. She becomes very flustered and hurridly tries to conceal it.)

Doctor: "Maybe we can talk about that next time."

Several themes were elucidated during that interview. First there was ready consensus on her dependency, her characterological defense as the helpless, but adorable baby. Her bringing the book into the interview was probably no coincidence. It indicated that she was prepared to talk about ghosts, the supernatural, and death. She seemed confused whether people can actually be wished dead, although she denied it. She felt unable to accept the death of her loved ones (or those upon whom she depended) both because of her guilt in having felt that she might be a causal force and because of her ensuing fear of being left alone. As a defense she thinks of her mother being as eternal as her concept of God, although consciously she is tormented by fears of her mortality. Her spontaneous association to her accidentally killing her parakeet is her anger at her mother, who "bugs her to death."

*   *   *

One week later—

Patient: "I hope I can put my family to rest. They're all dead and buried. My father's relatives." *Apparently there have been unfriendly ghosts floating around. Her expression leads me to assume that she has harbored very unpleasant thoughts toward her father's relations, all of whom are now dead.*

"My grandmother, grandfather, Aunt Mary, and my Great-Uncle Alfred, who was grandfather's brother. They all lived together, and our family went there on a rigid schedule every week. Tuesday from 7:00 to 9:00 p.m., Thursday after school I'd go with my mother and we'd all have dinner. The weekends! Saturday they all played cards from 7:00 to 9:00 p.m. and Sunday we'd be there from 2:00 p.m. to 8:00 p.m. Ugh!

"My grandmother expected me to be perfectly good. Otherwise she'd threaten to call the policeman and take me away. I'd scream whenever I saw a policeman. That's terrible to make a child fearful. Outside of that, grandma was harmless.

"Thursdays sometimes I escaped. Their landlord's daughter was only a little older than me. They were Italian. I said I loved spaghetti, so they let me eat there. No one liked grandpa—always, 'Don't touch this, it belongs to someone.' Aunt Mary was the drunk. When I was young they told me she was sick. So she was a chronic alcoholic. She had a lousy life, had to go to work at 13. My father was the black sheep of the family. He never went to school. During prohibition he ran liquor with a gun under his seat—cool. (She grins.) He was the oldest boy. When he was supposed to be in school, he got his brother to loan him his lamp so he could show his mother how industriously he was working in woodshop. He was such a rebel then. It's ironic, now he's so quiet. Is it old age? Or just poor health? He has that massive hernia, and he's terrified of surgery.

"Aunt Mary—I was her favorite. I couldn't stand her. She'd slobber all over me. I'd push her away. I regret not treating her better. She left me all her money when she died, her pension, insurance money, her jewelry. Altogether it came to $3000 and from it we buried her, so it was only a pittance."

Doctor: "But the gesture alone was enough to make you feel guilty?"

Patient: "I've thought of all the mean little tricks I used to pull on her, like putting rubber spiders on her pillow. She was terrified. A sad thing. She used to buy me little things—candy, or a bag of pistachio nuts. She was pretty when she was young, but she had an accident when drunk and her nose was smashed. Uncle Alfred had tuberculosis and diabetes. He used to make spending money buying bourbon and vermouth and selling Manhattans to Aunt Mary. Sordid.

"I wouldn't go near sick people. I recoil, even from my parents. Everyone hated each other. My grandmother died first, at 73, when I was twelve. We went to the funeral parlor. I said, 'It doesn't look like Grandma.' They'd left off her glasses. They took me up to touch her. It felt like partly unfrozen meat, soft outside, hard underneath. The next day when we were called to the cars at the funeral parlor, everyone kissed her. I got to the coffin and I couldn't kiss her. I got hysterical. My father had to drag me away. That cold, clammy, meat feeling!

"After grandma died, Mary moved into a boarding house and lived alone. I visited her once a week. Uncle Alfred got stoned, fractured his hip and had a ball and socket repair. Months later he was found unconscious in a subway station in insulin shock and with a fracture of the other hip. I didn't cry for him, or kiss him goodbye. His death had no affect on me.

"Then Mary died. It was tragic. She got drunk, and had D.T.'s. One day my father found her dead. She was buried alongside my grandmother. I *never* went back to visit that cemetery again. My grandfather died alone in Florida. That was the end of the family." *Not really; she left out her father.*

"I hate my father's family! The Bible says you're supposed to love your brother. All these years I've been carrying these feelings of guilt. I've never discussed it with anyone before." *It is the end of the hour. But I have forgotten neither the omission of her father nor my request that we discuss her embarrassment about the tampon case.*

* * *

For the first time she appeared ill at ease at the beginning of the next interview and was hesitant to speak.

Patient: "You take notes. My other psychiatrist didn't. If you have so many patients and don't take notes ——. You make me nervous when I don't talk. I once baby sat for a psychiatric resident. He never spoke to me. He was looking right through you, like he was turning your mind inside out." *Apparently she is beset with shame and guilt.*

"You said we should talk about that incident two weeks ago when I got so embarrassed about the tampons in my purse. That subject has always been embarrassing to me, that area, but even my body as a *whole*." *No doubt an unconscious double entendre.* "I was plump in high school, very self-conscious about my outward appearance." *Outward = breasts vs. inward = vagina?* "I'd cry about my weight and my mother would say, 'Then don't eat all that crap.' My constant complaint to her was, 'I'm ugly.' Actually I was conceited, really fishing for a compliment."

Doctor: "From your mother. Apparently you wanted your mother to approve of your body."

Patient: "My best friend was very pretty and got all the boys. She'd run through boys like I ran through nylons. I was always competitive with her—I had more intelligence. I've resented my mother. I'm flat chested like her, I wish I had more."

Doctor: "From your reaction to the tampons and what it implies, from your closeness to your mother and your wish to impress her with your body, I'm not sure *breasts* are what you wanted. What good would breasts do you with her?"

Patient: "It all comes back to me what I said. Jumping in bed with her if I was afraid of the dark. Hop in the middle—keep father from mother—the green Martians—envy—the night light. She didn't want me in bed any more."

Doctor: "You'll have to accept that your mother does love you, but you can't have her and it's not your fault. She's your mother and you're her daughter—it's circumstances—it's not your body to blame."

The patient begins to wheeze noticeably.

Doctor: "Maybe you should cry instead. Let it out."

Patient: "I cry very easily. Our neighbor Martin called me last night, 2:30 a.m. The kitten I gave him drowned in the toilet bowl." *She bursts into weeping, which, as it increases in volume, gradually replaces the wheezing.* Sobbing, she blurts out, "I did resent my father! I did wish him out of the way! He teased me, he frightened me! The three of us would be in the car and he'd kid me by driving down where the East River barricade was and pretending he couldn't stop the car. 'We'd all drown in the river.' I was terrified. Each time he'd do it."

Doctor: "That was a mean way to tease. Perhaps he resented you without realizing it, your closeness to his wife, your mother. He probably didn't realize it wasn't funny to you."

Patient: "I remember he'd delight in telling me while I was eating marshmellows, 'Why do you eat those poor little marshmellows? What did they ever do to you?' I used to cry. Hey, I've stopped wheezing!—I feel like I got something out of my system. Golly, I hope so. It just occurs to me we're going to New York for Christmas to see our folks. I wonder if I'll be self-conscious around them. It does seem creepy. Will I be thinking around mother, 'I want you'? And around my father will I be feeling guilty? Will I still want him out of the way? And I won't be able to see you for two weeks. Funny, I don't feel scared right now—just kind of an anticipation, like

I have to prove something to myself. I won't want to be that 'adorable' me of Thanksgiving."

✿　✿　✿

Two weeks later she returned with little trace of her little girlishness, but still smiling and friendly. Like the title of the Thomas Wolfe novel she began.

Patient: "Things have changed in New York. I was dying to come home (to Pittsburgh). I'm not part of my friends' lives any more. It's not the same. Our old closeness just wasn't there. A lot of them are engaged. I guess it's a cycle; you just can't stop it. But there was a real pang. It hurt. Fred said it would be that way. By the end of our visit I was just dying to get home."

Doctor: "This is the first time that you've used the word 'home,' referring to Pittsburgh, rather than New York. You seem to feel that something in you has died—you were just 'dying to get home.' "

Patient: "Seeing New York, the filth, the looks of it, the crumminess, even the people. I was seeing it as a complete stranger.

"We saw our relatives and got lots of presents. We had our cat with us. Half the time we stayed at my parents', half at his. That's not my home any more. Things don't stay the same.

"Fred was interested in calling you up, just to let you know he's interested. He asked me to tell you, so he doesn't need to call. I think he's a good husband now. I wouldn't trade him in for anything, not for all the tea in China. Cathy, my girlfriend who just got married, is having a baby. 'Secretly married in July'! The baby's coming in June. She was always the picture of sweetness and innocence. I want to have a baby now. Fred said we can't afford one now, so we'll continue with the diaphragm. I wasn't aware that I wanted a baby until I heard about Cathy. Fred says our first job is to get me well, then have a baby. How can you put a value system on it? Are we spoiled? It's nice being two only children!

"The three couples we saw, all old friends, are all engaged. We were still friendly, but less close and more mature. Not 'which discotheque are you going to Saturday night?' but which china and detergent. Domestic. Not little kiddish any more."

Doctor: "And you and your mother?"

Patient: "We had a nice time. There was nothing else. We gave her a slip and perfume. I didn't see that much of her." *I made no comment about that unconsciously voyeuristic remark.* "She worked during the day and we had company at night. The only apprehension I had was at Fred's, for an entirely different reason. They have a watchdog against robberies and burglaries, half Spitz, half Chow, and I was afraid for our cat. I got along fine with my mother-in-law. We talked. In fact all the relations with the families were pleasant. And the only wheezing I've had since I was here was on the night we were leaving Fred's family's for home. I wasn't sorry to go. I was apprehensive about the long drive home. But we took Route 22 back, the scenic route, and enjoyed the ride immensely. Right now I have no desire to go back. I don't want to make that trip again. What I'm thinking about is I'm having sixteen people for a New Year's Eve party at our place. Remember I told you I didn't know anyone in Pittsburgh? We started thinking of all the people we've met and know and we invited them and they're all coming."

Doctor: "Sounds like you're finishing one chapter of your life and starting the next. New York is closed?"

Patient: "Two or three nights ago I had a dream: Two of my pet cats were killed, I was told. Tipsy and Tiger. (Her associations) I was going to call mother to look out for them. They're males, the only ones that go out. Mother doesn't want any more kittens."

Doctor: "You said you were 'dying' to come home. The old you *is* dead—you and your husband, the two only children, the pets."

✱   ✱   ✱

Mr. S. F., the prep school graduate and manager of a supermarket, whose initial interview was the first example in this book, came to his third session friendly, but determined. He had seen that I was willing to engage him and his anger, that I was not afraid to confront him, and that I was still willing to help him.

Patient: "I called the uncle over the weekend and told him I was seeing a psychiatrist because the dermatologist said it would be helpful. He's all in favor of it. He calls me 'Sonny.'

"He told my wife that he's interested in me because of my messed up childhood. He'd been pleased that I'd taken on responsibilities the last couple of years. He has a great deal of money, from personal gifts from wealthy parishioners, and through wise investments. He's seventy-three and has retired as a priest. He gets a new Lincoln every year, but he won't lend me $400. He intends to leave everything to me. For a while I thought he was my father. Maybe I liked the image and respected his intelligence."

Doctor: "Have you ever asked him directly?"

Patient: "No. But he's the kind of a guy who would tell me; he never lies. If it were true, it would be an embarrassment to him, too, of overwhelming proportions, but he'd tell me the truth." *Then why has he never asked him? Obviously, there is some fear that prevents him, perhaps of learning the truth either way or of antagonizing his uncle and jeopardizing his inheritance.*

Doctor: "Then why have you never asked him?"

Patient: "I don't know. You have to remember that I'd tried to squelch all these thoughts until seeing you. I intend to visit him within the next couple weeks and ask him. My grandfather worked on the railroad for fifty years and boasted to my uncle that he never had a bankbook. My uncle told him that was nothing to boast about. My uncle always provided for my education and my mother gave me money when I was young. I took because I was given and I was never trained to do anything else. Now I've got to make my own break. My uncle aggravates me. I once made my own TV set and was proud of the accomplishment, even though I could get only one channel. My uncle saw it and said, 'I have a couple extra ones, take one.' I did, but it gave me no pleasure. I dislike him, but respect him. He's bright, speaks six languages, and has a Ph.D. and an LL.D."

Doctor: "You sound as though you dislike yourself even more for taking from him and have no self-respect."

Patient: "Terribly. Around him I was always treated to opulence. Obviously, his intention was to whet my appetite, to strive for material thrings. Instead I just got depressed. He sent me to an exclusive prep school. I was invited to the best homes in New England. After a while, I stopped accepting invitations, because I couldn't reciprocate. What did I have? A crummy, run-down dump with a foul-mouthed old lady in a wheelchair!"

Doctor: "You feel you have reason to be an angry man."

Patient: "I'm angry with myself even more than at anyone. Why did he show me nice things?"

Doctor: "You turn your anger on yourself. You feel guilty about your anger at your mother and uncle since they took care of you and you're afraid of jeopardizing your inheritance."

Patient: "The school used to send reports every week. If you flunked anything, you couldn't go out for the weekend. At the time I was dating the daughter of the psychiatry professor of the med school nearby. We had a date for the senior prom. That week I got a 75 on a military science and tactics test. It was passing. But my uncle decided that it was too low for me and asked the school to restrict me. I left the campus for the prom anyhow. I was furious at my uncle. I was caught and was busted from cadet major to private. And I graduated as a private, seventh in a class of 175."

Doctor: "So you rebelled at what you considered unfair treatment and you were severely punished."

Patient: "The same with my school-teaching. This kid had disrupted my class for a whole year. For a whole year I wanted to beat him. He was insolent, loud, and made trouble for other kids. One day he was being particularly obnoxious, even though I warned him many times before. So I cuffed him on the side of the head. It took him by surprise and he slipped off his seat. He was a tackle on the school football team and his father was a lieutenant on the local police department. The school board felt I should have exercised more restraint. I was suspended for three years! So I quit. I lost my temper once and I got put down for it."

Doctor: "So in both instances your anger seems justified and yet your punishment was excessive. Does this have anything to do with your wish to be a lawyer?"

Patient: "I thought I'd make a good attorney. I speak well. It's an exciting life, the drama of the courtroom. You're in contact with interesting people. I like the money. And law is interesting."

Doctor: "What field of law?"

Patient: (Laughs) "I intend to be a criminal trial lawyer. I'd defend criminals. Myself, huh?"

At the next hour the fiery redness of his face has paled to a pale pink, but neither of us comments about it.

Patient: "I thought I ought to fill you in with the details that brought on my present job circumstances. After my first marriage broke up, but before the divorce, I left my hometown and went to New York City. For a while, I worked as a chef and did a song or two in the Village. I played piano, occasionally did a soft shoe, and sang show tunes. I was happy there. I lived in one and a half rooms, but I was happy. It was probably the most relaxed time of my life. But I was corresponding with that married woman I'd been going with, who'd moved to Pittsburgh. She's about 27. I came to Pittsburgh to be around her. She claimed that one of her children, her little girl, was mine. That I don't believe. Even she would have no way of being sure. She lived in the suburbs and I got a job nearby. I followed her because she was the only one who gave me love and affection.

"I'd gotten a job doing systems analysis. Within a month or two, I'd devised a system of cutting the time of the process in half. My boss objected that no way could be superior to the company system. We got into an argument and I left. Meanwhile the woman had been taking great gobs of money from me. She would write checks like I've been doing now and she'd come to me to make them good. It was only after I left my job that I realized that she gave me what I'd thought was love and affection only when I had money. She just 'put out' for money. When I had no money she wasn't interested in seeing me. She's called me at my job even now looking for money; I've told her I have none.

"My first wife had found out about her somehow, had me followed, arrested, and fined. When she got the divorce from me, the court awarded her high alimony. I couldn't pay it—I didn't even earn as much as she was awarded! The court put me on probation for non-payment, so I left the state. Years later I learned that she had remarried and all the state charges against me had been dropped. That's another reason I have to be mad at my mother. She knew that I was no longer a fugitive and never told me. All those years I'd been avoiding jobs that might cause my being traced to Pittsburgh and my being discovered. I've been as furtive as a murderer. After all, it was only non-payment of alimony." *Was it really, to his conscience?*

"Now I've decided to go to law school full time. I'll have to save enough money over the next six months. Since I'd been out of school so long, the law school asked me to take a night course or two in the School of General Studies to prove myself. I got an A in expository writing. My uncle always wanted me to be a doctor. He'd sent another poor boy, who's now a famous surgeon. I don't know if he loved me. When I go to my uncle's, I become docile—my wife even notices. Everything is, 'Yes, Father Sam.' Whatever he says, 'Yes, Father Sam.'"

Doctor: "'Father Sam?' Sam is your name."

Patient: "He's Samuel I., I'm Samuel I., his father is Samuel I. Makes you think, huh?

"My wife is tough. You know she works, too, so I help with the housework. If I vacuum, she tells me what's wrong. 'It's for your own good.' She teaches in one school in the morning, at another in the afternoon. Enroute she stops at my store and riles me up by bringing up distasteful things. It may be her visits as well as the job, itself, that upset me. I told her that my doctor said I was crucifying myself. You've shown me what I'm doing, and that has helped. I wonder if I could take up your offer of medicine for my conscience?"

Doctor: "Sure." I prescribe Imipramine 25 mg t.i.d. and Thioridazine 25 mg h.s. and warn about side effects. *He probably needs a sign that I will give him something as much as he needs the anti-depressant and tranquilizing effects of the drugs.*

The following week, the patient appeared almost cheerful for the first time. The only evidence of his dermatitis was the old dark pigmentation.

Patient: (Pleased, proud) "I haven't used any salve for the last two weeks."

Doctor: "Two weeks? That's even before you had the medicine."

Patient: "That's right. But I didn't want to be over-optimistic. Incidentally, I haven't experienced any uncomfortable side-effects. I wanted to talk more about the circumstances of my job. An agency sent me on this particular job for a $500 fee. The owner of the supermarket, Mr. B., told me he'd pay it. Several months later I received a bill from the agency. Mr. B. had reneged on his offer. I never said anything, but it ate at me for a good long time."

Doctor: "Why did you never say anything?"

Patient: "There's more. The supervisor handed all the work over to me, 14 hours a day, every day, no lunch or supper break. The supervisor made $250 a week just for billing. I do everything for $165. The supervisor's always on my back; I was ready to deck him. And the girls are union-conscious, they bicker about when each is supposed to go to lunch. Then Mr. B. promised me a bonus at the end of the year and I never got it.

"I never looked for another job. My wife complained, 'You've had an education, yet you work for nothing, and holler at me on top of it.' After my visits with you, I can see the pattern of punishing myself with my conscience. I seem to thrive on hurting myself emotionally. But this Sunday I *didn't* do what I always do, worry about the week ahead, lying awake over the troubles I anticipate that haven't ever happened. I realized that mechanism was my conscience working on me, just to disturb my sleep and cause me mental turmoil. I said, 'The hell with it' and went right to sleep."

Doctor: "Good for *you!*" *Openly siding with his ego against his conscience.*

Patient: "Where did I get this conscience?"

Doctor: "A child isn't born with a conscience. Your mother had to tell you, 'No, you mustn't spill your milk on the floor.' 'No, you mustn't smear shit on the wall.' 'No, you mustn't tear leaves off the plant.' Pretty soon you took your mother's attitudes. The question is why you have adopted your mother's attitude as being so exasperated with you, rather than her being a benign and loving teacher."

Patient: "Did my mother love me? I could have been used as a lever between my mother and her brother. I may have been a vent for her troubles. Summers I was sent away to camp, winter the military prep school. And every chance I had to come home, I was out with a girl. When I was young my mother hired people to take me to the circus. My mother ran around with that guy from the time I was seven until I was fourteen. One thing, my mother gave me, money. . . . "

Doctor: "You've already told yourself that a whore gets that. You 'put out' for money." *His expression about the married woman—she only "put out" for him for money, when he thought it was love and affection.* "You 'put out' a show of affection to your mother. You 'put out' good grades and obedience to your uncle. Meanwhile you feel worthless, full of anger, full of shit, full of self-revulsion."

Patient: "That's the honest truth. I 'put out.' I've spent my life chasing after someone to love me. That's why I came to Pittsburgh, looking for love from that married woman. I know my wife loves me, otherwise she wouldn't put up with all this shit from me—unless she has a problem like mine. My life with her is harmonious if I don't cash those checks. But it makes me mad when she says, 'I told you so.' Then we fight and I have to be the one that makes up. Now I see why I have to be the one—I need to feel loved. You know my mother and my uncle used to say that to me, almost identically, 'See, if you'd done what I told you to. . . .'" *He connects his ambivalent feelings toward his wife with those he has toward his mother and his uncle.*

Chapter VII

DREAMS

IN brief psychotherapy, dream interpretation serves a function somewhat different than in classical psychoanalysis. There is less emphasis on the revelation of the patient's instinctual impulses and conflicts or their actual antecedents, the events of childhood that may be one source of the dream. While that aspect of dream analysis is not entirely neglected, much more use is made of the dream as a measure of the patient's ego, ego defenses, and conscience. Richness of condensation, imagination, inventiveness, humor, and allusion of the dreamwork itself, usually suggest that the dreamer is intelligent and often, though not always, possesses a potentially good ego, as well as a complex one. The latter impression is bolstered if the patient's ego defenses in various dreams are not stereotyped, and if they successfully ward off anxiety. Since Freud's postulate that dreams are wish-filling[8] seems to be accurate, most dreams in which the patient is thwarted, frustrated, disturbed, or made anxious represent the working of the patient's conscience. The nature and strength of his conscience can be gauged by the manner and degree to which he is thwarted. Freud wrote, "The wishes that are fulfilled in them (dreams) are invariably the ego's wishes." But he also added, "The . . . motive for counter-wish dreams is so obvious that it is easy to overlook it, as I did myself for some considerable time. There is a masochistic component in the sexual constitution of many people, which arises from the reversal of an aggressive, sadistic component into its opposite. Those who find their pleasure, not in having *physical* pain inflicted on them, but in humiliation and mental torture, may be described as 'mental masochists.' It will at once be seen that people of this kind can have counter-wish dreams and unpleasurable dreams, which are none the less wish-fulfillments since they satisfy their masochistic in-

133

clinations."[9] For the purposes of brief psychotherapy, the "plots" of dreams, the patient's instincts and ensuing conflicts, reveal mainly the source of his masochism. The method of resolution of those conflicts, the "literary form" of the dream, represent his ego defenses.[23] *Therefore, the manifest dream content shares equal importance with the latent dream meaning.*

Rapid-eye movement sleep research has corroborated many of Freud's ideas about dreaming and the dream process.[1-7, 20-22, 24-31] First, all doubt has been removed that everyone dreams, whether they remember it on usual wakening or not. Human beings dream approximately the same amount nightly, regardless of personality. That dreaming occurs under the heightened acuity of partial arousal tends to confirm the notion that the dream process, rather than expressing the senseless ramblings of a sleeping brain, represents very active cerebration of a high order. While the dream work may be expressed through any modality of the senses, most dream symbolism is visual, as proven by localized electrical brain activity. Nothing discovered so far contradicts any of Freud's postulates about dreaming and the dream process.

Unfortunately, up till the present time, there is no experimental way to validate Freud's methods of dream *interpretation,* except through the methods of psychoanalysis, itself. Some may argue that these demonstrations of dream analysis are empirical at best, and unworthy of scientific acceptance. Against this argument stands the fact that dream interpretation, using the dreamer's associations as a guide, often uncovers concealed impulses and forgotten actual past events which are later proven to be accurate. Moreover, the analysis of a series of a particular person's consecutive dreams, using the associative technique, reveals a logical progression of inter-connected feelings and ideas which provide internal validation for the correctness of the interpretation of those dreams. Since no better way exists for the understanding of dreams than Freud's, his associative method of interpretation is used in brief psychotherapy, with one addition. If the therapist exercises caution and restraint, he may, if he understands the patient's conflicts and defenses, tentatively use his *own* associations to the patient's manifest dream as an adjunct in comprehending the meaning of the dream *after* the dreamer's associations are exhausted. Once again, if the therapist's associations to a series of a patient's consecutive dreams reveal evidence of progression of thought and feeling, he may have more confidence in their accuracy. On the other hand, if his associations prove random, he had better stop relying on them entirely; he is not "tuned in" to his patient's unconscious thought processes.

This amendment to the associative technique of dream interpretation is not as wild as it appears. The best way to prove its respectability is by example, and the best example would be a well-known dream of a well-known dreamer, namely Freud's first specimen dream in *The Interpretation of Dreams:*[10]

PREAMBLE

During the summer of 1895 I had been giving psychoanalytic treatment to a young lady who was on very friendly terms with me and my family. It will be readily understood that a mixed relationship such as this may be a source of many disturbed feelings in a physician and particularly in a psychotherapist. While the physician's personal interest is greater, his authority is less; any failure would bring a threat to the old-established friendship with the patient's family. This treatment had ended in a partial success; the patient was relieved of her hysterical anxiety but did not lose all her somatic symptoms. At that time I was not yet quite clear in my mind as to the criteria indicating that a hysterical case history was finally closed, and I proposed a solution to the patient which she seemed unwilling to accept. While we were thus at variance, we had broken off the treatment for the summer vacation.— One day I had a visit from a junior colleague, one of my oldest friends, who had been staying with my patient, Irma, and her family at their country resort. I asked him how he had found her and he answered: "She's better, but not quite well." I was conscious that my friend Otto's words, or the tone in which he spoke them, annoyed me. I fancied I detected a reproof in them, such as to the effect that I had promised the patient too much; and, whether rightly or wrongly, I attributed the supposed fact of Otto's siding against me to the influence of my patient's relatives, who, as it seemed to me, had never looked with favour on the treatment. However, my disagreeable impression was not clear to me and I gave no outward sign of it. The same evening I wrote out Irma's case history, with the idea of giving it to Dr. M. (a common friend who was at that time the leading figure in our circle) in order to justify myself. That night (or more probably the next morning) I had the following dream, which I noted down immediately after waking.

Dream of July 23rd-24th, 1895

A large hall—numerous guests, whom we were receiving.—Among them was Irma. I at once took her on one side, as though to answer her letter and to reproach her for not having accepted my "solution" yet, I said to her: "If you still get pains, it's really only your fault." She replied: "If you only knew what pains I've got now in my throat and stomach and abdomen—it's choking me"—I was alarmed and looked at her. She looked pale and puffy. I thought to myself that after all I must be missing some organic trouble. I took her to the window and looked down her throat, and she showed signs of recalcitrance, like women with artificial dentures. I thought to myself that there was really no need for her to do that.—She then opened her mouth properly and on the right I found a big white patch; at another place I saw extensive whitish grey scabs upon some remarkable curly structures which were evidently modelled on the turbinal bones of the nose.—I at once called in Dr. M., and he repeated the examination and confirmed it. . . . Dr. M. looked quite different from usual; he was very pale, he walked with a limp and his chin was clean-shaven. . . . My friend Otto was now standing beside her as well, and my friend Leopold was percussing her through her bodice and saying: "She has a dull area low down on the left." He also indicated that a portion of the skin on the left shoulder was infiltrated. (I noticed this, just as he did, in spite of her dress.) . . . M. said: "There's no doubt it's an infection, but no matter; dysentery will supervene and the toxin will be eliminated." . . . We were directly aware, too, of the origin of the infection. Not long before when she was feeling unwell, my friend Otto had given her an injection of a preparation of propyl, propyls . . . propionic acid . . . trimethylamin (and I saw before me the formula for this printed in heavy type). . . . Injections of that sort ought not to be made so thoughtlessly. . . . And probably the syringe had not been clean.

Here follow my spontaneous asociations. 1. (3) "to reproach her for not having accepted my 'solution' yet." Freud's "solution" represents his seminal ejaculation. (The fact that it is set off by quotes would make it suspect, even if its meaning were otherwise not clear.) Since he reproaches her for not accepting his sexual advances, 1. (1) "numerous guests, whom we were receiving.— Among them was Irma" probably indicates the true meaning of "receiving": granting permission to *enter*. 1. (10) "She showed signs of recalcitrance" refers further to her reluctance to *open up* for him 1. (11) "I thought to myself that there was really no need for her to do that," after all, it's not as though she were a virgin; she is a widow. (My personal knowledge of Fliess and his theory of nasal sexuality makes it unfair to use 1. (15) "modeled on the turbinal bones of the nose," to verify that the aperture in question is Irma's genitals, since it is not a spontaneous association to the dream itself. However, that verification seems superfluous.) 1. (7) "She looked pale and puffy," following the sexual associations, refers to pregnancy. 1. (5) The pains in her throat, stomach and abdomen possibly refer to labor. 1. (13) The big white patch and scabs do suggest an infection, indeed, and, because of the location, no doubt venereal. 1. (25-27) " 'There's no doubt it's an infection, but no matter; dysentery will supervene and the toxin will be eliminated,' " refers to both the venereal disease and labor, possibly anal birth. 1. (28-33) Otto is blamed for the origin of both the infection and the pregnancy, with a "thoughtless" injection from his dirty "syringe." 1. (20-23) Freud is only an observer as Leopold "percusses" (fondles) Irma. The " 'dull area low down on the left' " and the infiltration of the left shoulder are displacements, and if added together rightfully become her left breast, which Freud admits noticing "in spite of her dress."

The meaning of the dream now seems clear. Freud experienced an erotic countertransference to his young widow patient and family acquaintance.[22] He was angry that she had not encouraged his attention, nor had she provided him sublimation for his sexual satisfaction through her recovery from illness. He recognized her need for sexual gratification, and at thirty-nine (his age at the time of the dream) he was envious and jealous of his younger, and probably more virile, colleague, Otto. He obtains sadistic pleasure in Irma's contracting a venereal disease from Otto, as well as a pregnancy under shameful conditions. While Freud admits partially his voyeuristic impulses, he denies any physical contact or intention. Instead he blames Otto. His defenses in the dream-work are denial, displacement, reaction formation, and projection. References to Freud's childhood in the dream are too obscure for further examination. His own associations would be necessary at this point, but not the kind that follow the dream. The presence of the elderly crippled consultant, the voyeurism, and the idea of anal birth suggest that the dream represents some forbidden sexual impulses from childhood.

No doubt Freud consciously recognized a great deal more about this dream than he described. "I myself know the points from which further trains of thought could be followed. But considerations which arise in the case of every dream of my own restrain me from pursuing my interpretative work. If anyone should feel tempted to express a hasty condemnation of my reticence, I would advise him to make the experiment of being franker than I am."[11]

Also, Freud inadvertently left clues in his choice of words and phrases that are indicative of his denied sexual wishes. For example, in giving his associations to Irma's being percussed in spite of her dress, he remembered a celebrated clinician who never made a physical examination of his patients except through their clothes. "Further than this I could not see. Frankly, I had no desire to penetrate more deeply at this point."[12] The play on words of both sentences is obvious. Even more striking are his unconscious references to pregnancy while writing of other subjects in his associations, such as, "Doctor M.'s fertility in producing far-fetched explanations,"[13] and two pages later, ". . . all my writings during the period of their gestation."[14] "The phlebitis brought me back once more to my wife, who had suffered from thrombosis during one of her pregnancies . . ."[15] followed by, "Irma's pains were the result of an injection with a dirty needle, like my old lady's phlebitis,"[16] means phlebitis equals pregnancy. Irma *is* in labor.

My point is not that Freud only partially interpreted his dream. As a matter of fact, his interpretation is correct at one level, my interpretation is correct at another level, and the never to be discovered childhood interpretation would make a third correct answer. Dreams, as condensation implies, can have meanings at several different levels.[17] The point that I do make is that the therapist can often make valid interpretations based on his own associations, after the dreamer's associations are exhausted. But he must be skeptical of his associations until they are validated by further material.

Having less temerity than Freud, I will present the dreams of my patients, rather than my own. They have the advantage of being recorded in the same language in which they were dreamed. The mental gymnastics of dreamwork, idioms of speech, puns, plays on words, double meanings, synonyms, homonyms, onomatopaia, rhymes, proper names and allusions from communication media, cannot be fully appreciated in translation. To interpret correctly a dream from another language and another culture is exceedingly difficult, even with the dreamer's associations.

My first example is the initial dream of a moderately obese, chronically depressed housewife in her early thirties. The mother of two children, she seeks outlets for her energies outside the home in ballet dancing and acting on the stage in semi-professional groups. She had been her father's favorite until his death during her early adolescence. She felt that she resembled him physically. Her mother, dead several years before treatment, was an emotionally cold person, who bestowed what little affection she had upon the patient's slightly older, but pretty and petite sister. The patient had made a loveless marriage, shortly after her sister's, and suspected that her chief endearment to her husband was her considerable inheritance. She suffered a severe chronic sinusitis and bronchitis, but in spite of repeated medical urging she would not give up smoking one or two packs of cigarettes a day. She objected to her obesity, but found it difficult to diet. The immediate reason for her referral was repeated marital strife.

Just preceding her recitation of the dream, she apologized for being attired in her blue rehearsal dress, and pulled down at the hem of her skirt, regretting its shortness over her fat thighs.

The dream itself was simple.

"Someone puts a small blue hippopotamus into a glass bowl." Her associations to the dream were rather constricted. The hippopotamus was a big animal, but it seemed to fit into the glass bowl. Period. I asked who the hippopotamus might represent. Since it was a large, fat animal, she thought it might be herself. Why that particular animal she could not fathom. When pressed about its being blue, she noted that she was wearing a blue dress, that her favorite color was blue, and, in fact, she had worn only blue apparel to my office during her several visits. I asked about the shape of the bowl. It was not a serving platter, ornate, carved or crystal dish; it could have been a fish bowl. (An interpretation of the dream could have been made at this point about her self-image and her exhibitionism, but it would have had little impact emotionally.)

My association at this point was very specific. I asked whether she remembered Walt Disney's full-length cartoon movie, *Fantasia,* which is re-released about every seven years. She lit up immediately and recalled one of the sequences, La Giaconda, The Dance of the Hours, performed by several hippopotami (color not remembered). What had made the sequence funny was the grotesque ludicrousness of those clumsy animals performing ballet. This immediately reminded her of her own dancing and she blushed as she realized her own concept of herself. I repeated her apology then about her thighs, which by its very statement had caused me to look at them while she was busily disclaiming any such intention. In fact, the way the dream was stated, "someone" placed the animal in the fishbowl for exhibition; it hadn't jumped in. She even denies any active part in her exhibitionism although her chief pleasures, ballet and the theater, are performed onstage for an audience! More important there was something masochistic being expressed in her exhibitionism. "Look at me, not because I am pretty, but because I am grotesque and fat. Then I can suffer from humiliation." I asked whether the humiliation might have something to do with her body, other than its fatness. Would a pink hippopotamus have been a girl? Was the blue perhaps to represent not only feeling cold and depressed, but also her wish that she might have been born a boy? (The impregnation phantasy, the animal being placed in a receptacle, did not seem relevant to pursue at this time.) The appropriateness of that question was rewarded with her fond memories of playing with her father's tools in the basement, even though she was forbidden to use them. She reminisced again about her father and her imitation of him, his ways, and mannerisms, and her feelings of loss after his death, but this time with tears.

The interpretation of the dream was aimed at producing an emotional response, rather than merely an intellectual one. A connection was demonstrated in vivo of her actions and her unconscious thoughts (in this instance, her denial of the wish to be looked at). While her wishes to be seen and to possess a penis were interpreted, more weight was placed on her need to *deny* her exhibitionism and on her masochistic manner of punishing herself for the forbidden wishes. Her identification with her father had already been apparent to her, but new dimensions had been added to it. Her feeling of emotional coldness and its implied wish for warmth was only touched upon.

Preferential treatment of material is unavoidable and the patient does not always indicate which path to follow. For the moment pursuit of her masochism seemed operationally useful. Considering her shame about her weight, it was cruel of her not to diet. And considering the severity of her sinusitis and bronchitis it was cruel of her to continue smoking. These observations led to examining her marital strife, where, as one would suspect, she was often the instigator and provocateur, for the unconscious purpose of denying herself love from her husband. This knowledge in turn helped her to see that she was a victim of *self-inflicted* deprivation and misery. The course of treatment would follow her need for punishment, her unconscious guilt, to its source.

In contrast to this rather stolid dream symbolism is the initial dream of a schizoid 26-year-old married woman, a college English instructor, who was referred in the sixth month of her pregnancy because of depression. She had marked ambivalence about her pregnancy, even though it had been planned. In college, she had had psychiatric counseling as a consequence of routine psychological testing, but felt she learned nothing. All her life she had consciously identified with her father, a quiet, intelligent salesman, who had graduated from law school and never practiced. Her mother seemed to be an anathema to the patient, who had not one positive thing to say about her. What could have been praise, had her tone of voice been different, was her ultimate defamation: "All she seems to be interested in is raising her children." The patient had a 23-year-old sister, "who is the opposite of me, talkative, poised, and outgoing," and an 18-year-old brother, of whose low intelligence and general ability the patient was contemptuous. Her relationship with her mother at the time of referral was confined to being told, with the patient's sullen acquiescence, what to wear, how to keep house, and how to run her life in general. Her goal of treatment was to stop hating everyone and everything. Her hatred had caused her to become increasingly withdrawn. While her life in reality was stunted and inhibited, her phantasy life was vivid, especially in her reading. She identified with two characters that she labeled "hebephrenic schizophrenics," the heroines of *Lisa and David* and *I Never Promised You a Rose Garden*. The patient's maternal grandmother had lived with the patient's family for seventeen years, and her mother seemed more concerned about her welfare than about her own husband's. Just prior to this initial dream of treatment, the patient and her husband visited her family and found them all feverishly working to complete four term papers for her brother, Dave, while he sat happily directing them in their chores.

"I had a very peculiar dream last night.

"I was walking down the street alone, holding white doves, like flowers, a whole bouquet. I was eating them. My face was in their feathers, that looked like feathery plants or clouds. They were beautiful and alive.

"One flew away. A lot of them were left. The one that had flown away got under a woman's foot, and she trampled it. It was horribly squashed. I felt so terrible that I let the others go. They flew away as doves, but returned as hawks, as though they still wanted me to eat them.

"I passed an old antique store, where I inquired for a cage. It was too small. But then they shriveled up and became brown, like dead flowers. It seemed very peculiar. I felt sad."

Her associations ran this way. Eating the birds tasted like dry cottage cheese that she had eaten the day before. The doves reminded her of peace. She and her husband were supporters of Senator McCarthy and had a large poster of the red, white, and blue peace bird. The woman's shoes were heavy oxfords, but she recognized neither the shoes nor the woman, of undetermined age. The feathery, cloudlike quality of the birds' plumage reminded her of the popular song, *Both Sides Now*, the words of which describe the singer's confusion and ignorance about the illusions and reality of clouds, love, and life. The metal cage seemed like cold hard reality in the midst of everything else that had an ethereal, almost spiritual quality. The plumage reminded her also of her hair when it had just been washed, clean and feathery. Eating the birds had given her a feeling of cannibalism, for which she could not account. She recalled that in writing poetry she had identified with sparrows, because they were drab brown. She felt plain and rarely used make-up. To her, being a bird also meant freedom. The words of an Emily Dickinson poem, comparing birds to people, came to her, "Hope is a thing with feathers." "I never combed my hair or took care of it." The bird that was squashed was dirty as well, having been ground into a mud puddle.

The initial association of dry cottage cheese seemed to incriminate her mother, the dispenser of tasteless, dehydrated milk. What had been a spiritual experience of peace and contentment, nursing at her breast, had become a source of rage on which her resentment and jealousy constantly fed itself. This seemed to be the essence of her bad introject. Some action of her mother had dashed her hopes to the ground, squashed them and soiled them. They lie now, like antiques or dead flowers, caged and inert. What was the action? Intercourse with her father? The arrival of her sister, brother, and grandmother who took her mother from her? ("Dove" is close to "Dave," her brother.)

I remarked that the dream suggested she'd been a happy, contented child at one time, nuzzling her mother. She replied that she had been breast fed, but had no memories of it, or of her brother or sister being nursed. She did remember her mother's seal coat in which she'd bury her face because of the soft, warm feeling. Because of the dead flowers in the dream, a genital symbol, I remarked that she seemed to have had romantic feeling for her mother at one time, had felt jilted first for her father and then for her grandmother, and had reacted with angry withdrawal and estrangement. Her guilt about her anger at her mother as well as the continued grudge had prevented her from making any mature affectionate relationship with her mother.

Intellectually, she felt that she had accepted my interpretation. I was skeptical, however, because there was no evidence of an emotional response. During the week, she spoke with her mother on the phone and told her how upset she had been at the family's doing her brother's work. Her mother in turn told her that she missed her. She brought a second dream.

"My mother went to bed with my father. Then my sister did. The room was enormous, with rows and rows of beds. My brother was lying on a bed, while I was sitting, waiting my turn with my father. My brother began to masturbate. I told him to stop, but he didn't, and milk, or rather colostrum came out."

Her breasts had begun oozing colostrum recently.

"It almost seemed that my brother was being a girl, his penis reacting like a breast. Something made me jealous on my recent visit home. My mother said that my father's favorite child had been my brother. I thought he was indifferent to all of us. I guess men prefer sons, and women daughters. I lost some respect for my father—I had felt that he was the epitome of morality—when I found he had written my brother's papers for him. Mother told me I had been her favorite and that she even spent more time with me after my sister was born. 'She just growed, like Topsy,' my mother said. I had always felt she preferred my sister's personality, friendly, and outgoing. I have a feeling of superiority to my brother."

My original interpretation seemed vindicated by the second dream. The second dream was a reversal. Her brother on the bed was not Dave, but rather the *patient,* herself, as evidenced by the colostrum emission. While she fancied everyone else was having intercourse with her *mother,* she lay in bed and masturbated, in frustration and anger. The patient responded by recalling not only the guilty masturbation, but the phantasy that accompanied it:

her mother finds her masturbating and yells at her, saying she is filthy. The phantasy has the element of both the repressed wish and its punishment, incestuous desires for her mother, denounced as being dirty. The patient felt that her mother was filthy, having intercourse with her father.

* * *

Skill in the composition of dreams seems to be directly related to intelligence and wit. Certainly the use of condensation in novel ways so that unique symbols represent meanings at several different levels at the same time cannot be performed by a simple mind. The so-called universal symbols may be useful to satirize psychiatry, but they have little value in dream interpretation. It is the personal symbol that communicates and gives dimensions of meaning and ambiguity which evoke emotional response. Emotional responses are essential to brief psychotherapy. Intellectual ones are deadening.

* * *

The author of the following dream is a 54-year-old married woman, the mother of two college graduates. She, herself, had never had an opportunity to go to college in her youth. She came from a poor family in New York, where her father, a strict autocrat within the household, worked as a cab driver. He was rarely home and, when he was, brutalized the family. Her mother was a little dumpy woman, who lived not only in quiet terror of her husband, but was also bullied by her youngest son, junior to the patient by two years. The patient also was frightened of her brother, who was almost always bigger than her and much tougher. She complained that her mother never protected her from him. But neither the patient nor her mother reported him to the father for fear of the severity of the punishment that would befall him. The patient spent her entire youth trying to get one word of praise or affection from her mother, in vain. She also wanted her mother to take better care of her own appearance, since the patient was ashamed of her and her heavy European accent. The only way in which the patient could get her mother's attention was to engage in dangerous childhood exploits, like climbing the Palisades along the Hudson or swimming beyond the patrolled limits of Rockaway Beach on the Atlantic Ocean. Then her mother would wail for someone to rescue her child. Her exploits included a teenage marriage that ended abruptly in a few weeks. Finally, she seemed to have been rescued by a young physician, who was then busily suturing accident cases in a hospital emergency room in order to survive during the Depression. Shortly after their marriage he even became a specialist in radiology, which no doubt should have pleased her mother even more. Unfortunately, the rescuer became the dragon; he was even more autocratic than her father had been before. They fought incessantly, he for dominance, she for freedom of expression. Their two daughters chose sides with the patient, and the husband became their common enemy. Meanwhile, the patient completely lost touch with her family. They had seldom corresponded after her wedding. Her mother died shortly after the birth of the patient's first child, and inexplicably she was not notified until after the funeral, supposedly to spare her suffering. Her father remarried and moved to Florida. An older sister married and disappeared into the West. The whereabouts of her older and younger brothers were equally uncertain. Her marriage shaky, the patient decided that when her daughters were grown she would have a career in teaching. With that in view, she had begun taking extension courses at the local university and at the time of her first interview was within a year of graduate school. An attractive woman, she was hesitant to use eye make-up or a wiglet, because they were "artificial, not a part of her real body." She tended to be plump, and during her adult life by her own estimation she had lost five hundred pounds, "the same twenty pounds about twenty-five times."

She began treatment when, in a fit of temper, her husband attempted suicide with sleeping pills. He refused psychiatric help, but she began therapy in hopes of understanding herself better, so that she might better cope with their relationship. After a short period of treatment, she began to realize how important her mother had been to her, and how her own apparent indifference was a response to jealousy of her mother's affection toward her father. She recalled her horror when she learned that babies were the product of intercourse. She could not believe that her mother would let her father do *that* to her. On Christmas Eve she reported the following dream.

> "I was lecturing. I kept saying, 'To perceive is to ———.' I wanted to say 'conceive,' but couldn't. So I said 'conceptualize.'"

Her association was to be frustrated at not being able to conceive, because she was post-menopausal. She had not realized the date of the dream until I reminded her, to which she responded, "Oh, the Immaculate Conception." She realized that it represented her wish that her mother had not had intercourse with her father, that the dream was a reversal, so that *she* was the informant. Three weeks later she dreamed.

> "I was living in a little room. I was a floozy, wearing sleazy clothes. I started making a sewing machine out of metal parts.
> "Then I was a wizened, skinny old lady and the sewing machine was now outdoors and bigger than a house. Next door were Japanese neighbors, who fought all the time. I told them, 'I messed up my life, don't you,' and gave them advice. I didn't know these people, I just loved the sound of my voice. One day we were outside. Parts of the machine would fall down. The Japanese man would climb on the roof to fix the parts on my orders. And one day the Japanese woman went inside and had a baby."

She had told her husband about the dream that morning and described building the machine, "but it kept losing screws and nuts." She realized the reference to male genitals, but could not decipher the symbolism. The seemingly virgin birth seemed obvious to her. She thought that the sewing machine represented her wish for better clothes in her youth, and a different identity, even if it were a lifetime task. To be thin was part of it. She remembered also that when her daughters were small, they had asked their father how their parents had met. He joked that she had been a dime-a-dance girl and he had saved her from a terrible fate. They would all laugh, and the patient would be angry. The Japanese male she considered the prototype of male dominance; for her to order him about would be to reverse her subservient position.

I inquired about the saying, "As ye *sow*, so shall ye reap." She, of course, then realized that the sewing machine was a giant impregnating machine. This stimulated further associations to "Japanese": little, yellow (cowardly), Hiroshima, radiation, her husband, the radiologist. The Japanese family was a replica of her parent's marriage and her own. Moreover, I pointed out to her that at the time of her marriage, as the doctor in the emergency room, her husband was literally a sewing machine. The over-determination of the sewing machine as a symbol represented condensation of her desire for new clothes, her longing for a different identity, and a wish for a penis and the doctor attached to it, all for her mother. Nor was I omitted from the dream. The patient pontificated without caring about people, her angry view of me and the treatment.

Immaculate conception dreams are not at all unusual, especially around Christmas time. One of the causes for depressive reactions at the Yuletide is the return of repressed feelings of anger, shame, and guilt attendant to the virgin birth. The feelings may emerge in the form of never having been given the gift that was really wanted for Christmas. Or they may be represented by nostalgia for the family reunion at the holiday. Pregnancy wishes, sibling rivalry, and envy over male supremacy represented by the male infant Jesus are other conflicts triggered by the twenty-fifth of December. The whole Christmas legend contains elements of almost every human conflict. But the most common reaction in women seems to revolve around the immaculate conception and virgin birth. Apparently, the only mother fit to worship is one unsullied by any male.*

Some time later, this same 54-year-old college student took her graduate record examinations for qualification for entrance into graduate school. Ruefully, she related that her conscience had really gotten the best of her during the examination. She thought she had completed the first part of her test only to discover upon

---

* One must marvel at the sagacity of the theologians two thousand years ago, who, flying in the face of scientific knowledge, recognized that no child, male or female, would worship a mother who had had intercourse even with her own husband. A Virgin Mother insures that idolatry of her will not give way to disillusionment and cynicism.

beginning the second part of her timed examination that the first part had another section on the back of the page. As a consequence, although her grades had been excellent, she scored very low and was not accepted at the University of Pittsburgh graduate school. Instead, she had to enroll at a school which she considered inferior for her graduate work in education. The following week she reported a dream.

> "It was a golf dream. I went to tee off on the first tee and it was bedlam. Young kids were milling all around while people were teeing off. In the middle of the first tee was a barbecue pit with a very tall chimney that obstructed the view from the tee. Everyone had to hit a blind shot over the pit. I felt annoyed and indignant. I drove off and knew that my ball was lost."

She had no associations to the dream other than to remind me that she golfed from spring to late fall and enjoyed it. Perhaps "teed off" was colloquial for anger, but she was not consciously aware of any anger. The dominant symbol in the dream was the barbecue pit and that brought absolutely nothing to her mind.

I asked whether the dream might have any meaning if "pit" were capitalized and spelled with two t's.

> "Ooh! Pitt! The tall chimney, the Cathedral of Learning. The young kids—my envy and jealousy of my youthful classmates. The golf course—I'm starting on my Master's course work, and Pitt stands in my way. The blind shot? I'm embarrassed to tell you. The graduate record exam is not the only reason I didn't get in at Pitt. I was taking a course from a blind professor and was doing very well. I asked him to write a letter of recommendation for me to submit to the graduate school. But shortly afterward he read a paper in Braille in class, a paper which he said was one of the best he had ever received. I felt that it was pompous, overly long, and tedious, and told him so. We got into a rather violent argument, actually. I was pretty vituperative. After class, I suddenly realized that if he read it in Braille, very possibly it had been his own paper, and I had really insulted him. So I really slit my own throat twice, once with that dumb mistake on the graduate record exam and then picking a stupid fight with the person who was supposed to

help me. My conscience was really working overtime. I have a vague recollection that in my dream my ball went out of bounds and into a haystack. I think the school that accepted me is a real "hayseed" place and I will be less than proud to have my Master's degree from there. But I can hardly complain, when I fully realize that I did it all to myself."

The story of a young woman's thwarted sexual desires toward her mother is enfolded in this dream of a very pretty 21-year-old college senior dramatics student. She entered treatment because of continued panic reactions at bedtime over a period of six months. The onset of her illness coincided with two events, a moderate flirtation with marijuana and an unsatisfactory initial attempt at intercourse with her boyfriend. During her panic reactions, she noticed increased heart rate, palpitation, alternating hot and cold feelings in her limbs, and fear of impending death. Two years before, her father, a minister, had had "a nervous breakdown" and resigned from the ministry. For some unknown reason she carried in her wallet a newspaper clipping of his resignation. She surmised that she was in love with her father and assumed that for that reason wanted only an intellectual relationship with boys. It soon became apparent, however, that it had been her mother who held her heart, and that at the age of three, when her brother was born, she had turned spitefully to her father for affection. She had a screen memory of being left alone in the house to fend for herself at the age of four. Her mother had fought with her father for many years prior to his breakdown. Since his illness her mother had attacks, to which the patient's were almost identical, though milder. Her mother informed the patient, shortly before the onset of her illness, that her father had been having an affair with another woman. The patient was disillusioned.

"I'm in an airplane alone, except for the stewardess. I asked whether I could see the pilot. She said I couldn't. I went up front anyhow. The pilot was drugged, doped, stoned—like on pot. I stayed and watched the landing.

"Then there was a flash of a scene at the base of the Matterhorn in the Alps. An old man was rummaging through old plane crashes. He looked up and spoke of a little boy who had died there. I assumed he'd once been a pilot, who survived an old crash. Now he was too old to go up again.

"The first pilot took off in another plane with passengers. I was on it, telling everyone that the pilot would crash his plane into the Matterhorn. We were flying over water. Our best chance would be to jump into the water, unless we hit one of the islands. Three of us held hands and jumped. Then suddenly I was the pilot and had a view of me, an evil looking woman at one side who kicked the escape hatch sardonically. She (I) went to the cockpit. I saw the Matterhorn. I headed the plane right for it and yelled, 'I hate you, Matterhorn!,' and crashed the plane right into it. I awoke."

Her immediate association was to note one thing immediately apparent and significant. "Matter" equaled "Mother." She had felt an incredible anger, hatred. What she feared most was death in a plane crash. Her mother had the same fear. "I figure the old pilot is you, a wise person; I assume he'd lost a plane in a crash and was now too old to go up again." I replied that I did not think I was *that* old. She understood the sexual meaning immediately and jokingly apologized. She had read somewhere that water was a symbol for mother. The hatch she felt was an allusion to birth. The two co-jumpers may have been her older sister and younger brother. The island brought back John Donne's lines, "No man is an island unto himself," so island meant man. She remembered that the stewardess was part of the crew, and indeed in the school productions she was often part of the crew (stagehands). The drugged pilot seemed to be clearly a reproduction of her reactions to marijuana. She recognized every role as her own (but one), a theatrical tour de force. The little boy who died may have represented death wishes toward her brother.

There seemed to be two views of her mother, one a secure haven for safety through regression, and the other a cold, forbidding, indestructible object against which even her rage is impotent. Her sadistic feelings toward her mother's genitals seem to be expressed in her kicking the hatch. She had tried to reassure herself that her father was safe; he was too old to "go up" again. That illusion was shattered when her mother told her that he had run off with another woman. He *could* go up again. That seemed to trigger her illness. In the dream her last act was to plunge her last "self," the phallic airplane against the mountain in futile fury, like Hamlet, dying, running the king through, shouting, "Here's an onion (union) for you."

Her reaction to the dream and to its interpretation was to understand intellectually but to have no feeling. "Nothing seems to penetrate," she complained. Apparently, I replied, she was a junior Matterhorn; nothing was supposed to sink in, as her boyfriend had ruefully discovered. She realized at that moment that she had been playing a role with her boyfriend. She was her mother, and he, her father. By seeing to it that entry was unpleasant, in fact painful, she had restored the phantasy that her mother never enjoyed intercourse and performed the act as a duty. She then confessed that she had omitted something from the dream. The old pilot had given the exact number of crashes on the mountain—sixty-nine. She had been embarrassed at her immediate thought, which she had sought to conceal. The only sexual contact she could figure two women having, since neither has a penis, was oral-genital.

Repetitive dreams are not uncommon.[18] In this particular dream series, one particular symbol is repeated, and the progression of the dreamwork leads to a résumé dream which is practically an encapsulation of the whole conflict. The dreamer is a 48-year-old married secretary, the mother of a 20-year-old son, who was referred because of a depressive and paranoid psychotic illness of almost a year's duration. The onset of her illness during menopause coincided with personnel changes at her office. Following the hiring of a 23-year-old attractive girl, the patient began having delusions of persecution and reference. She felt that the telephones were being tapped, that the office manager was conspiring to replace her, that the office personnel wouldn't eat her Christmas candy gift because they feared she had poisoned it, and that people were hinting that she was a lesbian. Several months prior to her being seen, but well after her illness had begun, her next oldest sister by two years had died suddenly of complications following a hysterectomy. They had not been on speaking terms since the sister's divorce and remarriage, supposedly because of their conflicting religious views on divorce. The patient's father, with whom she had been exceedingly close, died of heart disease when she was fourteen. Admittedly, she had never recovered from his loss; they had been inseparable. Often, she had accompanied him on trips where ordinarily one might expect a wife to be taken. Her mother, now partly senile, she remembered as always having been a cold, detached person. Her childhood memories were of her mother's pulling her hair and calling her a witch around age five or six. The patient recalled having reacted more to her mother's grief over her father's death than to her own. Her mother had remarried twice, the last time when the patient was in her thirties. The patient was not very close to her surviving siblings, a sister fifty-four and a brother forty-four. She recalled very little about her reactions to his birth. Her own marriage had been satisfying until her illness, when she became irritable and lost interest sexually. All her life she had had an aversion to anger and avoided it whenever she could. Her symptoms responded within several weeks to Amitriptyline and Trifluoperazine. She reported the following dreams.

> "It's about a dog. I was alone in the house and a dog came to the door—it was the same dog my husband and I had about fourteen years ago, a male beagle. Apparently I had this dog, neglected it, hadn't fed or watered it, or taken it out for a year. I thought he must be starving, not having had anything to eat for a year. He didn't look hungry. I let him go back out, but he came back later scratching at the door. I still didn't feed him; I don't know why. It kept bugging me that I kept wanting to give it something to eat, but I didn't."

She awoke, thought briefly about the dream, went back to sleep and dreamed again.

> "The same dog was there, only this time he was emaciated. Parts of his coat had fallen out, and he was weak and bony. I still neglected him. I was very upset. At that point my dead sister came in with a new little puppy. I was angry with her for bringing in a new puppy, while I'd neglected the one I already had.
> "I thought of giving the beagle some warm milk and started heating it. I looked for meat, but couldn't find any in the refrigerator. Then I found some in the freezer—it was soft. Then

I became frightened when I looked inside his mouth. It was all red and irritated; there were no teeth. Meanwhile, the milk on the stove had gotten too hot. I found myself going to pieces and I awoke."

She remembered that her son was about seven when they had the dog. She had wanted a female dog, because she felt they were better with children; they could take more abuse. They actually had bought a female cocker spaniel first, but it got distemper and died. She had always been afraid of strange dogs. A German shepherd had attacked her brother when he was small and only the intervention of a mailman had saved him. They had to get rid of the beagle because he snapped at children. The puppy made her think of babies. She couldn't get pregnant after her first delivery, although they had tried almost immediately afterward and from then on. She was concerned that she may have neglected her son unintentionally. She had worked since he was twelve and allowed that she didn't cook the same or care for the house as well afterward, and had to satisfy herself that she couldn't do too much about it. About the dog's lack of teeth, she remembered that her father had had all his teeth pulled because of pyorrhea three days before he died. The doctor had diagnosed his arm pains as arthritis coming from infected teeth. She herself, had lost a good deal of hair at age 9 from scarlet fever; her mother wouldn't come near her, for fear of transmitting it to her brother. When the doctor suggested putting her into the municipal hospital, her paternal grandmother agreed to take care of her. She remembered her grandmother trying to coax her to eat, and attempting to get her temperature down.

I told her that I felt that she was the dog, neglected by herself the past year, and feeling neglected by her mother during childhood. The scarlet fever memory typifies her feeling that her mother preferred her brother to her, and she felt guilty about her jealousy and rage. She made herself a male in the dream because this is what she felt her mother would have preferred. While the German shepherd mauled her brother, she herself was a weak dog with no teeth. In fact, she couldn't even tolerate a fight. Her pacifism seemed to be a reaction formation and denial of her rage. What she really wanted was her mother, the milk and meat.

She had turned to her father out of revenge, having felt neglected by her mother, but in reality probably wanting her mother all to herself.

Several weeks later she reported the following dream.

"We're having a family affair, my husband's family and my own, in two houses. I'm talking to all the people. I wanted my purse but couldn't find it. I had everyone look for it. My sister, the one who's dead, came with her first husband; they'd been reconciled.

"I was kissing everyone goodbye. I couldn't find my husband, or my coat, or purse. I left with my husband's brother, but without Frank, my purse, or my coat. We went trotting down the street, he pretending to be driving. He fell, and one of his teeth was knocked out. (She points to her canines.) I tried to put the tooth back in his mouth. He tried to kiss me. I pushed him away. I didn't want him to.

"I went on my way alone. I had to go through a big market. There were people outside. Two men in a meat truck were carrying meat into the store. A big black dog kept trying to get at the meat. Saliva was coming out of his mouth. The dog became angry at being kept away from the meat. He grabbed a little girl and threw her around like a rag doll. A woman, then a man tried to intervene. The dog killed the girl, the woman, and the man. The police came and shot the dog. Then a truck, like a garbage truck, took away the dog's body. Although I had been terribly upset by what the dog did, I didn't try to help because I'm petrified of dogs."

Her associations were sparse. She didn't know why she was dreaming about dogs. She couldn't fathom why the dream should have shifted from the happy occasion of the family reunion to the tragedy in the market. I asked whether there couldn't be another meaning to an "affair." She replied an "illicit romance." I said that the "affair" she seemed to want was with her mother and that she was willing to sacrifice everything, her identity and her marriage, for it. (Her coat, purse, and husband.) While she saw herself as weak and edentulous, she managed to snatch something from a male that gave her strength and potency. Thwarted from her goal, she'd strike out at bystanders in the family (father, sister, brother, mother) until her guilt caught up with her and her conscience disposed of her. Her father and sister actually had died. Because she feared such consequences, she controlled her temper completely.

She felt the anger, but found herself unable to express it. For the first time she was aware of her rage at her mother, "If I can't have what I want, being angry isn't going to get it for me." She had become aware during the past several weeks of erotic feelings toward me and saw similarities in the conflicts, not being able to have what she wanted, her anger, and her excessive control of it. She remembered her mother's washing her mouth out with soap if she used bad words. For the moment her mother's attitude prevailed, and no "bad words" came out. However, she complained that her desires for me kept her in constant torment. She tried to throw her arms around me. I told her that she had a rather unusual conscience. On one hand it would not allow her to say certain words, yet it entices her to have thoughts about me that torture her, and it allows her to enact them. She seemed to be behaving as inconsistently as she viewed her mother. She knew that her mother was having intercourse with her father. But the same mother washed her mouth out with soap for merely saying certain words. To the patient her mother's actions were certainly more wicked than her own. I compared her mother's idea of conscience with my own, in which any thoughts were permissible, but their enactment would have to follow an acceptable code of social behavior. And while I might admonish her for her rashness, there was no need for her to be tortured as a consequence. Self-restraint would do.

The last dream of the series indicated her beginning acceptance of the reality that little girls cannot expect to have their mothers; only their fathers can.

"I'm back in the neighborhood where I was raised. It was a Saturday evening and I was shopping alone. I was in a butcher shop. I got a slice of ham. At the check-out counter, the girl didn't wrap it and just put it in a bag. Then I went into another butcher shop. There were four butchers. They had cut too many steaks; some were unsold. They didn't want to keep them over the weekend. Somehow, like a game, they all started throwing those steaks at each other. One butcher threw a steak at me and I caught it. He said that I could keep it. The girl put it in the same bag with the ham, also unwrapped.

"I walked past a row of houses. My cousin Betty (my mother's sister's daughter, a year and a half older than me) came out and asked me to come in. I declined because I was in a hurry to get home. The juices from the meat, co-mingling, were saturating the bag. But a big dog came over. He was interested in me, not the juices from the meat. I was afraid of the dog and turned back to Betty's. The dog followed me and got his head inside the storm door, but I closed the inside door and the dog went away."

She recalled, of course, her previous dreams about meat and therefore, even though she was not entirely convinced of the correctness of the interpretation about the beef in the previous dreams, assumed that the steak was her mother. That it was unwrapped, she further assumed represented nudity, being unclothed. The game of the butchers reminded her of her feelings that men, as a rule, play fast and loose with women. The steak was only a plaything. She had no association to there being four butchers, her mother having been married only three times. The ham brought thoughts of an Easter meal several weeks hence, the Resurrection, and her own dead father. This led to her association that the ham (her father) and the steak (her mother) were lying together, naked, with their juices co-mingling (saturating the bag). She insisted, however, that in the dream the dog was interested in her, not in the contents of the bag she carried. Considering that the patient, herself, seemed to be the dog in the other dreams, that part of herself that she denied and projected onto the animal (envy, jealousy, greed, anger, curiosity, and frustration), this last dream apparently represented a primal scene in which the patient, as a small girl, was aroused by curiosity and sexual excitement into some kind of auto-erotic behavior (the dog was after her, not after the contents of the bag, and got part-way inside).

Only a short time afterward, the patient had another series of dreams which seemed to be about the same subject, expanded and clarified. The first two were the same night, the last two, a week later.

"I had just gone to bed when I heard a loud noise, perhaps from the basement. I went downstairs and opened the basement door. Cold air rushed out. Under the stairs, a cement block had fallen out. I got a ladder, put the block back, mixed up cement and patched it. I was pleased with my work."

The patient wakened from the dream, almost immediately fell asleep and dreamed again. "I was destitute; I had no money, no job, no place to stay. I was offered a job where I'd be expected to cook, clean, and take care of the others there. A woman showed me around. It was filthy dirty. In the next room, three men were lying on a bed watching TV, and all that work to be done! It irritated me.

"I was going to do the dishes. But where? There was a big bathtub, also filthy dirty. There was a big hole in the wall and when I looked inside, it was a big swimming pool with a ledge around it. On the far side was my father on his hands and knees. He said, 'If we clean this out, we could do the dishes here.' "

The only spontaneous association the patient had to the dream was that the missing block might be related to the treatment, that she was trying to find what the trouble was and remedy it. I replied that if that were the case, she certainly was avoiding looking at it, because she plugged up the wall without investigating further the sources of her *coldness* (the cold air in the dream and her symptom of sexual coldness). I asked whether she had any memories of noises at night as a child. She did not. I repeated the question, adding specifically whether noises emanated from her parents' bedroom. (The setting of the dream was certainly suggestive of such an event. Even her statement "under the stairs" could have been a voyeuristic play on words, "under her stares.") Again she denied such memories. Her avoidance in the dream was consistent with her memory.

However, since her second dream contained another hole in the wall which she pursued further, I also pursued the second dream further. Her spontaneous associations to the hole in the wall, which she then called a cave, where warmth, security, and her mother's womb. The only time she had been destitute was in childhood, and she really was expected to help with the housework, which she sometimes resented. She was puzzzled by the appearance of her father, whom she had never previously seen in a dream. She also wondered why he was on his hands and knees. Her only associations to such a position were supplication, prayer, and intercourse. I suggested that if that swimming pool did represent her mother's womb, it was certainly scornful and derisive of her to suggest in the dream that it was large enough to do the dishes, but was so dirty that it had to be cleaned. She agreed without feeling.

I told her that the dream contained a message similar to that of a vulgar joke. A girl and her father, in the family horse and wagon, are waylaid by outlaws. After a fruitless search for valuables, the bandits make off with the horse and wagon. The daughter triumphantly reveals to her father that she has concealed the family jewels inside her genitals to which he replies, "Smart girl. Too bad your mother wasn't here—we could have saved the horse and wagon!"

To this the very proper patient laughed heartily and replied with a joke in the same vein. A woman goes shopping for shoes, but forgets to wear underpants. The salesman, looking up from his task, murmurs, "I wish that were full of ice cream." That evening, indignant, the woman tells her husband of the incident. He retorts, "You didn't need shoes, and you should have worn panties and, and—who could eat so much ice cream?"

I ignored the oral-genital implications of her joke and merely commented on the affirmation of the idea that it was insulting to a woman to infer that her genitals were stretched into largeness by repeated intercourse. She giggled and brought forth another joke. A priest visits a sinner in hell. He is astounded to discover the sinner with a girl on his lap, and a goblet in his hand. The priest expresses astonishment. The sinner sadly laments, "Things aren't as they seem. The wine glass has a hole in the bottom and the girl doesn't." At this, the patient could barely contain her mirth.

I replied that she seemed to derive quite a bit of pleasure from the sinner's discomfort. Apparently, the source of her coldness was her anger at her mother's sexual activities with her three husbands, probably symbolized by her father's position by the pool. Her own coldness to her husband was an undoing of her mother's pleasure in intercourse, both an expressed wish that her mother had not enjoyed intercourse, and revenge on men for having despoiled her mother. "Recementing the block" guarded mother's genitals.

The following week she had two dreams.

> "I was back home. My older sister had lots of books. I wondered where she got them. She was putting them in the closet in my mother's bedroom. It was so cold in there. I thought that there was an air-conditioner there, but it turned out to be some kind of safe. I was curious about it and was going out in the hall to ask mother, when I tripped over a cord. I followed the cord; there was a vacuum cleaner in the hall. I was very annoyed and put it in my mother's bedroom. Her room was a mess. The floor was all dirty. I thought, 'I have the vacuum cleaner now, so I'll clean.' My father was there. I told him about the sweeper. He said, 'Why should you? You have enough to clean.'"

The books in her mother's closet immediately reminded her of the medical encyclopedia that was kept there. When she was sick in bed as a child, she was permitted to look through it. The book was full of pictures. There was a human body in the front of the book with color plates layered with muscles, blood vessels, nerves, organs, and a skeleton at the bottom. The musculature was the first plate. There was not a nude person. However, she was curious about the body and its functions. She had no other associations.

I commented that the coldness of the closet seemed similar to the two previous dreams, probably related to the same subject. And "safe" was a word similar to "security and warmth" from her previous womb dream. Very likely the "air-conditioner" was an "heir-conditioner." "Oh," she responded, "then that wasn't an electric cord, but an umbilical cord. But why a vacuum cleaner?"

"How does a vacuum cleaner work?"

"It sucks up the dirt. Sucks! My baby brother—that's what annoyed me in the dream."

"That is the source of your anger, your coldness, and your mis-trustfulness—your betrayal by your mother."

"But my problem is no different from other girls."

"It's the way you dealt with your problem. You forgot the source of your anger. You blamed it on your mother's pulling your hair and calling you a witch. In anger you probably provoked her from the time your brother was born until she finally retaliated with the name-calling and hair pulling."

"That makes sense. I've been angry with you for not responding to my romantic notions about you."

"Had I responded like your mother, we'd be in the same bind. What do you make of your having the vacuum and not using it?"

"I wanted to nurse my son, but I had no milk. Is it possible that your mind could do that, dry up your breasts?"

"Perhaps out of guilt at not wanting your brother to have any milk, you couldn't nurse your own son as punishment. Remember the dream about the hungry dog that you couldn't somehow feed?"

"I had another dream about a dog this week. I was back home, alone. I went to see my cousin, Alice, who lived across the street. She had company for dinner and was holding a woman's baby, about nine months old. None of them recognized me. Even Alice ignored me. I tried to think of some excuse to be there, like borrowing a cup of sugar, but I couldn't think of anything. I felt very uncomfortable being ignored.

"Everyone left. I offered to help Alice with the dishes. My husband came in. I remembered I put my key down somewhere and I couldn't find it.

"Then the scene changed. We were next door to our house, at Alice's grandmother's, still looking for the key. They had a small brown and white dog who didn't know me and kept barking at me. He wanted to go out and got entangled in my feet. I pushed him inside and got out myself.

"The scene changed again. I'm at an indoor swimming pool, still looking for the key. It's crowded. I ask if anyone found the key. No one did. My husband came in, all wet. He said a woman had a bathing cap full of water and threw it at him. He didn't know her, but thought I might. She was a little 'off her rocker.'"

Her only comments were about the repetitious symbols, the

dog and the swimming pool. I asked whether this dream might not be that of a little girl estranged from her family on account of a new baby, looking for the key to get over her feeling of alienation, asking to be recognized, offering to be helpful with the dishes. She thought it could be very possible. She also thought that she was the lady "off her rocker," but she didn't know what the bathing cap and water meant. I suggested that her revenge, wetting her husband, was intended for her father, for what he had been doing on his hands and knees in the previous swimming pool dream. What was the bathing cap, if not a big rubber? To a child the act of intercourse is interpreted as being urinated on. Therefore, the appropriate revenge is to wet the man. In that case, she responded, there must be an additional meaning to "the key." The key must be a penis. She must have wanted a penis, envying her father's, she said. However, her self-revelation brought forth no memories.

The chief functions of dream interpretation in brief psychotherapy are to make the patient aware of his unconscious thought processes, to connect his conscious behavior to motivations visible in his unconscious thoughts, to illustrate for him his defense mechanisms, and to demonstrate the role of his punitive conscience in thwarting his success in dreams and life. The style of interpretation should be calculated to elicit an emotional response from the patient rather than mere intellectual assent. The therapist's associations may be used cautiously after the dreamer's have been completed.

REFERENCES

1. Dement, W.: Dream recall and eye movements during sleep in schizophrenics and normals. *J. Nerv. Ment. Dis.*, 122:263-269, 1955.
2. Dement, W.: The effect of dream deprivation. *Science*, 131:1705-07, 1960.
3. Dement, W.: Discussion of Snyder, F.: Toward an evolutionary theory of dreaming. *Amer. J. Psychiat.*, 123:136-142, 1966.
4. Dement, W., and Wolpert, E. A.: The relation of eye movements, body mobility, and external stimuli to dream content. *J. Exp. Psychol.*, 55:543-53, 1958.
5. Ephron, H., and Carrington, P.: Ego functioning in rapid eye movement sleep: Implications for dream theory. In, Masserman, J. (ed.): *Science and Psychoanalysis*, vol. XI. New York, Grune & Stratton, 1967, pp. 75-102.

6. Fisher, C.: Psychoanalytic implications of recent research on sleep and dreaming. *J. Amer. Psychoanal. Assoc.*, 13:197-303, 1965.

7. Fisher, C.: Dreaming and sexuality. In, Loewenstein, R., Newman, L., Schur, M., and Solnit, A. (Eds.): *Psychoanalysis—A General Psychology: Essays in Honor of Heinz Hartman.* New York, International Universities Press, 1966, pp. 537-568.

8. Freud, S.: Papers on technique. *Op. cit.*, p. 122-133.

9. *Ibid.*, p. 159.

10. *Ibid.*, pp. 106-107.

11. *Ibid.*, p. 121.

12. *Ibid.*, p. 113.

13. *Ibid.*, p. 114.

14. *Ibid.*, p. 116.

15. *Ibid.*, p. 118.

16. *Ibid.*, p. 119.

17. *Ibid.*, p. 279.

18. *Ibid.*, p. 247.

19. Freud, S.: The ego and the id (1923). In, Strachey, J. (Ed.): *The Complete Psychological Works of Sigmund Freud,* the Standard Edition, vol. XIX. London, Hogarth Press, pp. 12-66, 1961.

20. Friedman, S., and Fisher, C.: On the presence of a rhythmic, diurnal, oral instinctual drive cycle in man. *J. Amer. Psychoanal. Assoc.*, 15:317-343, 1967.

21. Goodenough, D.: Discussions of Ephron, H., and Carrington, P.: Ego functioning in rapid eye movement sleep. In, Masserman, J. (Ed.): *Science and Psychoanalysis,* vol. XI. New York, Grune & Stratton, 1967.

22. Grinstein, Alexander: *On Sigmund Freud's Dreams.* Detroit, Wayne State University Press, 1968, p. 22.

23. Lewin, K.: The value of psychoanalytic literary criticism. *Psychiatric Communications,* 5:103-106, 1962.

24. Luce, G., and Segal, J.: *Sleep.* New York, Coward-McCann, 1966.

25. Roffwarg, H., Dement, W., and Fisher, C.: Preliminary observations of the sleep-dream pattern in neonates, infants, children, and adults. In Harms, E. (Ed.): *Monographs on Child Psychiatry.* New York, Pergamon Press, 1964, pp. 60-72.

26. Roffwarg, H., Muzio, J., and Dement, W.: Ontogenetic development of the human sleep-dream cycle. *Science,* 152:604-619, 1966.

27. Schur, M.: *The Id and the Regulatory Principles of Mental Functioning.* New York, International Universities Press, 1966.

28. Snyder, F.: The organismic state associated with dreaming. In, Greenfield, N., and Lewis, W. (Eds.): *Psychoanalysis and Current Biological Thought.* Madison, University of Wisconsin Press, 1965, pp. 275-316.

29. Snyder, F.: Toward an evolutionary theory of dreaming. *Amer. J. Psychiat.*, 123:121-136, 1966.

30. Stone, L.: *The Psychoanalytic Situation.* New York, International Universities Press, 1961.

31. Tauber, E.: Discussion of Ephron, H., and Carrington, P.: Ego functioning in rapid-eye movement sleep. In Masserman, J. (Ed.): *Science and Psychoanalysis,* vol. XI. New York, Grune & Stratton, 1967.

Chapter VIII

FAMILY THERAPY

THE confrontive technique is especially useful in a family setting. Very often an individual will become aware of his own conflicts and defenses when he sees similar conflicts and defenses exposed in other members of his family. The interaction of a group process serves to heighten awareness of feelings. In fact, the confrontative method with a family serves almost as a laboratory model, with the experimental evidence unfolding before everyone's eyes. It is very difficult to maintain denial, when more than one person confronts an individual with reality. Both intrapsychic and interpersonal processes emerge.

Ordinarily in group therapy (the family is a small group), the leader is relatively passive, intervening only when absolutely necessary. Interpretations are usually of a general nature. Confrontation is rare. Instead, the group leader's comments are frequently protective and supportive, since his intervention means that the group action has not been as constructive as he feels it might be.

In the confrontative method, the therapist is very active and alert for any opportunities to enlighten the group. Inconsistencies are questioned at once. The therapist does not hesitate to instruct in the most forceful way. It is not unusual for him to say, "You're wrong," or, "This is not consistent with what we know about human feelings and behavior," or, "This is what a child may feel under these circumstances." That does not mean that he only attacks aggressively. On occasion, it is necessary for him to protect just as aggressively, if for some reason a member of the family cannot withstand the group's confrontation. Usually, however, the cohesiveness and solidarity of the family bolster the ego of each member, just as in any group process. Very often, that very defense is the therapist's undoing, should the whole family align themselves against him.

All of these general statements will become clearer with actual clinical illustrations. Several initial family interviews will be presented with a minimum of editorial comment. The reader may decide that the interviews may have gone in other directions had he been in the therapist's place, and perhaps to better advantage. Hindsight is not being offered as an excuse, because were the interviews to be repeated, I would probably conduct them similarly again. The focus depends upon the therapist's personality and what he wants to accomplish.

Case Illustration: The first family interview is that of Miss J. M., a 14-year-old girl, and her parents, in their early forties. Miss M. was referred to me for consultation regarding a therapeutic abortion. A very small wisp of a girl with pale blonde hair, pale white skin, and pale blue eyes, she had a rather pale interview with me while her parents sat in the waiting room. Clearly, her intention in coming was the piece of paper excusing her from her pregnancy, like an excuse from gym. Her whole attitude was of penitence, as though she expected a great deal of stern moralizing from me. I assumed that she might have had that kind of response from her parents or from her family doctor and expected more of the same from me.

She had been dating an 18-year-old boy for six months. "I guess I made a mistake letting him go on—I don't know why—I thought he'd known better. It taught me a lesson." Everyone in school knew about her pregnancy, because she told her boyfriend in the hallway outside the doctor's crowded reception room. She described her mother as being "real hypertensive." Because her mother was easily upset, the patient rarely confided in her. Her father was a calm, quiet person, but she never talked much with him. There were three sisters, 21, 18, and 7. When asked about her relationship with them, she remembered her mother's story that the patient cried when told about the baby's coming. She, herself, felt that she had received a great deal of attention from her mother, who did not want her to start to school. The patient believed that her mother had another baby to keep her company. Miss M. had little reaction to my confrontation that her sister was now the same age as she was, when her mother had a baby the patient did not want; her unwanted baby was now both revenge on her mother for *her* baby and punishment for the patient for wanting revenge. She did admit that her mother had become very upset about her pregnancy. "Her blood pressure got awfully high. If it didn't go down, she'd have a cerebral hemorrhage. I worried about that." She had never been able to express anger or resentment to her mother. She denied ever wishing her mother harm. Her goal in life was to become a school teacher. Her life plans did not include marriage. She had no idea why she had so little interest in marriage. She showed no response to my comments about her masochism, her attempts to ruin her life as punishment for her bad thoughts toward her mother and sister. At that point in the consultation, I felt that for all the good the interview had done, I could have saved us both a great deal of time and energy had I just written her "gym excuse" and foregone my vain efforts to expose her sick conscience. After informing her that I wanted to speak with her parents in her presence, I asked whether she had any objections, whether there were areas that she wanted me to avoid, and whether there were things that she had forgotten to tell me. (Legally, as well as ethically, I had to discuss the situation with the parents of a minor.) She had no objections and nothing to add.

At first glance, it seemed apparent who wore the pants in their family. The mother was a tall, dyed-blonde woman, who strode confidently into my office, after a crisp greeting. The father was a small, completely bald-headed man, whose round rimless glasses gave him a wise-owlish look, undermined, however, by a very small, weak chin and a tiny mouth. He stammered a tentative, "Hello," and then scurried to look after the wraps left behind in the waiting room. His whole mien was a caricature of Casper Milquetoast. His wife set about to see that we were all comfortably seated so that we could begin the interview. She chose the chair I had been sitting in. I pulled up two others, while the patient remained sitting.

Mother: "May I sit here?"

Doctor: "Anywhere you like. First of all, I'd like to have some idea how you all see this problem so that we can discuss it. I hope we can speak freely."

Mother: "I'm sure I will. It's a problem I certainly don't understand. I kind of think it's my fault."

Doctor: "How's that?"

Mother: "Well, because I feel—my husband takes part responsibility for this—Janet is eighteen and the older girl, they were never permitted to go with older boys when they were that age. The girls take a lot of my time—I try to devote as much time as I could to them. As she grew up, I grew more relaxed—they grow up faster and you relax more with each child. She told me how old he was, that he was a nice boy, I said, 'You'll have to prove this to me.' We didn't permit him to go with her alone for a long while. One evening he asked if he could take her to a drive-in alone. He'd been coming to the house long enough that I felt I could trust him. From that day on I trusted him."

Doctor: "Well, what do you see as the problem?"

Mother: "I should have clamped down on it and said 'No, he was too old for her,' right in the very beginning."

Doctor: "And do you think that would have prevented her from doing what she did?"

Mother: "I believe so. When I said, 'No' to the other girls, they listened to me and I swear she would have done likewise. Now she won't see any more of him. That's it."

Doctor: (To father) "How do you see the problem?"

Father: "I agree with my wife. I should have stepped in. I was reluctant to—"

Mother: (Interrupting him) "I said to him, 'You'll have to help me here and take an upper hand, each girl is growing up faster.'"

Father: (Falls silent)

Doctor: "All three of you are approaching the problem from a different point of view than I am. The question in my mind is not why your daughter had intercourse. The question in my mind is why your daughter got pregnant. You all approach it from a moralistic point of view; this is not my point of view."

Mother: "Is that right?"

Father: (In a wee voice) "That's right."

Doctor: "Why did your daughter become pregnant? She could have had intercourse any number of times without getting pregnant. She knows about the birds and the bees, this is the twentieth century, and the young lady is intelligent."

Mother: "Right, 'Why?' I don't know."

Doctor: She doesn't know either; that's why I'm presenting the problem. It's something you all have to know, or it may be repeated not only in this fashion, but other ways."

168

Mother: "Right."

Doctor: "Okay. Let me pose a supposition. Suppose this pregnancy was not an accident, but unconsciously intentional. We know no attempt was made to prevent pregnancy. You have to ask yourselves, 'Why didn't she insist on using some kind of contraception, some kind of protection.'"

Mother: (Hopefully to daughter) "Because she didn't know about it?"

Patient: "I knew about it."

Doctor: (To parents) "Something inside her drove her to get pregnant in an attempt to ruin her life. I have seen many young ladies in similar situations and I have discovered that they *all* unconsciously *tried* to get pregnant. All three of you are approaching this pregnancy as though it is the crime. I say, 'This is not the crime; this is the punishment.' We have yet to discover what the crime is. Are you following my reasoning?"

Father: "I follow it all right, go on."

Doctor: "Let me ask some questions that may seem irrelevant. When your daughter was seven years old, you had another baby. Could you tell me about it? Her reactions?"

Mother: "I can't remember. When she first found out her mother was pregnant, she went into her room, closed the door and cried. She'd come home from school and found me in a maternity dress. I hadn't told her yet. She knew enough about pregnancy, she knew I was pregnant. She said, 'Mummy, you didn't tell me. You didn't tell me, Mummy,' and she went into her room, shut the door and cried. From that day on, I thought she had accepted it" (with a rather sudden sound of defeat).

Doctor: "Everything went underground. I presume she'd been babied quite a bit for seven years."

Mother: "That's true, she got a lot of attention. We did many things together as a whole family. With my pregnancy all that had to go down the drain. I was sick a lot."

Doctor: "So her relationship with you underwent a drastic change."

Mother: "Yes—a drastic change."

Doctor: "She was seven years old."

Mother: "Right."

Doctor: "But no longer the baby of the family."

Mother: "Right."

Doctor: "She tells me you were reluctant to let her go to school."

Mother: "Reluctant to let her go? (laughs heartily) Oh boy! that's true. The first morning she went out to catch the bus, I cried. First time I would be alone. I'd always had one of them with me at home."

Doctor: "Is it all right if I tell your mother why you thought she got pregnant?"

Patient: "Um-huh."

Doctor: "She thought you felt since she had gone to school you needed a new baby in the house to keep you company."

Mother: "No, that's not true."

Doctor: "Okay, but that's how she feels."

Mother: "I think that's a natural reaction for a child her age."

Doctor: "Yes, that the baby is a replacement. Get rid of this one, get another one."

Mother: "Right, natural."

Doctor: "Now think, how old is your baby daughter now."

Father: "Seven."

Doctor: "Doesn't that strike a responsive chord? Your seven year old daughter is exactly the same age as this daughter (nodding toward the patient) was when *you* had an unwanted pregnancy. I don't know if you both realize *how much* it means to a child when a new baby comes, if you realize what the child who has been succeeded feels toward her mother and the baby. Have you any notion of the kinds of thoughts that the child would have to her mother and the baby?"

Father: "I'm an only child."

Mother: "And I'm the youngest."

Doctor: "So neither of you would know." (To the patient) "Isn't it interesting, you see, your parents have not any experience, neither your mother nor your father, that would enable them to know what you must have gone through when the new baby came." (To the parents) "Well, I'll tell you, not only for you to know, but also for her, because otherwise she might feel she's peculiar. The older child usually wants to get rid of the baby, kill it, flush it down the toilet, chop it into pieces, get rid of it somehow. In addition, she'll resent the mother, and have similar angry thoughts toward her. Every child. She may not express it. It may go underground. She cried and that was the last you heard of it. But the feelings persisted and she felt guilty about them.

"Who was told first in the family of the pregnancy?"

Mother: "I was."

Doctor: "And what was your reaction?"

Mother: "I don't remember."

Doctor: (To patient) "Is it all right if you remind her?"

Patient: "She was upset—extremely—she had high blood pressure—she might have a cerebral hemorrhage."

Doctor: "And die?"

Patient: "And die."

Mother: "Oh—yeah—"

Doctor: "Her pregnancy, in her mind, threatened your death."

Mother: "Nobody told her that. I had to go to the doctor."

Doctor: "What you are seeing is revenge and punishment. Your daughter is enacting the guilt of her anger at her mother's pregnancy and her punishment is to try to ruin her life with hers. The act for which you are angry with her is not the crime, but the punishment. She is doing to herself what she wished on you. It's her life that would be ruined."

Mother: "She'd wanted it to happen to me."

Doctor: "And it's perfectly normal for the seven-year-old to have wanted it, that's what I'm trying to tell you today. Your daughter remembers nothing of it, she's obliterated it. She doesn't even remember her crying."

Mother: "Are we an unusual family?"

Doctor: "It happens all the time. That's why I'm trying to reassure you. Everything that happened, except for her guilty conscience, is perfectly normal. Some people accept these feelings as normal. And some kids carry their guilt around with them all their lives and ruin themselves. I'm trying to nip this in the bud. She's only fourteen. There are other ways to ruin her life. She can drop out of school. She can get on dope. She can marry a gambler, an alcoholic, a scoundrel. She can walk in front of a truck. I'm trying to get this out in the open now, so that she can work out her feelings about her guilty conscience and not have to ruin her life. You hear about mental hygiene, that's what I'm trying to do today. The letter to the doctor is a mechanical thing, over and done with; that's not what I'm concerned with. The meaning of this episode, I'm trying to help you, so it will never happen again, so you never have to walk into an office like this again. Now I've made quite a speech, what do you think?"

Father: "What do you suggest is the right thing to do, doctor?" (in a wee little voice).

Doctor: "There's the answer" (gesturing to the patient). "None of us has any direct control of the situation. All I ask of you is an open mind—to accept people's feelings. Anger is a normal feeling."

Mother: (Musing out loud) "Anger is a normal feeling—."

Doctor: "What's going on in your mind?"

Mother: "Have him (pointing to her husband) tell you about it."

Father: "What?"

Mother: "Because I objected to being pregnant. He says I built hatred up against him, because I was pregnant. You say that's normal?"

Doctor: "It's a reaction to certain feelings and circumstances. You had hatred over your pregnancy? Which?"

Mother: "The last one."

Doctor: "You didn't want to get pregnant?" (With surprise.)

Mother: "Uh-Uh" (shaking her head vehemently).

Doctor: (To patient) "How about that! She didn't want to get pregnant."

(To mother) "How did it happen? Or would you rather not discuss it in front of your daughter?"

Father: "It's better we don't discuss it."

Doctor: "How about that. She didn't want to get pregnant" (to patient, whose mouth is open with surprise).

Mother: "She knows that."

Doctor: "No, she didn't know that. She assumed you wanted the baby to take her place, because she's going off to school, remember."

Mother: (As though she has finally taken a definite stand and is getting a chance to relieve herself of a feeling long pent-up) "Well,—*I'll* tell you about it" (spoken slowly, deliberately, with a defiant glance at her husband). "Because she's old enough to know about the birds and the bees and I'll tell you why.

"We are Catholic. I wasn't a Catholic all my life. I'm a convert. Of course, after having had three children we felt that it was enough for us. And we—it's the law of the church—rhythm system is approved. So that's what we practice, because my husband said he could get it down pat."

Father: (Looks very uneasy, distressed, pale, glances apprehensively at his daughter, then at his wife. He seems to be frightened and angry at what he anticipates his wife will say.)

Doctor: (To wife) "May I caution you for a moment." (To husband) "You have already said you don't want to talk about this in front of your daughter. Is there going to be recrimination against your wife? I don't want that to happen. I would rather shut her up if that's going to happen."

Father: "No, it's all right."

Mother: "She knows what—rhythm system is."

Doctor: "But your husband may think there's something personal here that he'd rather not discuss."

Father: "No, it's all right."

Doctor: "Don't say it's all right if it isn't, because it will have to come out somewhere. I'd rather you said, 'No, shut up.'"

Father: (Laughs loudly)

Mother: "I will—."

Doctor: "I want to hear it and I'm sure your daughter does, but there may be reasons why it shouldn't be said." (I am being especially protective of the husband because not only does he seem quite passive, but his wife's venom is obviously dripping with her every word at this point.)

Father: "No, there are no particular reasons. It's okay" (very quietly).

Mother: "So—we—were convinced by a relative to—that it had worked with them and so we should try it. And it failed. And I said, when we started the rhythm system, I said, 'Don't you ever get me pregnant.'"

Doctor: "You knew that it wasn't 100% effective."

Mother: "But he assured me that he would be able to—get it down pat."

Doctor: "No one can 'get it down pat.'"

Mother: "Well, I mean, I—I love him and whatever he says goes" (she laughs loudly, but cheerlessly).

Doctor: "Obviously you didn't believe him."

Mother: "No. But he can—he has a way of making me believe things."

Doctor: (Turning to the patient) "Miss M.—, you are not

the only one, you are not the only one who is self-punitive in the family. Okay?"

Patient: (Nods, wide-eyed.)

Doctor: (To mother) "I am saying to you that you took an active part in this, that it was no more an accident for you than it was for her. I don't know why you need a cross to bear."

Mother: "So I got pregnant and I remind him of it" (surly).

Doctor: "Was that fair to do to him? You knew that it was going to happen. You're holding him responsible the same way that your daughter is holding fate responsible."

Mother: "Right."

Doctor: "You had just as much responsibility in getting pregnant."

Mother: "I believe it" (with sincerity).

Doctor: "You were playing Russian roulette, too."

Mother: "Right."

Doctor: "You've been taking it out on him all these years?"

Mother: "I have."

Doctor: "Isn't that unfair?"

Mother: "Now that you bring it out, it is. But it's the only way I have to express anger in the house. We're not allowed to raise our voices."

Father: "That's right. I guess it's my fault. I was raised with the idea that anger was unnatural. For you to say it's normal today is a new idea for me. In my family, we didn't raise our voices, just as my wife said. In fact we were told that anger was sinful and I've raised my family the same way. As you can see, I'm a very quiet, soft-spoken man. I keep my anger inside. I know that all these years it's been difficult for my wife to hold her anger in check, long before that last baby."

Doctor: (To mother) "What had you been angry about?"

Mother: "When I said I hadn't wanted a fourth child, I was thinking of my mother. She had ten children. There was no time for me (bitterly). She was so busy all the time. And she was cranky and irritable all the time with all the work. She died of high blood pressure—she had a stroke."

Doctor: "Exactly the way you felt you'd go—high blood pressure and a stroke—does the punishment fit the crime? Is *that* your cross to bear?"

Mother: "You mean that I might have had feelings of anger to my mother similar to the ones you pointed out that my daughter had to me? That really could be. I remember feeling guilty at times that I got so angry at my mother. That's the main reason I didn't want to have more children, myself. I wasn't going to have a big family like her. No time for me.

"And my seven-year-old is terribly spoiled. It's a big problem in our family. She demands constant attention. I guess it's hard for me to discipline her. I bend over backward being nice to her, because I feel guilty about not having wanted her."

Patient: "I always thought she was your favorite" (obviously shocked).

Mother: "No, honey, it's that I felt guilty about not having wanted her."

Father: "I can see that this thing is a problem for the whole family. Part of the problem is my fault. I can see that not expressing anger, feeling guilty about it, or holding it in, can cause trouble."

Mother: "You see! All that time you told me to learn to control my temper. Things are going to be different!"

Doctor: (Taking the wind out of her sails) "I hope so. Especially now that you should realize that much of the anger that you wanted to direct at your husband was really meant for your mother, that the pregnancy that you want to blame on him was, to a great degree, of your own making, to punish yourself for anger at her."

Mother: "I hadn't looked at it that way. From that point of view, I've been very unfair to my husband. He's been a scapegoat, then, for my mother" (chastened). "Then I've been using him. Truthfully, I haven't thought about my anger at my mother until just now—I haven't thought of it until it came up today—not since I was married. That's part of why I married when I did. My husband knows how anxious I was to leave home. This is the first time since we're married that I've consciously thought about, let alone expressed, any anger at my mother."

Doctor: "Then apparently everyone here today has to learn to accept these feelings as being human, your feelings and those of everyone else in the family. Our time is up. If you should feel the need to call me again, please feel free to do so. I feel that with this help you might be able to work things out yourself."

Father: "I've learned a lot today."

Mother: "I know I talk too much. But you got to me, too." (She begins writing the check for the visit and I comment that perhaps she feels that she is too aggressive, perhaps her husband could start writing the checks.)

Father: "I get what you're driving at. You don't just mean the checks."

Mother: "So do I. (To her husband) "I'll cooperate if you will. I must have been angry and guilty at my mother all these years. I guess all the time I've been complaining about you, I've really wanted to be the aggressive one."

(The patient takes up her mother's coat and helps her put it on.)

Doctor: "That's very nice. Maybe next time, though, you'll let your father do it. The union between husband and wife comes first, even if they seem to disagree at times. The child mustn't come between them, no matter how lovable she is. Let me hear from you how things are, okay?"

Patient: "Okay. Thanks—for everything."

Notice that many of the doctor's comments, seemingly directed at one person, were meant to be heard by another. The doctor talked a great deal, but it finally primed the pump. The problem of mother and child spanned three generations.

Case Illustration: Mrs. O.G., a 24-year-old woman, was referred because of self-induced starvation, abdominal pain, diarrhea, and vomiting without organic pathology. Normally weighing 105 pounds, she was now down to 75. Her loss of appetite extended for over a year. Two years prior to her consultation she had married for the first time. Her husband was compulsively frugal about food from the very start of their marriage. Nothing was to be thrown out; everything had to be consumed before it could be replaced. The patient at first resorted to shopping every day in small amounts. But she discovered that even then certain items spoiled. A loaf of bread lasted perhaps a week, and after the first two days became increasingly stale. No fresh bread could be purchased until the old loaf was finished. The patient tried, unsuccessfully, to change her husband's mind. He was adamant. The money that they saved on food would go toward the purchase of a home some day. She was unable to take a firm stand. Instead she resorted to the passive-aggressive weapon of a well-concealed hunger strike. As the food became tasteless, her appetite for all food diminished. Finally, when her family became alarmed and the family physician assessed the state of her cachexia, both an attorney and a psychiatrist were consulted. At the time of her initial visit, the patient had separated from her husband and had instituted divorce proceedings. However, her appetite continued to slacken apace and her weight melted away.

Mrs. G. had the appearance of concentration camp atrocity victim. Small in stature, her small brown eyes, sharp nose, and tiny mouth seemed isolated structures in a skull thinly covered with pasty white skin, dotted with pustules. Aside from her skeleton-frame, the only other noteworthy detail was a stomach bloated by hypoproteinemia. All she seemed to need was a sandwich board sign, reading, "My husband did this to me," for her attitude was that he was entirely to blame for her condition. Why she had not left him sooner, and why she had chosen this particular defense of turning anger inward upon herself were questions about which she had little interest.

Mrs. G. was one of twin daughters of upper middle class parents. She was not aware of any negative feelings toward her twin sister, but thought that the sister might be jealous of her. Her father owned a manufacturing plant and was away on business a good deal of the time, even before the birth of his children. Of recent years, his wife had started accompanying him. The patient's description of him was that he was "all business." He ran his family as though it were a small industrial office. Meal time and after dinner conversations were run like a board meeting, with agenda and voting. The patient accepted with quiet annoyance the aphorisms that he poured forth in the home. Mrs. G. did not seem to have a very clear picture of her mother, except that she missed having her around. She felt that since her marriage her mother had withdrawn from her and seemed rather cool at her returning home after her separation. The patient's other sister, older by four years, lived in another city and the patient was unreservedly and unashamedly envious of her mother's showering of attention on the sister's six-year-old daughter, the only grandchild. The patient had been the favorite of her mother's father, who had died while the patient was in college. On hearing of his death, the patient had a temper tantrum, throwing things and smashing furniture. He had been the one person she had loved. About five years prior to his death, he had made a very unhappy second marriage, which the family felt brought on the cardiac illness from which he died.

After several interviews I requested to see the patient's mother with her. Her mother was a very attractive, cool, detached woman who seemed quite vague about the whole situation.

Doctor: "Before we begin, I wonder if you could tell me how you see the problem."

Mother: "I really have no idea. I don't know what to tell you, I really don't" (in a faint, distant, controlled, uninvolved voice).

Patient: "I have a question. This is the first time I've seen that."

Doctor: "It's a tape recorder, because I'm not taking any notes, okay?"

Patient: "Oh, okay. I saw my mother look at it" (laughs).

Mother: "Problems? Really and truly, I can't tell you."

Doctor: "I'm not asking you to make a diagnosis. I'm asking you as a mother who has watched her daughter growing up."

Mother: "Really, I can't tell you. I feel a little guilty, sure—" (pauses).

Doctor: "Guilty? You make it sound as though you feel you have some part to play in this."

Mother: "I've got a big part to play in it. My daughter. Maybe we made a mistake. I couldn't do any different. First mistake was bringing children into the world, into *this* world. I can't tell you if it was how we treated them, I'm puzzled. A mystery."

Doctor: "What are your feelings about your daughter?"

Mother: (Annoyed, but very controlled and distant) "I love her. What else? Very concerned. I don't know what to do— husband and I both. We'd do anything."

Doctor: (To patient) "Tell me, is your mother this oblivious to problems? Is she bashful? Or what is it?"

Mother: "I must be oblivious."

Patient: (Tentatively) "I think my mother doesn't like to admit things to herself. She won't allow herself to think things over. She does what I do. She puts things behind her head and forgets them, she puts it away."

Mother: "I probably push things back. I'm a mother. I raise children. I can't tell you about the problem."

Doctor: (To patient) "I'm a psychiatrist and I'm completely baffled by your mother. I wonder how you react to it."

Patient "I think she's decided not to say anything. Cathy and I have told her things that have bothered us over the years. And now you're saying you don't know."

Mother: (Finally speaks up) "Dr. Lewin takes notes or has a recorder. I can't refer back to them. I've got a million things on my mind. I can't say specifically what bothers you."

Patient: "One thing Cathy and I have said, one thing, about Daddy, that everything is too much business, business, business. He was always out of town. That's one of the things you could have said." *Notice that she offers her mother a safe harbor by offering her father up for criticism.*

Mother: "It wasn't immediately on my mind. I've overlooked it. I've learned to live with it."

Doctor: (To patient) "It's interesting that your first complaint is about your father."

Patient: "Well, it includes her, too. The past couple months we went to Florida. It was a business trip. I never saw them. They golfed and went to dinner with people. They said it was business."

Doctor: "Was it that way when you were young? After all now, they probably feel you're a grown up young lady, able to fend for herself."

Patient: "Business came before we did. Mostly to my father."

Mother: "It was a way of life, a living. My husband was on the road. I knew I had to raise the children myself. He earned a living. We lived nice. He wasn't playing out there. I was home quite a bit."

Doctor: "Were you aware of any resentment being stuck there alone?"

Mother: "Yeah, sure. Until I got used to it. Then my children grew up and were away from home, I enjoyed it, going with him. I was glad I had *girls*. They're easier to raise. They're mine. Boys are tougher to handle."

Doctor: " 'Mine.' 'Tougher to handle.' You make them sound like possessions which are yours to manipulate and control."

Mother: "Maybe. Could be. Maybe that's why I had them, that's what I am. Never gave it any thought."

Doctor: "What kind of feelings did you notice among the children in growing up? For example, how much envy and jealousy did you see among the three of them?"

Mother: "A lot. I think that the twins didn't like their older sister."

Doctor: "What were the reasons?"

Mother: "I don't know. Maybe I gave her more attention than I gave them. I don't know" (becoming again more vague and detached).

Doctor: "We're talking ancient history?"

Mother: "A lot has transpired in fifteen, twenty years. The kids grew up, I got a granddaughter. I show more affection to her than to all three."

Doctor: "How come?"

Mother: "She's the baby."

Doctor: "What kind of an answer is that?"

Mother: "That always happens. Wait till you become a grandfather. You love your children, but—you spoil your grandchildren more. You love them and they return that love."

Doctor: "How much love did you get from your children?"

Mother: "I can't measure it."

Doctor: "You just did. You said a grandchild gives more love than a child."

Mother: "Yes. You have more love for your grandchild at times, for your husband at times, for your children at times."

Doctor: "Did they ever show it to you?"

Mother: "Yes."

Doctor: "How?"

Mother: "Do you want specifics? Do you want generalities?" (She is really very uncooperative.) "What do you want. They showed me respect. That's love. If I asked them to be home on time, they were."

Doctor: "Did they ever show you much affection?"

Mother: "I guess not."

Doctor: (To patient) "Is that true?"

Patient: "Um-huh. I don't think there was much affection shown."

Mother: "We aren't a kissing family."

Patient: "Not between you and Cathy and I."

Doctor: (To mother) "Do you think of yourself as a warm, affectionate person?"

Mother: "At times. At times, I'm pretty cold."

Doctor: "Have you any idea why?"

Mother: "I wasn't prepared today. I don't know what I'm working toward. The coldness is my character" (sighs). "I came prepared today *not* to talk; I really did."

Doctor: "How come?" (very softly and solicitous).

Mother: "I don't know. I'm afraid" (near tears).

Doctor: "Of what?"

Mother: "Of hurting her."

Doctor: "The other way is more harmful. It may hurt, but in the long run it will help. It's like opening a boil. There's the initial pain and then it's much better. Will you tell me about the coldness?"

Mother: "I really can't."

Doctor: "You decided to back off, not to cry, not to get involved."

Mother: (Weeping) "I don't know why I'm crying. I don't. I feel bad for her."

Doctor: "You seem to hold yourself accountable. I haven't said that."

Mother: "Parents aren't accountable for their child's unhappiness?"

Doctor: "We're talking about something specific: *Emptiness.* Your daughter is demonstrating her emptiness. She is becoming smaller and smaller. She's empty. What she is being fed is not filling her up. Somehow you seem to feel that you're the source of her emptiness."

Mother: "Well, I may have said it a few minutes ago. Probably we all need a lot of help. I'm mixed up, torn. Torn between my oldest and next two. And between the twins. Whose part I take is right or wrong? I'm sure I hugged one and not the other. Or bought one and not the other. There must have been mistakes made."

Doctor: "I'm not so certain that things are the way you say. I'm not so certain that the problem is in the mistakes of what you did and didn't do. We were on the right track, I think, when you began to cry about your emotional coldness."

Mother: "Until you said, 'cold'—I never really felt cold" (*she* said "cold" first, not I).

Doctor: (To patient) "Your mother is struggling very hard, deciding whether to open up to me or not. She's vacillating back and forth. She hasn't made up her mind. She started out today deciding she wasn't going to talk, but now she finds that she wants to talk. She's struggling with herself."

Mother: "I don't know what you want to hear. I don't know what you want me to tell you."

Doctor: "Exactly what it is that's troubling you about your emotional coldness."

Mother: "I don't think I'm cold—"

Doctor: "Your father was a different kind of person, I gather."

Mother: "She was the apple of his eye, I guess. I loved him very much—" (The patient and her mother spontaneously begin to weep.)

Patient: "It's all right, you know I cry when you talk about him."

Mother: "I always say, 'When they made him, they broke the mold.' He lived with us, Mother and Dad both, and we all adored him, both of them. We were a big family, seven of us in a small place, and we lived on top of each other. But we got along wonderful, all of us. That was when I started to leave my children. I could travel more. I loved it because they were there. I didn't have to get an outsider for my children. They were wonderful to them. They were wonderful to me. They adored my husband. One in a million. We lost him. He made a mistake and he knew it, too. That's what bothered us most at the end. Olive, thank God, was not home. Golly, he went fast. We called Cathy and told her he passed away, but we waited until we got up to school to tell Olive. We knew she'd take it hard and she did—"

Doctor: "What about your mother?"

Mother: "I was like her. She was good. She was sweet, warm. She took to my oldest daughter, Paula, like I take to my granddaughter. I know it. Paula was first born, her first grandchild. They adored her. They had four years of her before the twins were born and they took her, kept her, fed her. I had it very easy. Mother was ill a year. I took care of her—right after we moved to Pittsburgh. For a solid year she was in and out of the hospital. I learned to give her oxygen and shots. Her death, in a way, was a relief. Olive was 9 or 10."

Doctor: "You made a statement before that a grandparent gives more love to a grandchild than to her own child. Apparently you found this true with your first child. Were you aware of any reaction on your part, suddenly left out in the cold?"

Mother: "That's 29 years ago. I was left out in the cold *two* years ago."

Doctor: "What do you mean?"

Mother: "Well, after she was married" (nodding to the patient), "and Paula and her family moved away two months later, and my husband was working, going to the office every day. I was left with nothing to do. I went into a deep depression and my husband didn't know what happened. I didn't go out of the house." (To patient) "Do you know about this?" (cries).

Patient: "Of course I do!" (Impatiently) "I used to come over and you'd cry."

Mother: "I wondered if it could be change of life. My whole mental outlook. I talked with my doctor. He said I had to do what was best for me. I haven't completely solved the problem, but it's much better than it ever was. Husband and I have shared an awful lot and we've done an awful lot. Very close. I couldn't demand—my children were separate people—that was my resolution. My husband said I was making an extension of my family with Paula. In other words, she wasn't—I only took for herself until she moved away. I had Cathy come at that time and she was going through a very bad time. She didn't have it easy. She'd moved into her own apartment and we decided the children would do whatever they wanted. We had no—we couldn't stop them, if that's the way you want to put it."

Doctor: "So, after making the resolution, you find one of your children comes back. And what does she find? The wall that you had artificially constructed, to protect yourself before?"

Mother: "That's possible. Sure."

Doctor: "So you're faced now with the prospect of altering your defense a second time after going through all the pain of erecting the barriers the first time?"

Mother: "That's one way to look at it. I never thought of it that way. How long I built it up, I don't know. I don't mean I cut off my children entirely. I tried to be with them as much as possible."

Doctor: "You made the distinction. They are now separate; before they were yours. Remember before we even called attention to the terms you had used, that the children were extensions of yourself, that they were part of you."

Mother: "Um-huh, Um-huh."

Doctor: "They'd been under your control. Then two years ago they became separate. The cord was cut. Now the child comes back and finds the defenses that you have erected standing between you. Now you are faced with the prospect, if you break those defenses down, what will become of you? You know what you went through two years ago."

Mother: "That's right. I never thought of it that way. In a couple of years, if God is good to us, Olive will meet someone else and I'll be left alone. Could be."

Doctor: (To patient) "Do you understand what your mother will face, in her own mind, were she to alter her defenses again?"

Patient: "Um-huh. One time you said to me, 'How do I know maybe next year I'll be left alone again?' "

Mother: "Did I say that?"

Patient: "In the middle of one of our disagreements. I don't recall about what."

Doctor: (To mother) "Had you been aware of any feelings of bitterness or anger on your part toward the children?"

Mother: "Anger, maybe. Not bitterness. Not at their leaving."

Doctor: "Then why did you throw it up in an angry way that time?"

Mother: "I don't know. I think my anger is more at myself than at my children. Our sympathy is too great for Olive. She had a bad two years and we let her go into it. Not that we knew it would be wrong, or going to be that way. We're still afraid to say anything to Olive for fear of upsetting her."

Doctor: (To patient) "They must think that you're fragile, that you'll fall to pieces."

Mother: "She'll get diarrhea, that's what. Nervous. Throw up or something."

Doctor: "Those things do happen, don't they."

Mother: "They sure do. She got angry when I made an eye of round by her recipe and it was no good. She said, 'This is lousy.' "

Patient: "And you said, 'Next time we'll make it the way Paula makes it. Hers always turns out right.' "

Doctor: (To mother) "Do you understand that that was an expression of jealousy. 'You love Paula more than me!"

Mother: "It never entered my mind."

Doctor: "Are you oblivious to jealousy? Do you have any brothers or sisters?"

Mother: "I have one brother and one sister—my brother is older, my sister is younger. I'm the middle child."

Doctor: "Were you aware of any feelings of jealousy or envy toward them in growing up?"

Mother: "No. I was never jealous" (sharply).

Doctor: (Looking behind the mother) "I just wanted to check. There aren't any wings back there, so I presume you are human."

Patient: (Laughs loudly.)

Doctor: "For you to deny jealousy is almost like denying that you ever ate or slept. That's a normal human emotion common to every child. Even a dog, if you brought home a new puppy, would be jealous."

Mother: "Then I never recognized those feelings as such."

Doctor: (To patient) "Now you see why your mother is oblivious. You make a statement of jealousy and your mother doesn't get the message. You're not aware that your mother doesn't get that kind of message."

Patient: (To mother) "Didn't you know I was jealous?" (incredulous).

Mother: "I didn't know."

Doctor: You think that there has been communication between you, but it isn't always true. Your mother doesn't always understand. I'll bet that your mother doesn't know that there's jealousy among you three girls a great deal of the time."

Mother: "Towards me? I'm not that important."

Doctor: (Laughing) "You're not that important? You're the core. Why do you deny being important? Because she turned to your father? Did that deceive you? Why do you think she turned to your father? Because she preferred him?"

Mother: "No. He showed it to her, he gave her everything."

Doctor: "That's one reason."

Mother: "What's the other?"

Doctor: "Cathy?"

Mother: "That's a big thing. That I know."

Patient: "Cathy and I have been jealous of Paula, your affection toward her and not us."

Mother: "Yes, I recognize that."

Doctor: "She turned to her father for two reasons—she was pulled and she was pushed. Her jealousy at Cathy and her anger at you pushed her to her grandfather, and he was only too willing to take her."

Mother: "That's right. Absolutely."

Doctor: "It was anger at you. You have been the core of the situation from the beginning. Your father was only a substitute for you."

Mother: "I don't think I've been aware of it. Have I been too dumb to recognize it?"

Doctor: "Willingly oblivious."

Mother: "Willingly oblivious, yes."

Doctor: "She lost her foster mother when her grandfather died. That wasn't just her grandfather who died, it was her foster mother. Her returning from her newest foster mother, her husband, who turned out to be a wicked stepmother, is very similar to after her grandfather died; she's returning to her real mother."

Mother: "And I'm not there."

Doctor: "You weren't there then and you're not there now. One of the reasons she got married was to acquire a new family. She wouldn't have to depend on her old family. But her new family turned out to be not what she thought it was. So her grandfather died twice, so to speak."

Mother: "Well—then it all lies with me."

Doctor: "You make it sound like you're taking the blame. Why?"

Mother: "You say the core is here."

Doctor: "Yes, the core is there. But she can't have you. She can't have what she really wants: your 100% exclusive love and attention. She cannot have what she wants. Are we to blame you for not giving it to her?"

Mother: "It sure sounds like it. That's my own feeling."

Doctor: "That's because you feel you didn't want her enough in the first place. You're feeling guilty."

Mother: "Right. I have a guilt feeling about them. The whole thing. I was busy. Maybe I'm a cold person like you say."

Doctor: "How come you're emotionally cold? Your mother and father favored you, they lived with you. Or maybe it isn't the way it seems. Maybe you don't feel they favored you."

Mother: "Oh yes they did."

Doctor: "Maybe you feel you won their favor by being their nicest child."

Mother: "Oh! That could be. I hadn't thought of it that way."

Doctor: "You don't act like a favorite child. A favorite child ought to be warm, affectionate, and giving—overflowing with affection. You act like a child who has knocked herself out winning their favor because she wasn't the favored child. It doesn't add up."

Mother: "No, I was the favored child. I don't know why. Because I gave. I treated them well."

Patient: "Did they move in with you because Aunt Florence and Uncle Sid couldn't afford to take them?"

Mother: "No, they moved in with me because your Dad was to go in the Army and I was with three little babies. So they sold their house and moved in with me. Then the war was ended in a few weeks."

Doctor: "So we don't know whether their moving in with you was convenience or an act of love or—"

Mother: "No. Now I remember. I was always closer to my folks. My brother lived in the same town but wasn't as close—my sister married and went out of the city—though she wasn't very close. Months would go by and she didn't write or talk to them. My Dad was in financial difficulties and my husband helped him out. He gave him money—not lent—he never wanted it back. Maybe we bought them, too."

Doctor: "Not consciously."

Mother: "No, not consciously. Of course when I had the baby, my parents loved her and begged *me* to go out. Then my husband went to machine shop during the day. Goodyear Aircraft at night—1944."

Doctor: "I'm afraid we'll have to stop at this point. I feel so badly about interrupting because you have been talking very well, contrary to your original wish."

Mother: "You bring back memories, you talk."

Doctor: "I wonder if it would be possible to talk next week or another time."

Patient: "Oh we're going to be away."

Mother: "Well, so we'll arrange another time."

Doctor: "The three of us will talk, but more important the two of you can talk and communicate with one another. It's a family problem."

Mother: "It will be better getting things out in the open. Any time you say, we'll get together again."

However, the next interview was not so easily arranged. The following week, the patient had her divorce hearing. The next day she began vomiting and suddenly spiked a fever of 105 degrees. Her family physician hospitalized her at once and discovered a urinary tract infection. After massive doses of antibiotics, her fever abated, but not without causing fears for her survival. Her debilitation was pitiable, her weight under sixty pounds. During the acute state of her illness, the hospital staff was extremely attentive. Her period of convalescence, with special diet and considerable medication to correct protein and mineral deficiencies, saw a complete reversal of the attitudes of those caring for her. Medications were somehow forgotten, dietary supplements delayed, and instructions misinterpreted. The source of the difficulty seemed traceable to the patient's inability to express anger directly to the person responsible for it. She would complain to the resident about the physician, to the interne about the resident, to the doctors about the nurses, and to her family about everyone. Consequently, the staff responded in kind with massive passive resistance. Fortunately, she was discharged before matters worsened, although not before she was confronted with her inability to express anger through an intermediary.

After several interviews, a second consultation was arranged with her and her mother, *at her mother's request.* The patient was now a robust eighty-two pounds, but gaining weight steadily with good appetite and good spirits. She proudly related that she was speaking up to her father for the first time in her life, even openly disagreeing with him.

Doctor: "I wonder if we could take up where we left off."

Mother: "I don't recall exactly where we'd left off. We'd gone back quite a ways" (smiling and animated, a far cry from the vague, detached person at the previous interview).

Doctor: "You have your choice; either what's on your mind now, which is probably better, or we can go back where we were in 1944 with your husband in the factory."

Mother: "Well—let's start with now and see what we can do with what's going on right now. I personally feel that things have gone real well—I think."

Patient: (Nods enthusiastically.)

Mother: "Olive and I have done well together. We understand each other. We're both trying. I told her in the hospital whether we had that session with you where I was shocked into a lot of things or not, I have still been with her in constant attendance at the hospital because I love her and I want her to get well. We've done a lot of talking. A lot of talk—we had a lot of time. That's for the right now."

Doctor: "I'm a little skeptical about this. I'd call this a honeymoon. I'd like to see what happens when the honeymoon is over, how the relationship endures over a period of time."

Mother: "Sure. Definitely."

Doctor: "The main reason I'm skeptical is that I have not heard any anger coming out of your daughter directly at you."

Mother: "She hasn't heard any anger from me, either. Right now, it is the honeymoon, a lull. We're really satisfied with the way things are now. What will be, I really can't say—I'm hoping it will be for the best. I'll do everything in my power to make her happy."

Doctor: "I had the idea when you spoke to me on the phone you hadn't the intention of merely telling me how well things are going. Apparently there are other things you wanted to talk about."

Mother: "Well, primarily I wanted to talk about myself. Maybe I don't need help. Maybe I've had an awakening, and her process of getting well. Olive tells me we're alike—many times in the past couple weeks—I keep everything inside. I had one *tremendous* outburst. I told her; I had to."

Patient: "It has something to do with me, not the argument."

Mother: "It wasn't an argument. The subject wasn't Olive. It was an accumulation. All during her illness, I didn't break down once. This one night, I just *woosh*, I mean I really had a temper tantrum. *Never* in my life have I ever done that."

Patient: "It was about how Daddy was treating you. I get

the same thing. The subject wasn't me and it had nothing to do with me, but you hit into a problem that I hit into sometimes."

Mother: "That's right. Three weeks ago we were in the hospital lobby. He criticized me that I interrupt her too much, I don't let her talk enough. I didn't see myself doing that, but I thought I'll watch myself for it."

Doctor: (To the patient) "Is that true?"

Patient: "Not that I've been aware of."

Mother: "I wasn't aware of it either. It really hurt me, because I tried my best. Cathy came in and we went upstairs. I was down in the dumps when we got home. He said, 'Am I going to get the cold treatment?' I didn't know what to say. I hadn't been aware of suppressing her in any way. I said I wouldn't repeat what he said to Olive second hand. She'd have to hear it when we were all three together. Anytime I repeated something, it didn't come across right. All that week I was quiet and didn't discuss with him any of the things Olive and I said.

"Then the following week we were out to dinner. The daughter of friends of ours walked by with a young man I'd never met. She had a wild look on her face. The next morning she called me and asked me not to tell her parents that I'd seen her with this fellow that her parents didn't approve of. I gave her my word I wouldn't volunteer the information, but I wouldn't know what I'd do if they asked me directly. I advised her not to date the fellow if her parents were so much against him. I told her I wasn't qualified to give her advice. That evening after the hospital I told my husband about my conversation with the girl. He said, 'You gave her good advice, *but*'—he started to criticize me. "They're our friends. You have to tell them.' I said, 'I don't want to know any criticism. I feel I gave good advice, if you want to call her father, *you* do it!' I ran out of the room, banged my fists, threw myself on the floor. He walked in and I said, 'Shut Up!' hit my head on the floor and took me ten minutes to calm down, like a fifteen-year-old kid, or maybe younger. I seemed to have had it. I picked myself up. I scared him. I'd never done it before. *Never.* Never in my whole married life. I might have cried, but I never exploded like that. I threw myself on the sofa and I was so violent, I fell off. When I got up, I don't know what was wrong, I had no pain, I didn't even have a headache and I know I must have injured my hand. All those years I kept things in. I probably should have exploded years ago. I felt I'd seek help. I still love him."

Doctor: "What lay behind the temper tantrum. Could you specify the anger?"

Mother: "His criticism. I told him, 'Everything fine, *but—*.'"

Doctor: "What made you so angry? Does he always criticize you? Or you can't take criticism?"

Mother: "I don't know. I'd never been so aware of his being critical."

Patient: "He always seems to have to know a little bit more. That's the way I get it."

Mother: "It's true. He is a very detailed person—so many details you lose thread. It bothers me because he means so well. He wouldn't hurt any of us knowingly."

Doctor: "It makes you both angry and guilty, because he's not trying to be malicious."

Mother: "Right."

Patient: "Yes."

Mother: "That's the way it is."

Patient: "The same way it happens to me."

Doctor: "That's why your daughter said you've encountered a problem similar to hers. It wasn't about her; it was the same kind of problem she has. Does your husband hold himself up as the expert? Why is his opinion of the interpersonal processes between you and your friend's daughter supposed to be better than yours?"

Mother: "I don't know. That's one of the things that irked me. I felt I'd given her good advice. Maybe male advice is different."

Doctor: "Two aspects intrigue me: one, that his opinion is the expert's, and second, that his way of handling it was to stick directly to the truth and your way was to ignore the truth and pretend it never happened. I'm not saying whose is superior, I'm only noting the difference. The method that you use (to mother) is similar to the method you use (daughter) to ignore the truth, and, like you said last time, push things in the back of your head."

Mother: "That's true, that's the point. I remember now saying to him, and I used horrible language, vile language, 'I will not be caught up in somebody else's mess right now. I'm not capable of untangling somebody else's'—I used bad language—'when I'm just crawling out of my own. I no sooner brush mine off than it gets flung right back at me.' I went on and on. I got thirty-two years of anguish out of me."

Doctor: "Have you been aware of that anger before?"

Mother: "Oh-oh-oh, sure."

Doctor: "I don't mean itemized anger, I mean grudge. Simmering anger, festering anger, thirty-two years of anguish."

Mother: "Probably because he was so engrossed with business. He knows it. The past month he's been family minded."

Doctor: "What do you mean 'engrossed with business'?"

Mother: "Up to my depression two years ago, business came first. Many nights he didn't come home for dinner. Or birthdays or anniversaries would go by unnoticed. He told me he didn't have to buy me gifts for occasions. He'd buy them when he felt like it. As a result, I got very few gifts—until two years ago. I didn't care. It didn't bother me—."

Doctor: "Is your anger at him because of what you're telling me, or some grudge beneath this?"

Mother: "I can't really tell you. Truthfully. I've had a good life. I feel guilty complaining. I never wanted too much."

Doctor: "Last time here you defended him. 'Millions of men are on the road.'"

Mother: "Right."

Doctor: "Now you're suggesting you felt neglected."

Mother: "Maybe I wasn't aware of it then. A lot of things have happened since. He's tried his best."

Doctor: "What I've seen is a shifting of relationships. Last time this (nodding toward the patient) was 'odd man out' and you and your husband were a team. She complained of feeling ignored and left out. Now you two are closer together and united in being angry at your husband. The only anger you've both been able to show is at him and now he's 'odd man out.'"

Mother: "He feels it, too. He knows it. He's trying so hard to please us, he's tripping over himself, literally. He's trying to be so good, to please her and me that he's getting in his own way. We've already told him to relax—"

Patient: "He makes me nervous when we eat."

Mother: "He's not himself. It's a reversal, really a reversal. This is when I stop to think. He walks in the house at twenty minutes to six! This never happened. Eight, nine o'clock, he could be at the office till all hours. She knows."

Patient: "You've been telling me some stories. Daddy has every right to feel guilty. He did it. That's why he's running home early every night."

Mother: "He's trying to please, to change himself. He's not acting. He's trying with all his might (laughs), a comedy of errors."

Doctor: "What I'm impressed with, the male is now out, the females are together. I have seen this from generation to generation. I pointed out that you were the core of the situation, not the cause of the problem. Your child's primary relationship was with her mother. Remember, you also were a child and you had a mother. I wonder how close a relationship you had with your mother."

Mother: "You know we were very close."

Doctor: "No, I don't know that. I know that your father was 'one in a million' and 'they broke the mold when they made him,' but I don't really know what your relationship was with your mother."

Mother: "Very close."

Doctor: "Why did you leave her; why did you ever get married."

Mother: "Oh, I don't know. I think I fell in love. But we lived only two blocks away. I saw her every day."

Doctor: "So, your marriage didn't cause you to leave your mother."

Mother: "No. We were an extension of that family, the same that I caused in my older daughter's family. Same thing. I loved my mother and daddy being with me; when they lived with me. I don't say we didn't have arguments—and they were strict about the children. The oldest was spoiled by my mother, this one was spoiled by my father and Cathy was the odd man out. So you see, it does reflect back."

Doctor: "What was your reaction to your mother's death? You'd told me of the sense of relief on account of the oxygen and shots and all the rest."

Mother: "I missed her. Of course that was a terrible year. We were praying for her death, because she suffered so. And I had guilt feelings for wishing her dead. I know in my heart that I did everything for her I could. Olive doesn't remember her much."

Doctor: "How did you handle the mourning for your mother?"

Mother: "Mourning? The funeral?"

Doctor: "I don't know how long your mourning took, or if it was ever completed."

Mother: "Oh, you mean that?"

Doctor: (Turning to the patient) "I've been talking about this little girl who misses her Mommy." (Turning to the mother.) "And I don't know about this little girl who misses her Mommy."

Mother: "I don't know what to tell you" (stammers and starts several times). "I've told this to my girls. My mother gave me advice. She said, 'You want to gossip? Come to me. Tell me all about it; I'm not going to spread it. What goes in here stays in here. You don't have to gossip to anyone. I won't tell.' Olive, do you remember my saying that if you talk about your girlfriend to another girlfriend, she'll tell another?"

Patient: "Um-huh."

Mother: "We came to Pittsburgh. We don't have relatives here. I don't have anyone. Nobody. Mother was only with me a year before she died and I was without a girlfriend. It was tough. As a result, I probably missed my mother more than I knew. In fact, I still miss her. Twenty years and I'll miss her. She was a very smart woman."

Doctor: "Over the years you must have missed her a great deal." (Turning to the patient) "You realize your mother went through a depression two years ago and didn't even talk to a psychiatrist." (Back to the patient) "Certainly there must have been times then that you wanted to talk to somebody. But you followed your mother's advice: don't tell anybody but her."

Mother: "I do talk to my sister."

Patient: "I've remembered asking you, 'Have you talked things over with Aunt Alice?' She's your best friend and you don't even tell her everything."

Doctor: "When I asked you about the 'coldness' you brought up, I wondered at that time whether it was possible that you had turned off your feelings. I'm now wondering about your grief over your mother's death."

Mother: "I don't remember. My dad's death is in the foreground now, not my mother."

Doctor: "Do you think that your mourning consisted only of the funeral, as you implied before? Or the week that you sat 'Shiva?'"

Mother: "After that it quieted down."

Doctor: "It takes a long time getting over losing somebody. Is it possible that you haven't worked it out at all? After a week, you turned off the switch?"

Mother: "No, it took a little longer than that. It took about a month. We didn't have many acquaintances or friends in town. I think maybe not socializing, the mourning—."

Patient: "I remember she died and Mother was upset."

Mother: "It was the first Seder. She passed away on the morning of the first Seder. You're not allowed to sit Shiva during Passover. I forgot. Now I remember. So she said, I'll never forget, and this was when she was well, 'When I die, I don't want you to mourn me or sit Shiva for me.'"

Doctor: "Did you try to follow her instructions? As you followed her other instructions? I think she made a mistake. She was trying to save her child pain."

Mother: (In unison with me) "Save her child pain."

Doctor: "In reality you have to undergo that pain."

Mother: "I say the same thing to my kids. 'Don't mourn me, I've had a good life, happiness, three daughters—.'"

Doctor: "But the mourning is for the loss. You're not mourning for the dead person. You're mourning for the loss. The process that has to go on when people die is for the living to take something from them so that their monument is not the slab that sits on the grave, but something you've taken from the dead that lives on inside you. That's what the process of mourning is about. You have to re-integrate that person to take her as part of yourself, so that she'll live on inside you."

Mother: (Surprised) "Do people do that?"

Doctor: "That's what the process of mourning is supposed to be. If they do it successfully, that's what happens. Otherwise it's like a child losing a love-and-security blanket. It's put

in the ground, and it's gone, and you don't have anything."
(To the patient) "Haven't I talked to you about taking something inside?" (to both) "Remember we talked about 'emptiness?'"

Mother: "I never thought of it that way. I felt the loss all
these years."

Doctor: "The fact that you just now asked me, 'Do people
do that?' indicates that you don't believe that you have done
it."

Mother: "I haven't. I'm not aware of doing it."

Doctor: "So you're reliant on the people who are living for
your comfort emotionally. If your husband is away, you're alone.
I mean, *really* alone."

Mother: "I'll have to ask you again, when you asked whether I was cold, I don't know how you meant that."

Doctor: "Actually you have misquoted me. What I asked
you was, 'Do you think of yourself as a warm, affectionate
person?' And you replied, 'At times. At times I'm pretty cold.'
You're the one who said, 'Cold.'"

Mother: "I said it? Because maybe I don't show it. I feel,
but I don't show it."

Doctor: "Perhaps a better word would be 'emotionless.' Because the temper tantrum is the opposite, the eruption of a huge
feeling. Ordinarily, you're very controlled. No feelings show.
The surface is calm. We don't know what the currents are underneath. Maybe ripples."

Patient: "I can always tell she's holding it back."

Doctor: "You learned to do the same. Hold back, skirt
around, trying all kinds of ways not to express things directly,
perhaps through a third person."

Patient: "Right."

Doctor: (To mother) "Would it surprise you to learn that
you haven't worked out your feelings to your mother's death?
I suspect that is the problem."

Mother: "I never gave it a thought."

Doctor: (To mother) "Remember, what set off your illness
was the thought of everyone leaving you and your being left
alone. It's never entered your mind that you shouldn't be 'alone.'
Even if you were on a desert island and not another human

being were around there should be something inside keeping you company."

Mother: "I never thought of that in any way, shape, or form."

Doctor: "Is this starting to be clarified, this problem handed down from generation to generation, from mother to child?"

Patient: "Uh-huh."

Doctor: (To the patient) "Your father isn't the villain. There aren't any villains. He is the unfortunate male of the family where the important relationship is mother and child. You must be careful not to intrude yourself into your parent's marriage, because the unit is supposed to be husband-wife."

(To the mother) "Back to the question about your wanting help. I'd be very happy to see you both together again. What I'm wondering—is that enough? Would you like to talk to someone alone? In that case I could not see you."

Patient: "I think it's good for me."

Doctor: (To the mother) "I'd be happy to continue this relationship regardless of your seeing someone else, for the three of us to get together, in addition to your daughter's seeing me."

Mother: "I know a lot of things have been clarified."

Patient: "A lot of things you haven't mentioned. You say you're not angry at Daddy. Like when Daddy was away and you had to take us to get our tonsils out and no one helped you, you were angry, you told me."

Doctor: Your mother uses the technique you've learned. She tells her anger about the second party to a third party."

Mother: "At this point, I'm telling her my headaches and she has enough of her own. I've excused him, my husband, for what's in the past."

Doctor: "He did play an important part in helping you to retain the closeness with your family. There may have been few other husbands who would have been as willing as he to retain his in-laws. He allowed you to keep your mother although you were married."

Mother: "Right. Let's continue this, if Olive doesn't mind."

Patient: "This is valuable for me just listening."

Doctor: "She likes to be fed some of the time." (We arrange an appointment time.)

Patient: "I hear the same things coming from her that I feel."

Mother: "Everything I've said today I've already told her."

Doctor: "And everything you've said today she had told me about herself."

Patient: "That's how it's starting to dawn on me. I hear her and realize I feel the same way."

Mother: "It's a pleasure to see her eat. It's a pleasure to cook for her. She'll be all right now."

Patient: "I'm worried about Daddy not gaining weight now."

Mother: "I know." (Concerned) "He'll be all right."

Doctor: "Has he lost weight?"

Mother: "Tremendous."

Doctor: "Is he trading places, is he becoming Olive?"

Patient: "I was wondering the same thing. He's been complaining so much. He gets on the scale every day. Like I used to."

Doctor: "Perhaps you might bring it to his attention, the whole thing we discussed today, about shifts in the family relationship."

Patient: "He's looking for attention."

Mother: "He feels left out. It bothers the whole family."

Doctor: "Maybe it should be nipped in the bud."

Mother: "I've discussed it with Olive. I'm wary how to do it. We'll feel our way."

Chapter IX

LIFE CIRCUMSTANCES AND THERAPY

IN the course of therapy, events over which neither the patient nor the doctor have any control almost inevitably transpire and alter the entire direction of treatment. Vital decisions by other members of the patient's family, such as changing employment, moving the household to another location, birth of children, marriage, and divorce, may shatter whatever adjustments the patient had made previously. Catastrophes, such as sudden loss of financial security, severe organic illness, or crippling accident within the family can even unhinge a formerly stable personality. But, more commonly, such drastic changes in life circumstances merely interrupt the natural progression of the therapy by intruding external anxiety into a process already laden with tensions from intrapsychic conflicts. For the moment, the immediate external threat usually takes precedence in the patient's mind over those problems for which he had sought help originally. Should the external problem become a prolonged crisis, the original goal of therapy may face temporary abandonment. Brief therapy must be supplanted by a longer treatment relationship. The gravest consequences arise from the impending death and eventual death of an important love object, especially if that person had been the main source of the patient's introject. The process of separation and mourning causes shifts of identity that may lead to extrusion or externalization of the original introject, and temporary substitution of the therapist as an external replacement, a virtual "love and security blanket" which the patient can neither relinquish nor internalize. This may lead to prolonged dependency upon the therapy, the resolution of which is very difficult. Often it seems as though the patient has lost the ability to introject. No matter what phantasies the patient may erect of the doctor's perfection, ambivalence is inevitable and there is hardly a comparison between the actual transient significance of the doctor and the enormity of the previous relationship with the parent. Naturally, the patient is reluctant to replace his parent with a stranger. So he does nothing but drown his sorrow, like an alcoholic with his bottle, by depending on the presence of the doctor. The process can be even further delayed if the patient defends himself from the pain of loss by denial, a refusal to concede that he has lost the parent. The treatment of one such patient will be presented, not to offer solutions to the puzzle, but to demonstrate the complexity of intrapsychic mechanisms and interpersonal relationships which evolve from the death of a parent that prevent quick resolution of the original conflicts.

Case Illustration: Mrs. L.A. was a 29-year-old married woman who had been referred because of a marital sexual problem. It took the patient eight months to bring herself to call for an appointment. Her chief complaint at the time of the initial visit was feeling of insecurity that attended her being alone on the street, an insecurity intense enough to be called a phobia. That symptom had begun about eighteen months previously, after the patient fainted while watching a roller derby. At the time, she did not incriminate her emotions, but blamed the heat and a weight-reducing diet.

Mrs. A. was a tall, statuesque, green-eyed, sultry woman with jet-black hair, which she wore short, shaped close to her head in a fashion then current in high-style magazines. She had been married eight years and her sexual adjustment was never satisfactory to her. By mutual agreement they practiced withdrawal as a form of contraception and had intercourse about once every two or three months. She never experienced orgasm. Her attitude toward her husband was condescending. Although she felt that she loved him, and enjoyed his company, she felt superior to him in intelligence and sophistication. They had known each other since high school, but she was disappointed that neither of them had attended college. She had graduated high school with high honors and had aspired to be an attorney. Instead, she worked for eleven years as a secretary in a personnel office. Her mother liked her husband "the first day he walked in. That's why I married him." He had become an accountant but his job was still beneath her ambitions for him. Her mother, the head of an Italian household, was college educated. Her father, a retired laborer, had a second grade education. Their match had been arranged by her mother's adopted parents in Europe, against her mother's wishes. Her mother told the patient that they practiced withdrawal. The patient had an unmarried sister, five years her senior. The first-born had been a prematurely delivered son, dead at birth. The patient had no immediate desire to have children. She expressed little concern about her sexual adjustment as a cause for referral. Her physician seemed more heedful of it. She was unsure whether she wanted further visits.

The day after her initial visit her mother was found to have metastatic carcinoma of the spine. Roentgenography revealed a diffuse spread throughout the entire skeletal system. At the patient's second visit, the history of her phobia became clearer. Her mother had a simple mastectomy the summer before the onset of the phobia, and was being treated for "arthritis" of the back for several months. In February, her mother began having anginal chest pains. In March, the patient fainted at the roller derby. An attempt was made at the second visit to probe the intensity of her relationship with her mother. She was stoical.

Patient: "I love her very much. We've been close—but not abnormally so."

Doctor: "What do you mean, 'abnormally'? "

Patient: "Well, I didn't buy a house right next door to be close to her. She did help in decorating our house. Actually, since her operation, I've been preparing for her death. I don't object to death, but the suffering; she doesn't deserve it. She's been a wonderful wife and mother. She'll worry about making the family suffer. I'd like to feel Mother's going to a happier place. I vacillate. I guess I believe in nothingness. I'm doubtful there is a heaven. Nothing. I'll have grief and mourning. I guess I'm frightened."

Doctor: "Of what in particular?"

Patient: "Being alone, separated. I have the facade of a femme fatale. Inside I'm a shrinking violet. I went to a night class at Pitt in Italian and purposely sat in the first row. I was terrified. I had to prove to myself that I was different from when I sat in back of the room in grade school, frightened that the teacher would call on me.

"My sister will tell everyone in her office about Mother. She'll ask all those whose parents died of cancer all the gruesome details and get their sympathy. I don't like people looking cow-eyed. Mother has a lot of dignity. I want her to die with bearing. My sister will want to let people know what *she's* going through."

Doctor: "You don't seem to want to let even *you* know what you're going through."

Patient: (Disdainfully) "Should I cry at *La Traviata* or at the end of *La Boheme?* Corragio—courage—is what I want. I think, 'Which funeral home—what clothes to lay her out in—the burial place.' I almost wish it could happen overnight. My mother told my sister, 'You won't have your mother long.' She wouldn't tell me; she protects me. She doesn't spoil me. She should have sent me to college; she wanted to send my sister, but it would have been a struggle. Dad was a steelworker. They have a nice home. Maybe she felt I was strong. When we were little, she'd tell my sister, 'You're the cute type' and I wear a chignon because I was the 'sophisticated type.' My mother was unique—European—not the Southern Italian peasant type. She has a lot of refinement. Her marriage wasn't so wonderful. Daddy's not the kind of person you can talk to about world affairs. I always tried to please my mother and make life more interesting for her, take her to the opera and places to eat my father wouldn't know. I would prefer my mother to live than my father, if I had a choice."

At the next hour, while talking about her fear of driving and of mechanical devices, like washing machines, she suddenly interrupted herself.

Patient: "Around fourth grade, there was a girl in the desk in front of me, who'd reach behind and touch my clitoris. I'd do the same with her. We'd meet before and after school and do it. That went on for weeks until we decided it wasn't right. Then when I was twelve a girlfriend used to go into a kind of trance, not epilepsy; they called it 'petit mal.' When I fainted at the roller derby, my husband told me he thought I'd had a 'fit.' Tying in with the girl at school, I wonder if those rough babes in the roller derby impressed me as lesbians. Maybe that's what made me faint."

Were it not for the mother's impending death, therapy might

be relatively brief at this point, directed at her guilt over her incestuous, homosexual feelings toward her mother and over her jealousy and anger toward her sister and father. The process of separation and mourning and the working through of her ambivalence toward her mother would take time.

> *Patient:* "This week I had a tragic dream, but I couldn't remember it. Perhaps it was so sad, I didn't want to. Mother knitted all those baby things and she'll never see them used. She used to ask, 'Isn't it time you had children?' Now she says nothing, except to my sister, 'I guess they don't want children.' My sister and I are doing all the cooking for them. 'My poor girls.'"

She expressed anger at the family physician, because he "didn't know what to do for Mother. I thought, 'Don't you have some plan?' He offers no guidance." I commented that she was feeling helpless and angry at the doctor for his helplessness. She felt that the doctor was looking to her for moral guidance. She objected to "being talked down to" by the doctor. At her office banquet, her job was to pin flowers on employees with long years of service. This she found menial. She felt she should be a junior executive in place of some of the new young men to whom she felt far superior.

Meanwhile, her mother suffered a pathological hip fracture and was hospitalized under the effect of narcotics. Soon uremia developed and her mother became delirious, hardly a condition conducive to working out separation. The patient had nostalgia for the "marvelous Sunday dinners. Now we just go, clean the house, and make the beds. Everything's changed—there's not even salami in the refrigerator." She recalled for the first time her fear of her mother's temper. If the patient and her sister fought, "she'd come up and slap us wherever she chanced to hit—face, ear, behind. Once I wouldn't eat her soup. She hit me across the face. I'm not picky about food now. Her temper was as great as her affection."

> A month after treatment began, she remembered her first dreams, all the same night. "My husband and I are watching a man having an operation, a tonsillectomy. The seats in the amphitheater were small and my legs felt uncomfortable.

"My husband, my father and I were in a valley. It was huge and desolate, far from everything."

Her spontaneous association was "the valley of the shadow of death" of the Twenty-Third Psalm. The tonsillectomy reminded her of her own operation in a clinic office building that looked "decrepit, like the kind of place where you'd have an abortion." She had hemorrhaged, had been rushed to the hospital and transfused.

The tonsillectomy dream seemed to deny her mother's surgery. At the same time, the discomfort of her legs in the dream and the association of abortion suggest her own phantasies of castration, which she also sought to deny.

Almost miraculously, her mother emerged from her coma and returned home on steroid therapy. However, she was cranky, grumpy and irritable, to which the patient was unaccustomed. For the first time in her life she was unappreciated. When she washed her mother's hair, there was "too much shampoo" and the water was "too cold." She refused to see her mother's personality change at first, and instead accused the doctor of being grouchy. "You're no Norman Vincent Peale, you know. I'd like to hear nice things for a change."

At Thanksgiving, she had the following dream.

"It was a dentist's office (I hate dentists. I'm terrified of them). There was no chair. I had to climb on rungs on the wall, upside down, with my feet up. Mother was at the bottom, consternated at my fright. He tied my hands and feet to the rungs with a spool of thread. People in the reception room were watching. I felt excited and frightened. When the dentist first put me up, he lifted my dress. I had no underclothes on. 'You son of a bitch, put my dress down!' At the end of the dream, I began to cry."

A memory spontaneously escaped. "I was a little girl, maybe four or five. It was early on a Saturday morning. I walked into my parents' room. It was dark. I made out two bodies. My mother hollered for me to leave. Later, she said I shouldn't walk in with the door closed. It left an impression on my mind. Since my mother hollered, I felt that they were doing wrong."

The dream seemed to be a reversal. The patient was trussed like a turkey on exhibition, while everyone else was looking at her humiliation. Apparently she was, in actuality, angry at her father for what she considered a degrading act perpetrated on her mother.

Over the holiday, the patient and her husband were invited by an old high school friend to a "gay party," where they were the only "straights." She felt a burden, a black, unhappy, hopeless feeling. Shortly afterward she made an appointment with a gynecologist to be fitted for a diaphragm. He discovered a chronic cervicitis which he cauterized over a period of time before fitting her. She spoke to me of considering having an affair, because of her husband's lack of ardor. "I wouldn't feel guilty. Of course I'll have to choose a candidate." I commented on her cold-bloodedness. She replied that her husband made her feel neither desirable nor feminine, to which I inquired why she had chosen such a man. The only ecstatic sexual experience they had had was prior to their marriage, in five feet of water, some distance from her family on the beach. Was that the ecstacy, enacting a "primal scene" for her mother?

Mixed memories of her mother were returning. The patient had been her baby, pleasing, and appeasing her mother, never rebelling. Her mother was a "stormy" person. (this allusion appears later in a dream) The patient always sought her approval. Listening on the radio to the Metropolitan Opera, her mother opined that it would be nice to be an operatic singer. What did the patient want to be? An operatic singer. On the other hand, she recalled struggling against her mother's efforts to administer an enema and being slapped for her resistance, then being hugged. Her mother had shown her pictures from both their childhoods; the resemblance was "uncanny."

About this time, her husband began psychiatric treatment for his relative impotence; she envied him his doctor being a "Paisan." Although her phobia had diminished and was not incapacitating, it had not disappeared. Her phantasy was of fainting, being found by strangers and being taken to a hospital. This foundling phantasy was a replica of her own mother's adoption. Without any foundation in reality, the mother assumed that her real father had been an aristocrat and the patient felt that her own hands, different from her parents, were those of an aristocrat.

An incident terrified the patient. Her best friend invited her and her husband to dinner. Afterward, her friend got drunk, and in front of her own husband, the patient, and the patient's husband stripped off all her clothes and kissed the patient on the mouth. The patient's ensuing confusion and fright was abruptly cut short the next day by her mother's spiking a fever of 105 degrees, vomiting and developing jaundice. Within a week her mother lost her sphincter control, lapsed into coma, and quietly died. At the patient's next interview, I encouraged her expression of feelings related to her mother's death. Nothing was forthcoming; there was no overt grief. Unemotionally, she described the manner of her mother's death, her helping to choose a coffin, the funeral mass, and sorting through her clothes. Her only affect was anger expressed at her best friend's absence at the funeral. Within the following week, she experienced a flood of pleasant childhood memories, especially about her two "nippie-noonies" (pacifiers) that her mother carried for her when she was very young. Several nights she spoke in her sleep, waking her husband by asking, "Where's my water." It occurred to her that the date she learned of her mother's cancer was August fifteenth, The Feast of the Assumption. She stated emphatically, "I do not want to cry here," but could not explain her adamant position.

Over the next week she cried once, only briefly, when she needed the Italian word for lime in a crossword puzzle. Ordinarily, she would have phoned her mother. She felt that to cry would mean to be overwhelmed with grief, to be inundated in an unending flow of tears. She chose the alternative of stifling her sorrow. She consoled herself that her mother's death had ended her suffering, but was aghast at her memory as a child of wishing her mother dead for some long-forgotten reason. Also, a childhood memory of jealousy jolted her; her mother had given a little girl neighbor a small compact from her purse. With it came the realization that she had wanted sole possession of her mother and all that she had. This possessiveness seemed to extend to all her relationships. There was now a new boss in the office and the patient found herself daydreaming of becoming special to him. It suddenly occurred to her to tell me that although everyone else had kissed her moth-in the coffin, she, herself, did not even touch her. It reminded her of a scene in the motion picture, *The Three Faces of Eve*, in which a terror-stricken girl refuses to kiss her dead grandmother. Also, she took the crucifix from the coffin, but could not bring herself to hang it over her bed. In speaking of her mother, she still used the present tense. "It's almost as if she's away." I could not get her to talk about her fears of death.

At the next hour, she reported a dream in which she was invited to dinner and asked whether she could bring her mother along, since "she's been all alone since my father died and I hate to leave her." The naked wish to exchange her father's life for her mother's was no longer shocking to her; she readily admitted it, although she felt sorry for him. She spoke of superstition and the occult. She had been reading a book about demonology and exorcism, and was not quite sure whether she disbelieved or not. Memories of shame about her mother mortified her: her accent, her Catholicism in a Protestant neighborhood with Eastern Star Masonic mothers and daughters, her home-made-bread-and-salami-packed lunches when the other mothers packed peanut butter and jelly, her overweight. The realization that her mother would wear whatever outfit the patient liked, because she felt self-conscious that her daughters were embarrassed by her appearance, pained her. In another dream, her mother lay alive in bed, yelling at the patient's sister. The patient was glad that even in her coma her mother had yelled at everyone but her.

For her wedding anniversary celebration, she enticed her husband to a restaurant in a motel where her new boss was staying and invited him to join them for a drink. She described intercourse that night with her husband as being "successful." I confronted her with the selfish sexual gratification implied by her "successful" project and with her using her anniversary to further her own selfish aims in ingratiating herself with her new boss. She acknowledged both. She was aware of wanting her boss all to herself, just as she coveted her mother. She wanted her mother's sole attention always. Yet, she felt sorry for her sister when her mother put her arms around the patient. Her sister was not very aggressive and had no boyfriends. In childhood, her sister had fashioned a paper dress for her doll and the patient tore it up. Five years ago, the patient had gone to Atlantic City with her mother. "It was a delightful time, just the two of us—nothing to spoil it—one *pure* experience." Now the patient had a toothache and there was no one to rock her, to comfort her, to baby her.

A week later, she talked in her sleep again while her husband was watching the motion picture, *Bye-Bye Birdie,* on television in their bedroom. She sat bolt upright in bed and announced, "I have a birdie between my legs," then lay back asleep. When her husband informed her the next morning, she felt angry at herself for having said it. Until then, she had inwardly ridiculed my comments about her genitals being a source of anxiety for her. Now she could not argue with her own unconscious. She also had become painfully aware of her self-consciousness at a ginger ale commercial that was a parody of Bonnie and Clyde, cast entirely with girls. To her, it seemed overtly lesbian.

In succeeding weeks, she had several disturbing dreams.

"I am at the seashore, similar to Atlantic City. I seemed to be with my husband, my sister and an older woman on a vacation. I was so hungry I couldn't wait for dinner. There was a hot-dog stand, a high tower, I guess some kind of a phallic symbol. The older woman had a big pile of cotton candy on her plate. My order came, a hamburger—it was all messed up with a lot of stuff on it. Then I ordered cotton candy. My husband said to eat the candy first.

"Then I was suddenly crying to my mother. She had her arms around me. I told her how hard it was (tears came to her eyes briefly), and she said she understood. She said something that made me feel good about heaven, that there were no problems."

Hamburger reminded her of her German husband, who was from Hamburg. The cotton candy had an ethereal, ectoplasmic quality, that I suggested might be "essence of mother." The allusion to her "one pure experience" with her mother at Atlantic City seemed obvious to her. There seemed to be the message that her mother dead was still more satisfying to her than her husband alive. Perhaps after her own death she could rejoin her mother and be her baby again.

Her next dream was a reversal. Her mother was in bed, alive, swaddled in a sheet, like a mummy. The patient picked her up under one arm, when she suddenly felt that a man was going to murder her. In her associations she denied any awareness of her father's jealousy of her closeness to her mother. She had absolutely no doubt that her mother had loved her more than her sister or her father. Her attitude was that she should feel guilty only to her sister, who had lost her mother's affection.

She felt that her father had never had it to lose. "My mother used to pick on my father. They argued quite a bit, about almost anything. Nagging. If she happened to be in a picky mood, she criticized him or told him to shut up."

On August fifteenth she dreamed the following:

"Mother was ill at our family house. I was with her by myself. My Dad was supposed to come home at 11:30 as usual. I went downstairs in the basement to see if he'd come home. He was lying on the garage floor, dirty, sweating, with one arm severed at the shoulder. It was horrible. I picked him up in my arms. I had a feeling of desparation. My mother was sick upstairs and here was Dad. Also, I was repelled. Then I thought the railroad train caused the accident."

The scene of her holding her father reminded her of the Pieta, with the Blessed Mother taking Him down from the cross. She could not fathom the reason for the amputation. Her father had been the greatest help attending to her sick mother, turning her, giving her the bed pan, and feeding her. Why should he have an arm removed. Sarcastically she asked, "It's not going to be a penis, is it?" I reminded her that August fifteenth was the Feast of the Assumption, when the *Virgin* Mary was taken to heaven in body by Christ. I asked how she felt about her mother going to bed with her father, especially when she believed that there was no love for him. At first she denied even considering it. Her mother did not like sex. She had told the patient it was a wifely duty and nothing else. She recalled a second dream in which her mother was alive, but her father had died. The family was sitting around his casket when her father suddenly got out, entirely well, told everyone not to be upset and everyone carried on their normal conversation. When she was awake she had no doubt that she had wished him dead and had tried to undo it within the dream. She showed me several photographs of her family taken several years before. Only the patient and her mother were touching one another in each of the photographs. They had their heads together while the other members of the family were distanced from each other rather formally. She recalled being embarrassed to tell her friends in school that her father was a laborer; theirs were mostly professional people. Without meaning any disrespect, she regarded him as stupid. Her friends' fathers could help them with algebra. Her mother was her hero, not her father. I insisted that she must have resented his going to bed with her mother and probably hated him for what she considered sullying her goodness and purity. After all, the Feast of the Assumption took place only because of Mary's virginity, the Immaculate Conception. The amputation was his just dessert: castration. The patient responded with a memory of a conversation she had overheard in her teens and immediately forgot. Her mother was telling a friend how good her husband was at massaging her back, how good it made her feel. "He has such a nice touch with his hands. He gets to rubbing my back, and then before you know it ——," and the two dissolved in giggles. At that moment, she had been aghast that her mother was joking about intercourse pleasantly. The patient confessed that 98% of the time she merely pleased herself sexually during intercourse instead of sharing the experience with her husband. She wondered why she couldn't perform her "wifely duty," then realized she was parroting her mother.

At the next interview she reported three dreams.

"In my office, but not really my office, there was an interoffice memo: two wet spots on an envelope. I looked inside and threw it down in disgust and revulsion. There was an ejaculation inside. I was repulsed. I called one of the fellows in. He looked inside and said it was a discharge from a woman. 'No,' I disagreed, 'it's a sperm.' There was a rubber in the envelope, and maybe it had two black bands around it.

"My husband and I were travelling (we will this fall). There was a huge museum with antiquities, like a wine cellar, huge, with books, bookends, statues, even pianos. There were guards all around and lots of tourists. I wished my husband would steal something. I thought of old friends of ours, who had (not really).

"My new boss kissed me—nice—romantic. I always wanted to be kissed by a tall man."

Her husband had not had intercourse with her for weeks and she felt sexually frustrated. The black bands reminded her of mourning. I suggested that her revulsion about the ejaculation, "two wet spots," might refer to her mother's other two pregnancies, when her father did *not* use withdrawal. Her friends "stealing something" reminded her that they had just had a baby and she was considering doing the same, perhaps hoping that her husband might also "steal" one by not with-drawing. There was only one boss, her mother. A scene in the family kitchen came back to her. Her mother was fixing her hair and singing a ballad in Italian about a little girl who had a doll; the doll got old and was thrown in the trash pile. It was sad and had made her cry. On another occasion, her mother related the plot of an Italian play about a married sculptor and his model who pushed a statue on his wife, crushing her hands that had to be amputated. The final pathos was the handless mother being unable to accept a gift handed to her by her daughter. The patient suddenly realized that only her mother had ever been able to move her emotionally. She remonstrated with herself for not having spent enough time with her mother, for not having done enough. "I would like to relate the story of her death from beginning to end, but I can only do it here, and then it comes out only in bits and pieces." The previous week she had been searching for an evening gown for a dance and had called a place listed in the yellow pages of the phone book, only to be told that they made gowns solely for burial. It "shook her up" for two days, but did not free any of her grief. "I don't want to cry here. I don't like to show emotions anyhow. And this is a clinical atmosphere. You'd be sitting there, not com-forting me, letting me cry. It reminds me of that bunch in St. Louis who published that sex study" (Masters and Johnson). I commented that her association to thoughts of mourning of her mother seemed to be connected to sexual thoughts as well, that perhaps she feared revealing her sexual phantasies about her mother. As usual, she vigorously denied that any such thoughts ever existed.

However, the next week she reported a homosexual dream, "like a Fellini movie, very dirty.

"I'm going to a beauty parlor to have my hair done, but it wasn't a beauty parlor setting. A lot of wierdo hippies were walking around. One of the operators was a hard-looking, hand-some, striking Negro with a goatee. A girl is lying naked on her back on the floor. She had dark, long, black hair. She spread her legs. I looked at her vagina. She masturbated—she was eat-ing a hot dog—she touched the hot dog to her vagina and breathed a sigh of relief.

"Then a girl came up to me and said I was her customer. She was posing me on a table or ledge. As she touched me,

I felt myself becoming aroused. Then it was as though the dream were censored—she asked, 'Would you like to go for a walk?'

"I was calling a friend of mine who moved to California recently. I could hear the edge in my voice, 'You didn't send me your new address.' Then I was on my back porch with a man and a big dog. I thought, 'Oh, now beastiality with a big dog.' "

The patient had no associations except that she felt certain that the girl on the floor was she. She had to acknowledge her homosexual feelings, since they were obvious in the dream. The rest of the dream, including the masturbating scene, left her puzzled. I asked wasn't there someone who had just "gone West" (died), whose exact address was uncertain (her uncertainty about after-life and heaven). That led to her identifying the striking Negro as the devil. She could not fathom the allusion to the hot dog, except as one of those phallic symbols. I pointed out to her that in the dream she had unsuccessfully tried to avoid homosexuality by the use of the hot dog. Might she not be saying that were her husband more passionate, a hotter dog than he actually was, she could have satisfied her sexual urges toward her mother without being aware of them and without frustration. She allowed that the dog might have been a German Shepherd (her husband was German). A memory came to her of the pleasant relaxation of her mother's sponge-bathing her, and of her asking her mother, "Why do I have a yellow spot on the green of my eye?" Her mother replied that it was spaghetti juice. I asked, "And when you asked her about your genitals?" She remembered nothing.

During the next week, she had a "good cry" about her mother. Sitting alone, playing the piano, the patient thought of her mother preparing for her going, leaving each daughter a candelabrum. "Her being taken away—and I'd never see her again." Then she began thinking, "What is life all about? Why are we here?" That so frightened her that she stifled her feelings. The same night her sister called: she had been laid off from her job because her agency had lost two of its largest accounts. "My mother said that my sister walks around with a little black cloud." Several nights later she dreamed.

"I'm going to the doctor. I supposed it was to see you, but it was like a department store ladies' room or a terminal with lots of seats and benches. A female sat next to me and had men's shoes on. I thought, 'A lesbian.' Then my husband was with me and the girl, walking past a woman's shoe store. The girl was never offensive, but talked about homosexuality. I was getting sexually aroused, I walked rubbing my legs together, so I'd have a climax."

There were no associations. I asked whether the female who was in the doctor's office, had on men's shoes, and spoke of homosexuality might not represent me, a maternal substitute? She replied that two nights before she had dreamed about being at my office, reclining, and I had bent down and lightly kissed her on the lips. With the dream came an explanation that she was very frustrated sexually, had approached her husband, and he had been unable to have an erection. "I am attracted to you. Right now you're the only man in my life I could be attracted to. Stripping one's soul is worse than stripping one's body. The only involvement one can have with a psychiatrist is phantasy." (She had no specific phantasies in mind) I asked about her walking with her legs together. Her mother had been critical of her walking with her feet too far apart. I assumed that her gait was an avoidance of sexual arousal and asked about her phantasies during masturbation. At other interviews that same question lay unanswered. This time she replied vehemently, but she replied,

"Jesus Christ! These are thoughts you shouldn't have to tell anyone! I'm in a movie theater with a man. We start love play. I remove all my clothes under the raincoat. Oh, for Christ's sake! He stimulates my clitoris—I'm getting angry I have to tell you this—we leave the balcony. I ask the usher—he's colored—if there's a place we could screw. The man opens my raincoat and shows the usher my body. We tell the usher he can watch. We go screw in an alcove.—I must be an exhibitionist—he ejaculates in me and I climax.

"Then there's another one. I'm on a beach by myself. Several guys come along. I have intercourse with all of them. Also a dog.

"These all started when I was thirteen or fourteen, reading *True Confession Magazine*. I'd get aroused, lay on my stomach on the floor and put a lead pencil in me."

I asked about the theater and the exhibitionism in terms of

seeing her parents or imagining them having intercourse. There were no memories of either.

The next week she came dressed in a very mannish pants suit with a stylish urchin's cap. She was armed with her diary from age twelve, the essence of which was her complaints of not having a boyfriend. By protesting that she really wanted boys then, she was trying to refute my interpretations of her sexual desires for her mother. Contract negotiations were being held at her office and she had to run for coffee a dozen times a day, a menial task. She complained that she was not in the limelight any more.

By the following week, she had corrected that. Her boss made a pass at her. I doubted that it would have happened without some kind of encouragement from her. It represented acting out at several levels against her husband and me, especially because of her anger at my interpreting her homosexual feelings toward her mother and at my lack of response to those same feelings toward me. She tried to interrupt my comments, and when I continued she apologized, "Sorry, I didn't mean to cut you off," which was also obviously interpreted. She related a dream to which she had no spontaneous associations.

"I am in a cemetery in a drab line of people along a hillside, but I am not sad. There was a path over an access of lawn. Perhaps I was looking for a tombstone. Then in the valley I saw two human figures, representing tombstones, of dark plaster and somewhat abstract, bent and not together, exactly like bookends.

"The scene changes, and Mother, Mary Lou and I are kneeling in church (father never went with us).

"Then I'm a bride, taking part in an *annual* marriage. I had on an ice blue wedding gown and red ballet slippers with draw strings like a raffia rope, untied and dirty and dusty. 'Lulu,' my sister said, "the wedding is about to begin and you're getting all dusty and dirty."

I asked whether she was familiar with the fairy tale and the movie on which it was based, *The Red Shoes*. "Of course, Moira Shearer, the girl who couldn't stop dancing—My God! that's the scene in the dream! Is that *my compulsion?* My mother? That over and over I keep wanting to marry my mother? Like the annual Tom Thumb wedding the kids used to hold in the church. Very good, Dr. Lewin." She controlled her emotions at that point, and made it an intellectual exercise for which she graded me accordingly. I commented that it was interesting that, like bookends which never meet because of the books between them, she had separated her parents from one another for all eternity.

At the next interview, she reported that her gynecologist told her that he had found an enlargement of one ovary at her previous visit, but that it had returned to normal size. "So it's not cancer. I wasn't one hundred per cent pleased. I want to have him say some day, 'You're perfect.' I thought of cancer and my mother. I'm too young to die. Is my love for my mother abnormal in degree? I hate myself for having this problem, thinking of her as my lover. I wish my husband and I were straightened out." The previous night she had had a dream.

"My husband and I were invited to my girlfriend's for dinner (the one who'd gone out West, I dreamed of before). I went to the bathroom to urinate. She took me aside and whispered, 'You urinate so much. You should go to a doctor. It's a psychological problem.' She made some wretched Syrian (?) dinner. I didn't recognize anything but kidney beans.

"I was in the apartment alone. The further back I went, the prettier the apartment became. There was a window with sheer white curtains, but outside was a black ugly fire escape and the 'el' (elevated train). Then a girl came in (she's an acquaintance who once complained about her bottom being pinched at a 'gay bar' by another girl). She wanted to use the bathroom to straighten her girdle." I asked her associations about urination and kidney (beans).

"I remember wondering, when I was ten or eleven years old, why I couldn't urinate standing up. It seemed so much easier for a man to urinate. A woman has to take her girdle down and she has to wipe herself afterward. I remember in elementary school there were no doors on the ladies' room commode. We never wiped ourselves. Until last year, I always wiped from back to front. A woman at the office had a kidney infection and she told me that her doctor warned her that infection could be started with germs carried forward that way. My mother wiped from back to front. Why doesn't somebody warn women about that? We never learned it in hygiene in school. It reminds me of old ladies, spreading their legs and reaching back to wipe themselves. It's ugly and dirty looking. An area for eliminating wastes. Until I was ten years old or so, I didn't really know where urine came out from. I wish I could remember more details about that episode of standing up to urinate. Maybe it was later, maybe when reading *True Confession Magazine.* That would have been twelve or thirteen. Something sexual about standing up, being a man. Curiosity, no fear. I think I tried it only once and it wasn't comfortable. I had to straddle the toilet, whereas a man stands in front of it. That's all I can recall."

I asked when she learned about ejaculation, if at ten she had so much confusion even about her own urination. She couldn't remember, but it seemed well into her teens and long after learning about intercourse. It seemed clear then that when she first had phantasies about her parents' having intercourse, she must have assumed that her father urinated into her mother. While she had no specific memories, she agreed that it sounded very likely. I asked whether, in any event, for her mother to have intercourse, a dirty act, was not indeed the road to "el" (hell). She had never considered it consciously.

During the next week, she had dreams on successive nights. In the first, she was in a hotel and heard a dance or wedding downstairs. When she came downstairs to investigate, her boss kissed her. She awoke feeling guilty and frustrated.

In the next night's dream, the male homosexual friend from her high school days was carrying her up the front steps of her family's house, as though they had just been married and he was carrying his bride over the threshold. The last dream found her on the steep street (nicknamed Cardiac Hill) leading to Pitt Stadium with her boss and the public relations man from her office. The latter was doing comical things. They took a flannel bathrobe, soaked it in a tub of water, and the fellow was supposed to put it on. She and her boss were supposed to make fun of him running up the hill in the wet robe in the freezing cold, and take a humorous picture of him for a newspaper article he was writing.

In reality, her boss had called her the night before about a certain office form. She felt that it was odd that he would call her home, and she assumed that it had been a pretext to hear her voice. Her phantasy was that he had an uncontrollable yearning for her. I confronted her with the phantasy that lay just beneath that one, that it was her mother who loved her more than anyone else in the world. In the dream she interrupts the wedding and "the boss" kisses her. Being married to a homosexual male was as close as she had come in a manifest dream content to marrying another woman. She responded by recognizing the bathrobe in the dream as one she had given her father for Christmas. She and "the boss" were not only ridiculing the public relations man (she realized the implication of "relation") but were endangering his health by tempting pneumonia or a heart attack. Why that man? She felt he was becoming wise to the boss's attraction to her. "He knows too much. He's no dumdum. He's seen us looking at each other." The similarity between her phantasied office triangle and her family triangle was striking. And the night before the interview she had opened up the package of Christmas cards she had ordered months before. On the card was a picture of the Virgin Mother, and the patient was astounded to see a resemblance to her own mother. The dream of Cardiac Hill convinced her that she really did have deadly impusles toward her father. At the same instant, she expressed awareness of anger at her mother for the first time. "She should have sent me to college. I was smart enough to be college material. It wasn't intentional, just ignorance on her part. To her, a girl went to college only to become a teacher, and for some reason she despised what she considered a typical teacher's personality, naggy, dull, old-maidish and unintelligent."

At the next interview, she complained of a horrible week at the office, thinking about her boss romantically and feeling guilty. I confronted her with the sadistic nature of her conscience, which, instead of prohibiting even the possibility of such a romance, encouraged the phantasy and then tortured her for it. She described a vivid dream from mid-week.

"My husband and I lived in a provincial farmhouse with lots of levels. We were showing it to my sister and my father. Outside, sparks flashed in the sky all around—frightening. We ran outside. The next house was a quarter of a mile away with a tree nearby. The tree had no leaves; it had been cut by tree surgeons. A bolt of lightning struck the tree, which fell on the house. We realized that the sparks were from a huge storm and tornado. There were black funnels everywhere in the sky. I ran down the street. There was no panic. Instead, it seemed to be a festive occasion, a parade, with little children dressed in black. Each time they opened their mouths, little puffs of black smoke came out, similar in shape to the tornado funnels."

She had no associations, except recalling vaguely that there had been a tornado near her community in childhood. I reminded her that she had described her mother as a stormy person, that the storm may have represented her presence. I also reminded her of her dream many weeks before of her father's amputation, likening it to the amputated tree. "Before our very first appointment I told my husband that the psychiatrist would tell me I hated my mother. When a child says, 'I wish you were dead'—I said it only once and I don't recall when or why —she doesn't really mean it. I always had a bad temper. I suppose some children are placid." I indicated that in the dream the children, with the smoke coming from their mouths, would be worthy some day of being full-grown storms like their mothers. At the end of the hour, I told her of my intention to be away for ten days, two months hence (I customarily tell my patients of my vacation plans as soon as I have made them and encourage them to discuss their feelings about my leaving from then on).

During the next week, the patient noticed herself becoming more relaxed at the office. She repeated to me the story of her mother's arranged marriage to her father. "Everyone knew that Daddy wasn't the right person for her." She had thought about my comments about her conscience and found them interesting and thought-provoking. She felt that over the years she had adopted many of her mother's petty grievances, prejudices, and grudges as her own, such as her disdain of Negroes, uneducated people, and Southern Italians. Fifteen years ago a good friend of her parents died and the widow did not ask the patient's father to be a pallbearer. Her mother abruptly and irrevocably terminated the friendship. The patient wondered whether she had adopted her mother's conscience as her own, along with all her other attitudes, including her vindictiveness. She had dreamed.

"Little balls, like eggs, or egg yolks were coming down from the sky. I was trying to catch them in my mouth, bite, and chew them. But I couldn't, because each one was slippery and would slide back and forth." Her associations were eggs, ovulation, conception, and babies. She might have been ovulating, herself, when she dreamed; the stage of her menstrual cycle was appropriate. She had received Christmas cards from her friends and it seemed almost everyone was pregnant. She would be thirty soon. Her mother had told her babies came from the moon. Now she realized it fit the notion of Immaculate Conception. "You know, it was a long time before I knew that the baby was in its mother's stomach." At first she was bewildered when I inquired, "Stomach?," but then it dawned on her that at one time she must have believed that babies grew in the mother's stomach, and naturally the seed had to be planted through the mouth. How else does anything get into the stomach? She had no conscious memories of fallatio phantasies.

The following week she grumbled, "I've been carrying anger all week. Mother is dead." Her friend, who had not paid her condolence call, had had a miscarriage and the patient did not visit her in the hospital. The patient had her and her husband for dinner. When her friend tearfully inquired why she had not visited her, the patient responded, "Don't you dare cry. Blow your nose and we'll talk about it." She told her friend of her own anger at her friend's unresponsiveness after her mother's death. At that moment, the patient felt a marvelous surge of relief, unburdening the anger which ordinarily she would have nursed indefinitely, as her mother might have. But the next night she regressed. She and her husband were discussing whether cancer patients should be told the true nature of their illness. He felt that they should. She found herself becoming so angry that she felt like striking him. She threw a book of matches at him. She felt furious with him and furious that her mother had died, while he lived. She found herself hating Man. "This week I even hated Frederick Chopin." She had had five dreams and forgotten them all (an act of defiance and anger at me?). All she could recall was that in one dream she was going to be married to the Greek millionaire, Onassis. I responded, "That would make *you* Jaqueline Kennedy, the world's most famous widow—if *you* are the famous widow, then your father wasn't married to the person who died; you were 'The one who lost her spouse.'" She said nothing and looked even more sullen. I continued, "If you're angry with me, tell me outright as you did with your friend. Are you

afraid I won't like you or try to help you any more?" She
whined that she was being unjustly accused, and furiously
pulled down the edge of her miniskirt. Immediately I continued, "Now you're trying to deny your anger, just as you're
trying to hide your exhibitionism. You walked in acknowledging your anger, and wearing a stylish haircut, heavy eye make-
up and a miniskirt obviously meant to draw attention to you,
and now you pull down your skirt as though by doing so you
can deny and undo it all, exhibitionism and anger. You don't
want to be told about *your* cancer, your anger that's eating at
you. You're saying, 'Look at what I want you to look at, but not
at what I'm trying to conceal!' " The patient was aghast at what
I said and probably at the vigor with which it was said. She
half-whispered, "I couldn't say what I feel. I couldn't say, 'I
wish you were dead.' My God! Who would I depend on?"
Quietly and deliberately I answered, "Did you hear what
you said? That was confirmation that you *do* believe that your
anger is deadly. Your mother *is* dead. You're convinced that it
was the result of your half-forgotten wish, slow-acting." "Still,
I can't express that feeling of anger toward you. Oh, my poor
husband! He'll really get it this week." I asked her first to consider which of us two was truly more expendable to her; she
could easily find another psychiatrist. But, more important,
it was time that she realized that her angry wishes were harmless, not fatal. She merely preferred the guilt of phantasied
omnipotence to the almost completely helpless feeling of her
childhood self.

At the following session she related two dreams.

"Mother was in bed. I was upstairs complaining to my sister
how hard I worked at the office. I was sitting in an overstuffed
chair and began urinating into it. I thought, 'How ridiculous—
I'm too busy to go to the bathroom.'

"I had an adopted oriental girl, age six or seven. At first I
didn't like her and ignored her. I thought, 'She's not like a cat
that you can give away.' All of a sudden I loved her and
wanted to become a mother to her. I had the child against my
breast. I opened my blouse and she sucked on one breast. I became sexually excited and woke up."

She had seen a television commercial for helping deprived
children, among them oriental girls. Perhaps she had an urge to
suck on her mother's breast at that age, but she had no mem-

ories and it was merely a guess. She recalled our previous discussion about urination being equated in a child's mind with ejaculation. She recalled a dream a few days later.

"I'm drinking a warm Pepsi from the bottle. It didn't satisfy my thirst. I drank a Coke and noticed a crack in the neck of the bottle. I wondered if I swallowed glass. Little pieces were in my mouth. I spit them out, but they didn't hurt."

Her mother always served Royal Crown Cola. Her mother's friend, who had offered mothering since her mother's death, served Pepsi-Cola. She assumed that the bottles were phallic symbols or breast symbols or both. Obviously, she rejected the ministration of her mother's friend in real life. Was the last part oral impregnation?

The next time a dream series was described, it was a resume of her illness.

"My husband and I and a group of people are all mounting horses (in real life I avoid them out of fear). I had a small horse. I was furious at my husband because I didn't know how to mount and he wasn't there to show me. Then I was in the grandstand with people. The horses were going around the track and we were supposed to grade them. I had nowhere to put the paper. I tried to write on my lap. Everyone was finished but me, and I hadn't even started to write.

"I was in a room with my boss. A party was going on. He kissed me. Someone came in and we had to break our embrace. I decided I would make love with him. Everyone left and I expected him to kiss me, but he said that there was no time now.

"The setting seemed to be *Romeo and Juliet*. There was another girl with me and a fellow. We were *all* going to make love. We ended up in a bedroom. I was aroused. The girl began undressing, but I undressed first. The fellow made love to me and ejaculated in me (the first time I ever dreamed that)."

She commented, "They were all nice, sexy dreams, just situations without any guilt." She had felt sexually aroused all week. She began talking about the dreams. "Everyone had finished and I hadn't filled out my form."

I commented, "Oh, *that's* what you were doing? You couldn't fill out a form and you couldn't mount, and you needed instruction from a male."

"That all fits in with what we've been talking about, just as you've said. Somehow I must have wanted to become pregnant or make my mother pregnant when I was small. Now I understand about the animals going around the track—it was the roller derby where I fainted—they were animals. The night of that dream I watched wrestling and they had women wrestlers. I didn't want to watch and yet I watched. I felt frightened and depressed—I actually did think about the roller derby and lesbians, watching two women wrestling. I'd never been convinced about these feelings until now. There isn't any doubt in my mind about my physical love for my mother."

I replied, "The fact that *I* consider astounding is your refusal to mourn her death by what amounts to a virtual denial of her death. For all the excessive closeness that you claim to have had with your mother, you still need her as an actual external object, like a love and security blanket. For some reason you don't have her inside to keep with you. Instead you must maintain the fiction that she is alive, here or somewhere. You need her actual physical presence."

"I know you're right. There is one thing left. Mother had put away fine linens for my sister and me to split between us. I haven't been able to go ahead and do it. If I don't take those things from her house—well, if I do take those things, then Mother's not there anymore. But why isn't she 'inside', as you put it?"

I reminded her of her dreams of her father's amputation on the Feast of the Assumption, her wish for Immaculate Conception, and her anger at her mother's being sullied. "Imagine how Romeo would have felt had he discovered that Juliet had another lover? She told you that intercourse was a wifely duty, yet you overheard her tell her friend about his back massages, 'And then the first thing you know—', giggle, giggle. You refused to keep your mother inside because of your anger at her infidelity to you, anger that you nexer expressed to her for fear of losing her love."

DEATH OF A PARENT

Therapy is much more difficult with a patient who has lost one or both parents. No matter how incisive one's interpretations are about the preposterousness of the infantile omnipotence of phantasies, they are overbalanced by the fact that the parent is, indeed dead. As the man on the Manhattan street corner, snapping his fingers in order to keep tigers away, dismisses disbelievers, "Well, you ain't seen no tigers, have you?" the orphaned patient can retort, "I wished them dead and they're dead. *Prove* I didn't do it." That kind of guilt is exceedingly hard to overcome. The introjected sadistic conscience is implacable. Moreover, it is much more complicated to alter an introject when one must deal only with memories and phantasies about that individual. The actual day to day living with a person makes it more possible to weigh one's preconceived, distorted notions from childhood about that person against the reality of that person as he appears to the patient's adult view, clarified through therapy. Would the parent react differently if the patient were to modify his own emotional responses? This testing is impossible with a ghost.

Chapter X

TERMINATION AND LEAVE-TAKING

WHEN the goals set in the initial interview have been met, the therapy is over. Obviously, if clear-cut goals have not been agreed upon at the beginning of therapy, it will be virtually impossible to determine when the treatment has been completed. The absence of goals commonly agreed upon initially is one of the main causes of interminable treatment. Should the doctor decide arbitrarily that the patient is well enough to leave, he would be making an autocratic decision that would immediately infantilize the patient, resulting in either passive compliance, defiant rebellion, or most commonly, regression with recurrence of symptoms.

Termination should be a joint decision, arrived at almost simultaneously by both patient and doctor. The only possible method of termination that preserves the patient's autonomy is one that has been pre-arranged by common consent at the onset of therapy. Should the patient decide unilaterally that the treatment is over, the doctor must rely on the same pre-arranged condition: have the goals been met? If the goals have not been met, then the wish for termination must be exposed as a resistance and be analyzed. If the goals have been met, the treatment is over, and the doctor should ask himself why he had not recognized that fact himself. Counter-transference resistances are just as real as those of transference. Often, like the story of Scheherazade, the patient's tales and personality are so intriguing that the doctor is reluctant to see him go. Although in our current culture there are seldom shortages of patients, the physician may unconsciously be reluctant to have an empty hour in his schedule, even for a week. Also, he may consider it a chore to take on a new patient, meaning a whole new set of information to learn and to integrate and a different personality with whom to interact. Most important, the ending of therapy is difficult both for patient and doctor because of their feelings attendant to leave-taking. *Termination is not always synonymous with leave-taking. The therapy is over when the goals have been met. However, that does not necessarily signify that the patient and doctor will discontinue the interviews forthwith. Before the interviews can be discontinued, the relationship which the patient has made with the doctor must be resolved.* In brief psychotherapy, this is not identical with the resolution of transference in psychoanalysis. In brief therapy, not enough time has elapsed for the relationship to have attained the strength nor the complexity of an analytic transference. Likewise, in the resolution of the relationship in brief therapy, not all aspects of the transference can be examined. One aspect of the relationship is crucial, whatever the mode of treatment. Has the patient introjected his therapist to the extent of replacing his sadistic conscience with the model afforded by the therapist? If that introjection has not taken place, there will be more likelihood of symptom recurrence at some future time. The dictum that a lack of introjection of the therapist means a bad prognosis is not absolute. During the course of therapy, the patient may have regrouped his old defenses or added new ones that would enable him to avoid anxiety and depression. Introjection of the therapist increases the probability of longer lasting emotional well-being for the patient.

At the onset of the therapy, the doctor is only an external object to the patient. His actual physical presence or its direct implication by his voice on the telephone is necessary for the patient to feel his attendance. At first, the doctor is viewed as a neutral external object, like a piece of furniture in an unfamiliar room, emotionally colored only with those feelings that the patient has brought with him. However, the confrontative technique of brief psychotherapy quickly converts the therapist in the patient's eyes into an emotionally charged object of ambivalence. Soon, the doctor's benign aspect emerges and the patient perceives him as an ally against his own sadistic conscience. At that point, the doctor is an external loved object, an entity distinctly separate from the patient's self, no more internalized than a love-and-security-blanket is for a small child. Just as that blanket gives the child a feeling of security, well-being, and placidity, and its removal produces insecurity, tension, and anxiety, so the patient becomes dependent upon the doctor's actual presence and the promise of the continuance of that presence through regular interviews.

The threat of loss of that presence creates anxiety usually inversely proportionate in amount to the maturity and ego-strength of the patient. The regressed, poorly organized patient may become frenzied with the doctor's absence and therefore will require frequent interviews. Often, he will telephone the doctor between visits just to hear his voice. On the other hand, the more mature person will merely "look forward" to his next visit. As the therapy progresses, the patient's old introjected sadistic conscience is identified as a malignant force and is separated from the patient's self. The therapist has served as a model for a healthier conscience, admonishing the patient to do better, yet never hurting the patient for mere torture's sake, accepting all his thoughts and feelings as human and not requiring punishment, cautioning him about the consequences of his actions, while helping him to consider alternatives, and guiding him toward the fulfillments of his goals without hurting himself or other people. Inevitably, the patient develops positive feelings at some level for his doctor, and if unable to give love, at least wishes that the doctor will love him. The termination of therapy poses a threat to the source of that love. Rarely do patient and doctor see each other, even accidentally, outside the confines of the office. The nature of their relationship assures that they have no social acquaintanceship. When the interviews cease, they will likely never see each other again. To all intents and purposes the doctor will be dead. In miniature, the leave-taking in psychotherapy is a replica of the death of the patient's objects of love, especially his parents.

The basic anxiety created by the death of loved ones is abandonment. The death of loved ones is probably the single most difficult thing to accept in growing up, only possibly equalled by thoughts of the dissolution of one's self. Even the analysis of a patient's own death usually reveals fears of eternal loneliness, death being seen as a permanent, complete abandonment. Undoubtedly the concept of a life after death in almost all the world's religions is meant to offer reassurance of a final togetherness. Heaven is conceived as a place of permanent reunion, eternal bliss, a denial of the desolation of death. There is no equivalent of heaven in psychotherapy. What is offered is more real, though in a sense spiritual. While the external object of the doctor will die when the interviews end (and indeed some day the doctor will, in reality, die), the patient has an opportunity to incorporate whatever is worthwhile of the doctor before he goes, so what he may take the doctor with him. The memorial to the dead is not the slab of marble or granite that stands on his grave, but rather that part of him that lives on in the minds and hearts of those who admired, respected, and loved him. If the patient wants to keep anything of the doctor, he must learn to introject him, to take him inside, to convert him from an external object into a part of himself.

LEAVE TAKING—INTERVIEWS

Case Illustration: Miss A.B., a college professor of chemistry, was a 30-year-old large woman, who came into treatment because of polymorphous perverse sexual behavior, which she, herself, recognized as a symptom of identity confusion. "Perhaps it all boils down to sex. Am I making a wreck of myself? I seem to be unsure of what's right and wrong. I go to bed with anybody, but I can't bring myself to go to bed with someone I love. Perhaps I'm a lesbian. I identify with men; I think I don't seem to get along with women. If any woman treats me with kindness, I love it, but I spoil it. I don't want to continue to treat myself like garbage and make garbage of my experiences. I'm starved for mothering." Her doubts were of long standing, but her immediate problem was an imminent sexual relationship with a female student. Over the previous five years, she had had several years of psychotherapy, one experience lasting for two years, mainly to relieve her guilt about masturbation. Her therapy had been interrupted by her moving to other cities in pursuit of her academic career. She had lived alone since college, in keeping with her schizoid personality. Part of her withdrawal, however, was facilitated by her continual provocation of people who showed her affection. She had two brothers, four years her senior and her junior. She was consciously aware of jealousy toward her younger brother, "a beautiful blonde, curly-haired pet," and of her resentment of her parents, especially her mother, for his being favored.

She was not aware of the enormity of her guilt attendant to those feelings, or of the nature of her sadistic conscience. With those I confronted her at the initial interview, with the self-destructiveness of her sexual activity and her over-eating (not only was she grossly overweight, but she had had surgery for a ruptured disc and had been warned that overweight would be disastrous for her spine), and her alienation from her family and friends through her provocative behavior. Her conscience was ensuring that she got none of the mothering that she craved.

At the onset of treatment, she tried many ploys designed to thwart, frustrate, irritate, and provoke me. Frequently, she would invoke statements from previous doctors that would either contradict what I said or, in agreement, that would out-do what I said. Interpretations were met with stony silence, sarcasm, or burlesqued acceptance. She forgot all her dreams. My only reaction was continued confrontation that her conscience was trying to drive me away so that she would not get my help. She retorted that men were gullible, that she could pull the wool over their eyes. "I act helpless and foolish and I laugh at their trying to help me." After several weeks of unsuccessfully attempting to provoke me, she gave it up, and we proceeded to resolve some of her guilt feelings. She began writing to her family and visited with them. After she stopped her acting-out, her overeating, drinking, and homosexual behavior, she decided that she had attained the goals she had set for treatment. Her leave-taking was rather abrupt, one session to be exact.

She spoke of her excitement, apprehension, and exhilaration at leaving. "I'm feeling well and doing well. This sad feeling—nostalgia perhaps—leaving someone who's been good to you, someone you've come to admire and respect—I might never see you again. It's so—final. I feel that I've left a little bit of myself behind and replaced it. On the way here today, I ran across a funeral procession. I thought of my grandmother's funeral when I was seventeen. I remember having an idea of what I'd lost and felt sorry for myself. The only person who loved me had died. My loveableness was dead. I certainly haven't been very loveable since. Maybe there is more to this symbolism of death. Perhaps it signifies, too, the death of all the bitter feelings to my mother, and not just the death of *our* relationship here. I'd been aware of the rage inside me, but not that I'd driven people away. Now I feel able to be open to people, to give myself. It sounds corny, but I feel that maybe I could be loveable again. Maybe our *relationship* is over, ended, and dead, but I can be alive again, like you."

INTROJECTION

The concept of introjection has always been well known to religionists in terms of their gods. The evangelist exhorts his congregation, "Take Jesus inside yourself; let him fill your soul." The Twenty-Third Psalm intones, "Yea, though I walk through the valley of the shadow of death,I will fear no evil, for Thou art with me." Somehow it seems difficult for most people to substitute a humanistic view for the religious one. The doctor is no god, nor does he pretend to be one. Yet the principles of psychiatry and religion, in their essence, stripped of jargon, dogma, and ritual, are identical: do not to your fellow man that which you would not have him do unto you. The doctor stands for that credo and with it tries to replace the sadistic conscience of his neurotic, masochistic patient. For a patient to have insight into the nature of his infantile conflicts is not enough. There is no honor in being the smartest neurotic on the block. The standards by which the patient judges himself must be altered. At least temporarily, the doctor serves as a healthier, kinder, more consistent, more compassionate, more firm conscience that the patient had when he first came into treatment. When the patient first adopted his punitive conscience, he was young, frightened by his own impulses and impulsiveness, and unsure that he could prevent himself from harming others. He gave his conscience complete reign, virtual dictatorship to assure order. The dictatorial conscience strengthened itself and could not be dislodged, even when the need for dictatorship had passed. Presumably, growth, experience, and judgment could now enable the patient to channel his impulses, but his conscience had retained its control in an infantile, self-punitive, stereotyped manner. To *remove* that conscience would lead to chaos. Impulses would go unchecked. The only healthy solution would be to *replace* that sadistic conscience, first with the introject of the doctor, and then hopefully, perhaps even some time after the therapy has ended, with an introject of the "good parent."

The healthy solution, introjection of the doctor as a conscience, seems rather obvious. Unfortunately, its enactment is neither predictable nor controllable. Even when a patient recognizes his need for a better conscience and really wants to replace his own conscience with the doctor, he has no notion how to proceed. Worse yet, the doctor cannot describe the steps by which the patient might effect such an introjection.

The best that the doctor can do in abetting introjection is to help the patient to resolve his negative feelings toward him. Ambivalence seems to impede adult introjection. Therefore, when the therapy is over, and leave-taking commences, the patient must be helped to resolve the resurgence of anger toward the doctor attendant to termination. In small measures, such anger arises in the course of therapy each time there is an interruption of treatment caused by the doctor's absence, whether by illness or by vacation. An alert therapist will have encouraged his patient to express his separation anger on those occasions, in anticipation of their final separation. (The expression of separation anger after vacations is so common in my own practice that it almost seems that I need a vacation more after a week following my return than did when I left! I am accustomed to announce my vacations to my patients as soon as I have definitely arranged my plans, no matter how far in advance. My patients are asked then to express whatever feelings they have about my leaving. Those feelings are pursued after my return. Most patients are hesitant to express negative feelings prior to my departure. Even the least regressed people are fearful of the omnipotence of their thoughts and wishes. Rarely will anyone relate hostile fears or wishes, such as thoughts of my plane crashing, until after my safe return. Then comes the deluge.) That the doctor will actually voluntarily absent himself is often viewed by the patient, at least on one level, as a betrayal. The patient is bereft in time of need. At the same time, at another level, the doctor's absence is an unspoken compliment to the patient's ego, an act of confidence in the patient's ability to care for himself. After all, one of the prime goals of any good parent is the enablement of his children to fend for themselves eventually. The doctor's aim is similar for his patients, to make himself dispensable. The positive aspects of separation from therapy should not be ignored. But the negative aspects of separation, and the loss of faith brought on by betrayal, deserve immediate attention. Once again, the patient must be encouraged to express his anger in any way short of physical violence, without any kind of reprisal. In the encouragement of the patient's expression of anger, the interviews near the end of treatment are similar to those near the beginning of treatment. Once again, the separation anger would be likened, if possible, to that time of betrayal in childhood when the patient spewed out his previously good introject in exchange for the sadistic one he has retained.

LOSS OF FAITH AND EXTERNALIZATION

Case Illustration: Mr. R.N., a 28-year-old junior executive, came into treatment as a consequence of a series of disastrous relationships with women. He sought relief for his immediate depressive reaction, but he also wanted to search for the source of his neurotic entanglements. He had been estranged from his family since adolescence, several years after the birth of his younger sister. His mother especially bore the brunt of his wrath, which was expressed in a passive aggressive fashion. Whatever his mother wished of him, he did exactly the opposite, in his choice of friends, schooling, and career. Having been raised in a rather Orthodox Jewish home, he dated only non-Jewish girls, much to his mother's chagrin. Consciously, he perceived his behavior as a resistance to his mother's domination of the household. He viewed his father as a weak, ineffectual man, henpecked and brow-beaten, unable to defend himself, let alone his son, from his wife's hysterical outbursts of temper. His family had wanted the patient to become a physician. He decided to become a writer. But after two years in the service, four years of college, and a large collection of rejection slips, he compromised his principles and went into business management. He had lived apart from his family that whole time.

His hostility to his mother was apparent from the beginning of treatment. Paradoxically, he had considered himself a "Momma's boy" all during his childhood. Not only was he close to her, but he heeded her every word, ascribed to her every idea, and tried to fulfill her every wish. Without being asked he would help with the household chores, basking in the warmth of her praise for such monumental tasks as regularly scrubbing all the floors in the house at the age of nine. Exactly when the drastic change in his attitude to his mother took place was not clear in his mind. Vaguely, he connected the change with the family's moving from their old home when he was thirteen, two years after the birth of his sister. He recalled becoming frightened at that time of the darkness in his room and the shadows on the wall.

From his young adulthood on, his relationships with women were of a definite pattern. He would begin dating one girl almost exclusively, become enamored of her, and decide he was in love, only to be deceived and jilted after a few weeks. All of the girls whom he dated had certain qualities in common. They were pretty, not Jewish, had had previous unhappy affairs with older married men, and gave ample evidence that that they were still interested in another man while the patient was falling in love with them. The patient maintained complete obliviousness to their apparent infidelity until the moment that they openly revealed their faithlessness by returning to their original lovers. His trust was so implicit that in his marriage plans he often incurred large debts, such as leasing an apartment and making bank loans.

He had been in treatment for some time, when by chance during an interview a small metal object slipped out between the buttons of his shirt. At the moment, he had been discussing his feelings concerning his most recent debacle. He was in the process of paying off debts incurred by a therapeutic abortion of his most recent girlfriend. The fact that the surgeon had to sign a death certificate for the fetus made him suspect that the pregnancy might not have been his. He had been intimate with the girl for the first time only two months before, and the death certificate was evidence that the pregnancy was at least four months old and therefore not his. Confronted with this most recent deception, he was bitterly denouncing the duplicity of women and his own naive willingness to believe, when the small metal object slipped out from under his shirt. When I inquired about the metal object, he seemed reluctant to discuss it, disclaiming it as a stylish form of medallion that some young men were wearing at the time. It was just a "tiki," a good luck charm. "I don't wear a 'Mezuzah.'" (A Jewish amulet containing scripture.) When pressed, he related that he had begun wearing it after a particularly painful love affair had ended two years before. Originally, it had been suspended on a leather strap. When the strap broke the patient replaced it with a metal chain from an old necklace of his sister. For many years he had worn a Mezuzah, but it no longer represented something in which he believed. Now he wore his tiki constantly, into the shower, in bed, even during intercourse.

I suggested that his tiki seemed much more than a modish medallion. Rather it seemed to be an amulet, a good luck charm, a pagan symbol, his own golden calf, a symbol of anti-institutionalism, against religion, marriage, and perhaps the therapy as well. He agreed that he considered himself "anti-institution." He was more than non-religious; he was anti-religious. He'd never seen a good marriage and doubted that such a thing existed. He complained about the Army. "You can't even wear your hair the way you want." What he seemed to complain about was his lack of control over his environment and his being constantly dominated by others.

I asked to have a closer look at his amulet. It was a free-formed unpolished silver object, about 4 inches long and two inches wide, rather amoeboid, but with a pinching in at the middle that suggested the waistline of a human figure. There was no question, however, that two small polished disks on the upper part of the "torso" represented female breasts. I confronted him with the feminine nature of his amulet and suggested that this was, perhaps, his new foster mother, a substitute for his own for whom he had lost faith. This amulet was like a love-and-security-blanket, an externalization of what should have been inside himself.

He replied, "I can't have faith in any institutions or in any persons. I was very religious when young, but that was only a symbol of faith in my mother. Since she believed in it, I did. I recall that even at the age of five or six I fasted on Yom Kippur. I remember laying Tfillin (applying the phylacteries, a Jewish prayer ritual) even after my Bar Mitzvah. Then a year or so later I chucked the whole thing. I guess I had tolerated everything, my parents' bickering, the birth of my sister, my mother's domineering, until I had 'become a man.' I had anticipated that things would be different after my manhood, perhaps that my mother and father would accede to my wishes and that while my sister would just be a child, my status would be enhanced. I kept the faith until I realized that my symbolic manhood had changed nothing. The only difference was an added burden; I could be counted on for a 'Minyan' (it requires ten adult males to offer the daily prayers). I couldn't vote, drive the car, or achieve any sexual rewards. Attaining the age of twenty-one was a more prestigious arrival into manhood; I could drive, vote, and drink. The whole idea of religion and Bar Mitzvah was a hoax. My mother had led me on. That's when I stopped wearing the Mezuzah and chucked the whole thing. Today just seems to be a culmination of the revelations here the last couple of weeks. I haven't ingested my mother. I've externalized her. I remember for a long time feeling pessimistic about having something of my mother inside me, insuring that I'd be like her. Feeling that she's external and not really a part of me makes me feel more confident, secure, and optimistic. Yet I know that my feelings toward her tie in with my behavior with girls. I rush head-long into a relationship, then I feel honorbound to make my committments. Like an innocent lamb, I feel that if she slaughters me, it's her fault. What a risk, opening myself to a girl I don't know at all! Maybe some day I'll find someone who doesn't harm me. I embarrass myself before my friends, put myself in debt, jeopardize my job through neglect, all for a girl who deceives me. I get into these situations, but no one holds a gun to my head. I act with malice toward myself. If there's another bitch in the world, I'll find her!"

* * *

What seems to happen in the introjection of a bad mother is first the development of feelings of anger toward the mother by the child, whatever the source of his frustration or loss of faith. This anger seems to be projected onto the mother and then reintrojected as a "bad mother," replacing the previously adored loved object, the previously unambivalently worshipped good mother. An example of the process was described symbolically in the chapter of dreams in which the schizoid young woman dreamed of nuzzling the white doves which flew away, only to return as hawks. Parents are often innocent and ignorant of their part in converting the previously good introject into a bad introject. Unintentional frustrations of children occur so often in their growing up, that it is virtually impossible to avoid ambivalent reactions to parents. The fact that good introjects ever occur seems almost miraculous.*

AMBIVALENCE AND INTROJECTION

Nevertheless, in leave-taking in therapy, all efforts are directed at reversing the processes of introjection. Allowing anger to be ventilated by the patient to the object of his ambivalent feelings permits him to retain his feelings of affection, respect, and admiration for his doctor, relatively free of his negative attitudes. If this were not permitted to happen, whatever introjection of the therapist might take place would be no better than the introject of the bad mother that the patient brought into therapy originally. From this standpoint, the leave-taking is the most crucial part of the therapy, far more important than the mere attainment of the goal agreed upon by the patient and his doctor at the beginning of treatment. Hopefully, the moment of the attainment of the goals of treatment will closely coincide with the resolution of leave-taking. Unless the patient is told otherwise, he will usually assume that leave-taking represents dissolution of his relationship with his doctor, a weakening of ties. Actually, it is an invigoration of the relationship; the doctor, representing a model of healthy conscience, becomes a part of the patient's personality. Hopefully, this introjection will be transient, allowing the patient to re-introject his own good parent some time in the future. Should that final introjection not take place after the therapy is over, the patient could do worse than to keep the doctor as his conscience indefinitely. That model would guide him toward finding the best, most efficient, usually safest path in life, would stay with him through privations, and would assure him that he is accepted. The patient's previous conscience had taken him by the most difficult, dangerous, circuitous routes, ig-

---

* I strongly recommend, for a more technical discussion of this process, Hans W. Loewald's paper, "Internalization, Separation, Mourning and the Superego." *Psychoanalytic Quarterly*, 31:483-504, 1962.

nored his discomfort, often deserted him in the times of trouble into which it had led him, and criticized him to the point of self-hatred.

There are times in which the anger of leave-taking is apparent neither to the patient nor to the doctor, even in dream-interpretation. If anger is dealt with sufficiently early in treatment, it poses less of a problem upon termination and leave-taking. An example of this phenomenon is Mrs. O.A., the 23-year-old gamin with asthma from New York, who, after a dozen visits had been totally asymptomatic and had seemed to have made a healthy transition from being her mother's baby to becoming a grown-up in her own household in Pittsburgh. I had just returned from a nine-day vacation, my first since she had begun therapy. She had expressed intentions, before I left, of getting a job, preferably as a teacher's assistant, since she enjoyed working with children and was still forty credits shy of a teacher's certificate in Pennsylvania.

Patient: "Everything worked out well for me. Dr. S. (her general practitioner) was away on vacation the same time you were, and I hadn't the slightest fright of what would happen if I were to get sick.

"I had had a difficult time finding a job that I wanted with children. It's right in the middle of the school year. Lo and behold, a job appeared on my very doorstep. Lorraine, my upstairs neighbor, works at the hospital. Her sister had been staying with her, but went back home, so she needed a baby-sitter. Not only am I getting paid adequately, considering no expenses of transportation or lunches, but the job has therapeutic value. I'm a temporary mother to a child, and you know how much I want a baby. I've even gained four pounds from having to prepare meals all day. You can see I don't even look scrawny any more. I work from seven to four-thirty and either I bring the baby down while I do my housework, or bring my ironing up. Jeanie is a year old and a real darling.

"I've made all these decisions about staying in Pittsburgh and getting my teacher's certificate. I find I miss my old friends in New York less and less. As a consequence of depending less on my mother and on my girlfriends, my husband and I have grown much closer.

"I'm not worried about my reaction when I have to give up

taking care of Jeanie. As a teenager, I took care of a little neighbor boy almost four years. I realize that she's not mine and it's only temporary. Everything's going so well. Basically, my neighbor and I agree on how to raise children, so there are no conflicts in my looking after her daughter.

"I've had many dreams while you were gone, but I remember only two. In the first my mother-in-law called to tell me Aunt Dolly died. I guess it has something to do with giving up my mother. I seemed able to take it all right. It wasn't traumatic at all. Of course, in the dream it was only Aunt Dolly, but when the time comes for my folks, I feel I'll be able to survive all right. It doesn't hold the terror it used to for me. I think that the second dream is even more significant. It was a Carvel Stand, I guess they call it Dairy Queen in Pittsburgh; you know, they sell soft ice cream. It was at Penn and Negley and my husband and I were eating *soft* ice cream (laughing). So the milk wasn't very cold. That is the very first time that I've had a dream since moving here that the locale was Pittsburgh, not New York. Isn't that great! I feel like I'm 'unhooked' from some habits—not only my mother and New York, but my doctor made me throw away my nebulizer a couple of weeks ago. Poof! right into the rubbish can. That's the best move he ever made. Before, I'd be panicked if I were without it in my purse, even for a minute. I'm free."

Doctor: "How did you feel about both your doctors' being away?"

Patient: "Three months ago I'd probably been frantic. But now I didn't miss you at all. I just wished you had a nice time. In fact, it crystallized a feeling that's been growing the last month or so. I feel I no longer need you. Please don't misunderstand. I've grown very fond of you and I like talking to you. I guess I could let myself keep coming forever. But the need is gone. I've learned a lot from you, mainly not to beat myself. You know, this sounds funny (she hunches her shoulders up and giggles), but now I like me. I thought about this and told my husband. I haven't changed my personality at all or assimilated yours, but I'm somehow kinder to myself. The only way to say it is the way I just did: I like myself better. And I realize now, you're not a love-and-security blanket that I have to have around, like that old nebulizer. You may not be aware of it, but I think it's impossible to come here and talk with you and not take some of you with me. I know I'm going to miss talking to you, but I know also that you'll be with me wherever we go."

✿ ✿ ✿

The termination of treatment of Mrs. B. K., the 32-year-old phobic housewife, also was without angry incident. After a few interviews, the patient began taking swimming lessons at night at the local "Y." She had had a life-long fear of water. As she was leaving her first lesson, a man whom she and her husband had known for many years offered her a ride home, which she accepted. Subsequently, she began to have romantic daydreams about the man. However, she did not reveal her phantasies to me until the following week, when after her next lesson he proffered a ride home again. This time, he suggested the development of a more intimate relationship between them, and she found herself pondering whether to accede. Somewhat alarmed at her thinking, rather foreign to what she considered her real nature, she quickly told me about her phantasies.

Patient: "Since coming here, I've come to the realization that I've been walking around dissatisfied, feeling unappreciated. I've never felt I had a legitimate right to have an affair. Basically, my husband is a good person and we have a great deal in common. But he led me to believe, when he courted me, in attentiveness and love, things that you see in the movies, a romantic idealization. You sort of legalized my dissatisfaction. Your attitude picked me up, as though you were saying, 'You have a legitimate right to be dissatisfied.' I've never actually dismissed an affair as a solution to my problem. In fact, I'd never seriously considered it enough to accept or dismiss it until now. I know that I'm vulnerable to anyone's giving me attention. I'm alert to living, breathing men around me. Now a man comes along and doesn't think I have male qualities." *Apparently an allusion to my confronting her with her sexual desires for her mother.* "He admires my femininity."

Doctor: "Is he single or married?"

Patient: "He's married."

Doctor: "Then exactly what would the future hold for you?"

Patient: "He doesn't intend to leave his wife, I'm sure. We'd just have a clandestine relationship; I presume a sexual one."

Doctor: "Would that satisfy your needs? Would you feel loved and cherished or would you feel used?"

Patient: "Obviously, I couldn't be his sole love. There would be his wife."

Doctor: "How would that be better than what you have now?"

Patient: "At least someone would pay attention to me. Dave knows I'm attracted to the man. Dave could have taken a half hour off from work to pick me up at the pool. Instead, he encouraged me to get a ride from the fellow. This last time we sat in the car in front of my house talking for forty-five minutes; I wonder what my baby sitter thought. I told Dave. He said I was a big girl and I could make my own decisions."

Doctor: "Isn't this a dangerous game that you're playing? I can understand your dissatisfaction and your feeling unappreciated and unloved. But this man doesn't seem to offer you what you need and crave, to be loved more than anyone else in his life. And you are jeopardizing your marriage. Once destroyed, it can't be put together again. What will you have then? There's nothing wrong with daydreams, but enacting them can destroy your life."

As she left the interview she reached out impulsively and touched my hand. I responded by saying that we didn't have time to discuss it at that moment, so that the meaning of her need to touch me would have to be examined at the next hour.

She immediately launched into that examination at the onset of the next interview.

Patient: "The implications of my making a point of touching your hand—when I spoke about my—'boyfriend,' you really wanted to help me. You showed concern that I'd hurt myself. Obviously, your opinion of me wasn't so terrible; your attitude showed that plainly. I just can't accept what you're saying: you have to accept what you have. I hope I'd be able to have an affair, to be free enough, not be inhibited."

Doctor: "Some inhibitions are constructive, some destructive. I assume that what you wanted from me, for which you've turned to this man, is stroking, like your mother used to do. You haven't had much stroking lately."

Patient: "Stroking. I couldn't sleep for several nights in a row, thinking about my decision regarding the affair. I was so exhausted that I didn't feel like going to the opera with the family, as we usually do. But Dave went. Apparently the opera was exceptionally brilliantly done. His comment to me was, 'It was a perfect evening. Too bad you weren't there.' My mother said, 'I missed you. It wasn't the same without you.' That encapsulates the whole problem. The sexual implications I don't accept. But the other part of it—it's a perfect example of my not being prepared for this kind of marriage by my early life. My mother led me to believe that I could expect more.

"Last night after swimming, the fellow" *(she had been careful never to name him. Apparently she was protecting him by anonymity)* "picked me up again. He wanted to get physical. I didn't, not because of Dave, and not because of the man's wife. I realized that I wouldn't be any different in this fellow's life—just replaceable—like in Dave's life. You tore down my last feeling of desirability. You didn't mean to."

Doctor: "By questioning your future with an affair? By responding to your touching my hand only with an analysis?"

Patient: "Both."

Doctor: "My not responding to you physically is no reflection on your desirability. This is a reality you have to accept: you're my patient and I'm your doctor, exactly as she's your mother and you're her daughter. It doesn't matter how pretty, charming, intelligent, and lovable you might be. The circumstances of life, reality, sometimes dictate that you can't have exactly what you want, whether you are old, young, tall, short, thin, fat, male, female, smart, dumb, ugly, pretty, dull, witty, anything."

Patient: "That's hard to accept."

Doctor: "I know. But we *all* have to learn to accept reality."

Patient: "I realize that I have to find other solutions. I know that I have too much time on my hands. Friday I had an appointment with a young woman at Pitt in the counselling department. We got along great. The conversation was so stimulating that we talked for two hours and I got a parking ticket. I've become hungry for closer relationships. My illness is better" *(notice, she said, "better," not "gone")*. "I can eat in restaurants without fussing over the silverware, for example. And I'm enjoying people like I used to. I'm the girl I was ten years ago. The answer is to work with people again. I guess you'd say that I need to be stroked again. I'll get my Master's in Guidance. I can get a fellowship. It means a full year of

school. Then I'll teach full time. Right now I guess I've regressed a lot. In a fog of non-existence—I've been impatient
and egocentric. I feel a great urgency to get involved with
other people. I don't feel the need to come here any more.
If I need you, can I call you?"

Doctor: "Of course." *While I am not completely certain of
her introjection, I feel that accepting termination is a calculated risk. To insist upon her continuation would be autocratic
and destructive to her self-confidence. That she decided against
enacting her conflict in an affair for the reason that she gave is
a sign of a healthy conscience.*

PATHOLOGICAL INTROJECTION

Benevolent introjections are not easily brought about, especially in adult life. Yet the longitudinal histories of patients with
emotional illness often reveal pathological introjection that occurs in adult life, even in relatively healthy, stable people. Providing that the circumstances and stresses are qualitatively and
quantitatively appropriate, a good introject can be replaced by a
malignant one rather easily.

Case Illustration: Mr. I.D., a 46-year-old man, was referred
for treatment because of chronic alcoholism and a persistent
obsession that he had a venereal disease. He suffered dysuria
and urinary frequency, as well. The son of lower middle-
class West Virginia small-town parents, he had strongly identified in his youth with a prosperous great-uncle who operated
a large hardware store in his hometown. His father was irre-
sponsible, living mainly on a family inheritance. Diligently the
patient followed his uncle's precepts to "work hard, save your
money, live cleanly, and keep your nose to the grind-stone."
Under his tutelage, the patient became the town scholar,
worked his way through college, and graduated at the top of his
class, a member of Phi Beta Kappa. Upon graduation, he began working for one of the country's largest industrial complexes and by steps achieved a prominent position in its personnel department. He assumed the care of his parents, not
only providing them with financial assistance but also making
such decisions for them as to where and how they should live.
In essence, he had reversed the role of child and parent. The

patient married and moved his own home according to the dictates of the company for which he worked, and he only occasionally visited his hometown to see that all was well. His visits to his parents were rather perfunctory. The bulk of his time he would spend with his great-uncle, reminiscing about old times, attending sporting events, and comparing business practices. Then tragedy struck. At the age of sixty-five, his bachelor great-uncle married. Not only did he marry, but he married a woman with a tarnished reputation as a promiscuous gold-digger. Looking back, the patient remarked, "That was the start of my downfall. My uncle started doing everything that he'd spent his whole life telling me not to do. He bought a large fancy house and furnished it extravagantly. He bought a huge air-conditioned automobile. His step-daughter he sent to a fancy private school. All the things he'd railed against, self-indulgence, extravagance, living beyond his means. Everyone in the family asked me to talk to him, to change his mind. I felt that it was none of my business, so I never said a word, but I regret it to this day. That's when I began drinking. Now my uncle's over seventy and he can hardly walk, a broken man."

Clearly, the man he had formerly worshipped was now a fallen idol. The man he had proudly introjected in his youth was now a figure of scorn and derision. The patient's self-esteem plummeted apace with his estimate of his uncle. What had fed and sustained him was now bitter poison. Even the patient's symptoms were in part a reflection of his anger at his uncle for selling his principles for a second childhood fling at sexuality. Only by a transient introjection of the therapist was the patient able to reintegrate his previous personality.

Case Illustration: The stability of an introject is not dependent alone upon the fate of the model of the introject. Mrs. L.M., an attractive 40-year-old executive secretary, was the personification of efficiency, dependability, responsibility, and maturity. She emulated her hard-working, kind, compassionate, loving, giving immigrant parents, who devoted a great deal of their energies and personal resources in helping those less fortunate. The patient, herself, was extremely active in civic and civil rights groups, even though at times it earned her the unpopularity of her peers and siblings. Her youngest brother, the only male child, had been spoiled by fawning relatives. Exceedingly dependent and infantilized, he rarely did an honest day's work and seemed always to be overwhelmed by ill-fortune. So accustomed was his family to his constant misfortunes that they referred to him always as "Poor Don," never just "Don." After the death of his father, his mother subsidized Don from her own meager inheritance. Members of the family would bring him food and perform all kinds of personal services for him. No one ever asked anything of him or expected anything from him. On the other hand, his older sister was the pillar of the family, caring for the needy, visiting the sick, bringing cheer to the disheartened, and helping to solve everyone's problems, never requesting any help for her own, which were far from trivial. Her husband had been chronically invalided and sexually impotent many years with a progressive muscular dystrophy. Aside from his government pension, she was the sole bread winner, raising a son and a daughter. Now both her children were to be married, which would leave the patient alone with her slowly dying husband, confined nightly to their apartment. To this and to sexual abstinence she had painfully reconciled herself. During the rather hectic last days of planning for her daughter's wedding, she developed a cystitis and an ascending pyelonephritis with fever, pain, and urinary frequency. However, she continued to function at her job while undergoing treatment. Then one day, without any justification, a paranoid secretary in her office publicly accused the patient of having an affair with her husband and threatened to call the patient's husband. That afternoon the patient left work and took to her bed. Ordinarily calm and good humored, she began crying piteously. She called her urologist and insisted upon immediate hospitalization. She summoned all her relatives to her bedside and wailed for their help. The next day she developed urinary incontinence and her family and physician considered psychiatric hospitalization because of her severe regression. Fortunately, there was enough healthy ego to respond when the psychiatrist addressed her as "Poor Don" and confronted her with her sudden incorporation of her baby brother. She had, indeed, become a caricature of that infantile character. It was as though she suddenly had had enough of the burdens of her grown up self and was willing to assume the identity of her helpless, dependent baby brother. With-

in a few hours, all of her symptoms disappeared and she re-
assumed her usual self.

*   *   *

These examples serve to demonstrate the ease with which malignant introjects can be substituted for healthy ones. Unfortunately, the reverse is not so simple. To displace a sadistic conscience, the result of an introjection in early childhood, is probably the most difficult feat of psychotherapy.

I know of only one positive suggestion that can be made directly to the patient in order to assist the displacement of his
sadistic conscience by the model of conscience afforded by the
therapist, and that suggestion is an awkward, crude contrivance.
I offer it now apologetically, because I know of no better method.
Only after the patient has shown awareness that his own conscience is sadistic and has asked my help to replace it, do I suggest
that hereafter, when confronted by decisions of conscience, he
ask himself, "What would my doctor think of this situation?
How would he feel about it, and how would he react to it." By
this time, I am not merely a phantom figure of transference to
him, but a real person with a code of ethics that the patient has
come to recognize. I admit that I am not necessarily worthy to be
his permanent conscience, but without doubt my code of ethics is
superior to the sick conscience that has plagued him and caused
his self-hatred. During the brief course of therapy, I have tried to
guide him, to keep him from hurting himself and others. I have
accepted all of his thoughts, feelings, and wishes without criticism, but have not tolerated any enactment of those thoughts,
feelings, or wishes that would be harmful. In the course of therapy I may have admonished him, and perhaps may have even
hurt his feelings, but only for constructive purposes. Never have
I hurt him for the sake of pleasure in his suffering. In all of these
ways I am at least superior to the defective conscience he brought
into therapy with him. By preferentially responding to what he
considers my conscience, he must ignore his own. The only power a conscience possesses is in being heeded. Just as a conditioned
reflex can be extinguished gradually, so a conscience can be weak-
ened by not responding to its stimulation. At first, the patient
may find it difficult to be consciously on guard all his waking

hours in order to adhere to what he considers my code of ethics. Gradually the process becomes automatic and less burdensome. In no way does the patient alter his personality nor imitate mine, except in the area of conscience. When that transaction is completed, his self-hatred is replaced by acceptance, his insecurity, by self-confidence. *Only then* can he throw away his love-and-security blanket and terminate our interviews. That decision is mutual, but it is usually proposed by the patient. In conclusion I wish him well and remind him that his future, as well as mine, is unknown to us. Should he ever decide for any reason that he wanted to see me again, be it in a week, a month, a year, or twenty years, he would be welcome; and he knows my telephone number.

REFERENCE

1. Loewald, H.: Internalization, separation, mourning, and the superego. *Psychoanalytic Quart.*, 31:483-504, 1962.

Chapter XI

RESULTS AND SUMMARY

THE CASE FOR FOLLOW-UP

ASSESSING the results of psychotherapy is a tricky business. To begin with, most psychiatrists do not even know the results of therapy beyond their last visit with the patient. Assuming that the doctor can recognize progress from the patient's interactions with other people and with the doctor in interviews, from his dreams, from his own statements about himself, his feelings, and his conflicts, assuming all that, the doctor still cannot foretell what the patient will be like a year from their last interview, or for that matter, even the very next day. He has no certitude of the permanence of the apparent result of therapy. The fact that the patient may never call him again consitutes no proof of his well-being. Possibly he remains well. But possibly his symptoms may recur and he decides to live with them in quiet desperation. Possibly he may consult another psychiatrist and, for a variety of reasons, never let his original doctor know. What creates this state of uncertainty is the refusal of psychiatrists, in general, to do follow-ups on their patients. In no other branch of the healing sciences is this true. The basis of any empirical treatment depends upon the knowledge of what effects any given procedure produces. How can one ascertain the most effective method of therapy, when the long-lasting results of all forms of therapy are unproved suppositions? If Freud's patients, when he was using hypnosis with Breuer in the 1890's, had not been followed after their "cures," Freud would not have learned of the recurrence of their symptoms, and hypnosis would have been espoused as a panacea for the world's emotional ills. The history of medicine is replete with worthless treatments, once hailed and respected. Time is the best test, and that is the exact test excluded from psychiatric use.

In their defense, psychiatrists have valid reasons for their refusal to do follow-up studies. To make inquiries about a patient's life after the treatment relationship is over is an intrusion of his privacy. Moreover, it tends to recall old transference relationships that had been resolved prior to the termination of treatment. It tends to encourage dependency feelings; it might even be viewed by a patient as a seduction back into treatment. On the other hand, to my way of thinking, if such a flimsy stress could produce such destructive consequences, the patient's resolution of his conflicts is not very stable and his ego defenses are not very solid. That state of affairs hardly speaks well for the effectiveness of his treatment. The vicissitudes of life produce much greater stresses with which a patient should be expected to cope, especially after analytic therapy. If a follow-up phone call or note is enough to disturb the status quo, woe be unto the patient.

Follow-up can and should be a regular part of termination. I see nothing wrong in asking patients to let me know how things are going in their life after the treatment is over. In fact, I regularly get in touch with patients a month or two after even single consultations. So far I have not experienced any of the terrible consequences that other psychiatrists have predicted The single common response has been ego-syntonic. Without execption, the patients have been pleased that I cared enough to call, and my interest enhanced their feelings of worth. Not once was my intrusion openly resented, nor was there any indication of reluctance or passive resistance to my inquiry. No former patient has asked for an appointment at the time of my call or afterward. Therefore, I would urge my colleagues to reconsider their position regarding psychiatric follow-up. The dangers are not as real as they have been painted.

Whether the information obtained from these conversations is entirely accurate is a moot question. Probably there is some tendency for patients to magnify the good and minimize the bad, to salve their own feelings and those of their former therapist. However, it is unlikely that they would completely fabricate the state of their well-being. In this regard it follows the general direction of follow-ups in any branch of medicine. One would certainly agree that even a telephone follow-up with a severe diabetic successfully controlled by insulin and diet would be far different than that of a diabetic treated with vinegar and honey. It would be difficult to conceal hyperglycemic acidotic coma, even if the patient wanted to please his doctor. All in all, even a casual follow-up is better than no follow-up.

The matter of follow-up aside, evaluating the results of any form of psychotherapy is difficult. Eysenck is not the only one who who has raised the specter of the incidence of spontaneous remission of emotional illness.[2, 8, 36] He estimated that one-third to two-thirds of all psychiatric illnesses resolve themselves completely or partially without treatment. He maintains that psychotherapy receives undeserved credit for almost any results. Goldstein followed a group of patients who had been seen only for intake interviews, placed on a waiting list, and who never had therapy at all. He discovered that a large proportion of them had symptomatic improvement proportionate to their expectations of help from their intended treatment at the time of their initial contact.[12] Presumably, this "expectation factor" would have been operative had the patients been in continued therapy during the same period of time that they had languished on a waiting list.[10] Once again, psychotherapy should not have been credited for their improvement. Spontaneous remission and patient expectancy seem to achieve results uncomfortably similar to those that any form of psychotherapy affords, whether the form is analytic, or non-analytic (deconditioning, hypnosis, drugs, mechanical, etc.).

Before we psychiatrists sink into a nihilistic despond over the presumed ineffectiveness of any sort of psychotherapy, we had better examine just exactly what "spontaneous remission" entails. Spontaneous remission merely indicates a return of a level of emotional comfort compatible with continued existence. It does not necessarily mean an improved resolution of conflicts, ego growth, or maturation. Most often it means a continuing miserable, but bearable fate. Future illness can easily recur. For example, one condition statistically favorable for spontaneous remission is post-partum depression. After three to six months, most women recover their previous state of emotional health even without therapy. However, successful psychotherapy not only could shorten the course of their illnesses, but also it could enable the patients both to resolve the conflicts that led to their illnesses and to improve their interpersonal relationships with the members of their families, leading to emotional growth and opportunities for fulfillment for all. Moreover, future illness could be prevented. That kind of a result is infinitely superior to "spontaneous remission."

Case Illustration: Mrs. R. V., a 27-year-old housewife, was referred because of a depressive reaction, which began the first week after the birth of her son, her second child. Five years before she had given birth to a daughter without incident. This time, she experienced anorexia, apathy, sleeplessness, tearfulness, bouts of acute anxiety, hopelessness, and helplessness. Her obstetrician first treated her with reassurance, then mild tranquilizers. As her depression deepened, he added antidepressants. Nothing happened, except that her depression worsened. By the time she was referred to a psychiatrist, after eight weeks of gradually progressive illness, she not only felt desperately ill, but she was unable to function as a wife and mother. Furthermore, she felt that her husband was unresponsive to her illness and unfeeling toward her, showing her no sympathy, merely encouraging her to "pull herself together." She felt that he showered attention on his sister and neglected her. The patient entertained thoughts of divorce, and so threatened her husband.

At her initial interview, it became apparent that most of the patient's suffering was masochistic. Her unconscious guilt seemed to center around feelings of jealousy toward her brother, coincidentally five years her junior, and anger toward her mother for constantly babying him. The eldest child, she was the recipient of responsibilities without added privilege, and often was asked to take care of the brother in her mother's absence. Unaware of her obvious bitterness, she related how at seventeen there had been an explosion in the family home while she was in the shower. Stark naked, unmindful of her own burns, she had led her unharmed brother to safety from the burning house. Summoned home from a card party by a neighbor, her mother rushed onto the scene, screaming, "My baby! How is my baby?" The patient's well-being was only an after-thought. The patient worked her way through college with the aid of a scholastic scholarship. Her brother, a poor student, was sent by the family. Her good performance was taken for granted, as was his poor one. She was rewarded by her mother's not worrying about her. "My Ruthie is a responsible girl, I don't have to worry about her," was her mother's version of compliment. "I don't know what my Sammy would do, if I didn't look after him," was her mother's complaint about her son. As a result, the grown-up daughter was ignored, and the baby, babied. After the first hour, the patient began to realize that part of her anger at her husband for being neglected was really meant for her own mother. The crime of which he was being accused was identical with that of her mother.

The husband was seen with the patient after the first hour as an adjunct to her therapy. Interestingly, he had a problem identical to his wife's with his older sister's being favored by his mother. Unconsciously, he *had* been giving his sister an unwarranted amount of attention, far beyond anything that his affection for her would have required. He was merely currying favor from his mother. Actually, he considered his sister spoiled and egocentric and preferred to avoid her, were it not for his fear of antagonizing his mother. Out of shame, the husband had never revealed the situation to his wife before.

Within a day after the initial interview, the patient's symptoms had diminished. Within two weeks, they were gone. Both the patient and her husband, giving each other courage, had discussed their complaints with their respective mothers, which led to a more open, honest, and comfortable relationship with both families. The patient's treatment lasted for less than two months, the last half of which she spent helping her daughter to work out feelings of anger toward her and jealousy toward her new brother. Three families and three generations benefitted from a new relationship with one another.

Not all cases of post-partum depression work out with such far-reaching results. But most of them do with brief psychotherapy of a confrontative type. Without treatment, probably the patient described above would had some kind of spontaneous remission, but not at the level she achieved with psychotherapy, nor with the same rapidity. Were it to be tabulated statistically, however, both results would have been identical: "Markedly improved." Obviously anecdotal descriptions must be annotated to any result of therapy, along with the accepted descriptions of markedly improved, improved, unchanged, or worse.

In 1967, the American Psychoanalytic Association released their findings of a long-term sociologic and statistical study of the results of treatment by psychoanalysis and analytic psychotherapy. While ninety-seven per cent of the patients were judged by their therapists to have improved in total functioning and an equal number of patients felt that they had benefitted, the over all rate of symptom "cure" was only twenty-seven per cent, discouragingly close to Eysenck's predicted spontaneous cure rate of thirty-three per cent. Incidentally, over seventy-eight per cent of the three thousand odd cases reported had attended college or graduate school, certainly a very selective patient population. Forty-five per cent of those patients were in treatment from two to four years or more.

GOOD RESULTS

With these findings as a standard, and my own long-term cases as a control (although obviously the total numbers are much smaller in my practice, they are relatively comparable), my results are at least as good as those reported by the American Psychoanalytic Association, and in terms of symptom cure, superior to them. Moreover, *the results are achieved at a fraction of the cost to the patient in time and money compared to standard long term psychotherapy*. Not only have I used this method successfully in my private practice, but I have used it with almost equal success at the Staunton Clinic, a low cost psychiatric unit of the Department of Psychiatry of the School of Medicine, University of Pittsburgh. Most of the patients there come from low socio-economic classes, with high school education or less. Regular analytic long term psychotherapy has fared notoriously poorly with this kind of patient population at low cost clinics. Experimental models should be tried. Confrontative therapy works. Furthermore, even *relatively* inexperienced therapists can be trained rapidly to perform this kind of brief therapy. I have supervised junior and senior medical students in this method of brief therapy for over five years and they obtain results similar to my own. Nothing spurs the enthusiasm of medical students more than therapeutic success, especially in psychotherapy, where the techniques of therapy are usually a complete mystery to them. Whatever criticisms the readers of this book may have, they are not keener or crueler than those of medical students. Disbelievers can be convinced only by results. The results of this method are good.

ADMONITION

Before we are carried away on wings of song, let us examine the fate of the very first patient described in this book, Mr. S.F., the Navy demolition man with neurodermatitis. At the end of his first month of treatment, he received his bill, which he paid by check by return mail. His skin had completely cleared and everything was fine, everything that is, except that his check bounced because of insufficient funds. Also he moved and left no forwarding address. In other words, my attempt to alter his corrupt and sadistic conscience was a complete failure. To list the result as "markedly improved," which his skin was, would be statistically correct, but morally dishonest. In truth, he is unchanged. Very likely his dermatitis will recur, and if not, his conscience will see that he suffers in some other fashion. Why then, knowing in advance the failure of his therapy, did I not only include his case for presentation, but place it in premier position, where it was impossible to escape notice? It was done for exactly that reason, not to escape notice. Obviously, when anyone presents an experimental method which he suggests for general use, unintentionally he chooses his best cases in order to convince the skeptics. Let no one be deceived into thinking that this confrontative method of brief psychotherapy is uniformly and unreservedly effective. I never promised you a rose garden.

FLEXIBILITY

Not everyone can be helped by this method or perhaps any method of psychotherapy, brief or otherwise. The two most dependable criteria for successful prognosis using this method are the same ones noted by Malan:[20] the ability of the therapist to grasp the patient's conflicts quickly, and the patient's willingness and ability to utilize interpretations. If, at the initial interview, the patient shows no reaction to interpretations, one should assume that the confrontative method of therapy will be ineffective. This assumption can be confirmed if the patient comes to his second interview without having worked on the interpretations from the first hour. The doctor must find another method, if possible, to help the patient. Those unresponsive to confrontative technique might utilize counselling, supportive care, drugs, or group therapy.

Case Illustration: Mr. Z.F., a 47-year-old businessman, was referred by his gastroenterologist because of chronic aerophagia and eructation. The patient complained of burping continuously six to eight hours a day for almost three months. His wife was a dietician. Naturally, she blamed his eating habits and placed him on a low residue diet, avoiding salads and salad dressing, ketchup, spices, pickles, and coffee. It gave him only partial relief. When pressed for the circumstances of the onset of his illness, he related that he had been negotiating several very large leases about which he had become increasingly concerned. If the leases were not signed, he might lose the investors in his shopping center and his financial support would crumble. When I tried to get at his feelings, I learned to my dismay that not only was he not conversant with them but he did not even know what feelings were. Such things as anger, jealousy, greed, fear, anxiety, and depression were only words to which he could not relate in any way. He was not denying them; he had not even defined them. He could speak only in terms of physical symptoms. "I've had trouble with my stomach for fifteen, twenty years, maybe more. If I get a cold, it settles in my stomach. When I fast for a holiday, I break out in a cold sweat and vomit gall." His whole life was wrapped up in his work. His work was an obsessional defense. He never examined his interpersonal relations and was not interested in starting to now. All he wanted was relief for his stomach. The leasing contracts had finally been negotiated and signed several days prior to his interview, but his symptoms had not abated.

The interview was not very old when I realized that confrontative therapy was not for this patient. He wanted symptomatic relief and avoidance of psychological investigation. He had consented to this interview only to mollify his doctor. The obvious solution was to join him in his obsessive defensiveness with a regimen of more stringent obsessionality. I told him that with the signing of his contracts he could expect his symptoms to recede gradually. But to expedite his improvement I suggested the following regime:

1. Continue his low residue diet (I did not want to undercut his wife).

2. After each meal chew two tablets of simethicone (a defrothicant) and then chew a stick of pepsin chewing gum for exactly five minutes.

3. After dinner sip slowly one ounce of brandy or Drambuie (a Scotch liqueur).

4. Walk around the block during the evening at least once.

I assured him that he would feel much better within two to three days, and I wanted him to call me in one week. Furthermore, if he ever felt in the future that he had had any feelings that he wanted to discuss with me, not to hesitate to call. In four days he called me delightedly to tell me that his symptoms had cleared up completely within two days and that he felt wonderful. He asked if there would be any harm in his using the treatment in the future if his symptoms ever recurred. I assured him that it would be perfectly safe and I reminded him of my availability.

Some may scoff at my use of obsessional magic and ritual. My position is that the treatment must be modified to suit the patient. If what he is willing to accept coincides with what he needs, if it is ego-syntonic and in no way regressive, then I am all for it even if it represents a method antithetical to the one I prefer. For this patient, I believe that confrontative therapy, or any insightful psychotherapy, would have been a fiasco. To disturb his rigid, and previously successful obsessional defenses would needlessly and uselessly cause him severe psychic trauma, all for a little gas.

REAPPRAISAL OF BRIEF PSYCHOTHERAPY

The current wave of the community mental health movement not only threatens to swamp existing facilities, but may isolate psychoanalysis once again from psychiatry and from medicine. Bellak writes, "Psychoanalysis faces the danger that, under the pressure of enormous public need, there will be a reversion to the pre-analytic days of the common sense approach, the purely humane approach, which will involve the loss of the advantages of the valuable hypothesis that Freud applied."[4] Aldrich similarly warns, "Community psychiatry puts a new premium on efficiency in psychotherapy. Unless effective brief methods based on psychodynamic principles are developed, the practical application of the theoretical advances of the last half century may be jeopardized by consequences of the increasing public demand for psychotherapeutic care."[1] He espouses altering our attitudes about psychoanalysis and short term therapy.

> "For psychoanalysis to help evolve brief psychotherapeutic procedures may require the exposure of some of its traditional and cherished assumptions to a more unprotected review than has been the case thus far. An example of an assumption that requires review is the assumption that the results obtained in 'long term' psychotherapy will inevitably be better and more lasting than the results obtained in short-term therapy. Although this assumption is based more on anecdote than on evidence, it is deeply entrenched and defended as if it were established fact.
>
> "Contributing to the persistence of this assumption is a tendency to dismiss any improvement that occurs early in the course of planned long-term treatment as 'a flight into health,' 'a transference cure,' or simply evidence that the patient is not prepared to enter a more intensive phase of treatment. Instead of encouraging the patient to use his ego resources to consolidate and extend unanticipated early gains, therapists often act as if they believed that autonomous maturing and conflict-resolving processes cease functioning when psychotherapy begins, and that improvement not directly accounted for by resolution of unconscious conflict cannot be sustained without continuing therapy.
>
> "Another deterrent to the development of brief methods is the assumption that they would be more dangerous than conventional 'long-term' treatment. Planned brief therapy presumably would be more dangerous because it would require more therapist intervention, with a greater risk of inaccurate or premature interpretation. The adverse consequences of this type of error, however, have not been as well documented as tradition would suggest; furthermore, the consequences of er-

roneous interpretation in the framework of psychoanalysis may be quite different from the consequences of erroneous interpretation in the less intensive relationship of psychotherapy."

Sloane finds common denominators in the varied approaches to brief therapy, specifically psychoanalytic, behavioral, and Rogerian: 1) the relationship between the patient and therapist; 2) a conversational content; and 3) techniques such as interpretation, counterconditioning, and reward. Whatever the method, it seems likely "that psychotherapy is dominated by the beliefs of the therapist and that the outcome of therapy is mediated by the success with which he can get his patient to share them."[33] But weaving through the thread of every brief psychotherapy method is the idea of *positive transference*. Describing the psychoanalytic view of brief therapy, Gillman focuses on a "strong positive transference towards an understanding, accepting therapist who does not react like other important figures in the patient's experience."[3] Sifneos was even more deliberate in excluding anything but positive transference. "The therapist encourages the establishment of rapport with the patient and tries early to create a therapeutic alliance. He utilizes the patient's positive transference feelings explicitly as the main therapeutic tool. His specific goal is to concentrate on a circumscribed area of unresolved emotional conflicts underlying the patient's symptoms. He actively bypasses character traits such as masochism, excessive passivity, and dependence which give rise to therapeutic complications."[29] In other words he utilizes transference, but does not resolve the transference. That seems to be the hallmark of all forms of brief therapy, whether analytic, behavioral, Rogerian or any other: utilize positive transference and stay away from transference interpretations; avoid negative transference like the plague. Except for children's residential treatment centers in California and John Rosen's work with psychotic patients in the East, no one else in the United States performs brief psychotherapy utilizing negative transference and vigorous interpretation of it.

The rationalization behind the avoidance of negative transference is that it is dangerous to the patient and to a rapid resolution of therapy. It is neither. It is avoided for one obvious reason. It is unpleasant. It is unpleasant both to the patient and to the doctor. It is especially unpleasant to the doctor, who derives a good deal of ego satisfaction from the continuing experience of patients' trying to please him, to win his favor and approval, to praise him and to extol his virtues. By the end of the day, it is difficult not to believe them, especially when all of his patients feel similarly. Positive transference is a huge game based on an idealized phantasy that encourages dependency and apple-polishing. The doctor's satisfaction from the game has been described. The patient's pay-off is his avoidance of his unpleasant self and his unpleasant feelings. For both patient and doctor, positive transference is a narcissistic delusion. If the doctor really stands for reality, then he must "tell it like it is." That means that the patient must be faced with his negative, as well as his positive, feelings. All feelings are human. To examine only one side is no more mature than to reassure a child that he will never die. Eventually, each of us must face bitter truths. Sugar-coating them does not prepare us to accept them.

Unfortunately, not all therapists are willing to face some bitter truths about themselves. We are not as all-wise, all-knowing, omniscient and omnipotent as the phantasies of positive transference would have us believe. We make our share of mistakes; our judgment is not perfect; things do not always go as we plan; we catch colds and we cannot protect others from catching colds. What should be reassuring to patients is sometimes disconcerting to doctors; we are as human as they. We get cranky some days; sometimes we are stubborn, and on occasion, even dense. Hopefully most times we are not. Sloane lists some of the attributes of a good therapist: "understanding, empathy, flexibility, and a respect for the dignity and integrity of the patient . . . genuineness, unconditional positive regard . . . warmth, tolerance, and acceptance."[33] It is relatively easy to exhibit these qualities toward someone who lavishes praise on your head merely for being allowed to enter your office and to pay you for listening to him. Not everyone can behave that same way when being ignored, or being heaped with derision, scorn, abuse, and denigration.

Even without negative transference, brief therapy is no picnic. Campbell makes that clear in his comments:

"I would caution here against the tendency to equate short-er therapy with easier therapy. Even though few of the patient's maladaptive patterns can be traced explicitly through their genesis and development during brief therapy, the therapist can hardly point the way if for him, too, the road remains in utter darkness. Rather, the therapist must make a rapid assessment of the patient's personality structure and of his ways of responding to conflict. The therapist's formulation of the dynamic factors involved direct the content and the styles of his maneuvers in each session. His aim is to translate his insights about the patient's behavior into a message that is tolerable, meaningful, and practicable for that patient."[6]

Psychiatrists, as a general rule, underestimate what is tolerable for a patient. Patients' egos are much more resilient than most doctors give them credit for. If psychiatrists would come down from their ivory towers, they would also find that patients even with only average intelligence can understand complex ideas when they are not made abstract and abstruse by jargon. A man does not have to have a superior intelligence or a college education to comprehend that he has made himself a lifelong victim of his guilty conscience. And he can accept almost any impulse when it is presented as a conflict attended by guilt. "You must be very upset that you want to injure your brother in a fit of jealousy" is acceptable, whereas, "You hate your brother," is a painful, unacceptable condemnation. Likewise, "You must feel very badly that the person you've come to for help seems so inept" leads to a continued relationship, but, "You think I'm stupid" does not. The patient cannot help his hating. That is part of what brought him to seek help. He needs to find out that it is possible to dislike someone and still work with him in the expectation that his feelings may change, that something likeable will ensue. What should emerge is his dignity and uniqueness as an individual, separate from his doctor, but equal as a human being.

Alan Gregg put it rather well.

"First, psychiatry along with the other natural sciences leads to a life of reason. It explains what must otherwise excite fear, disgust, superstition, anxiety, or frustration. It breaks the clinches we otherwise get into with life and all the unnecessary, blind, infighting.

"In the second place, by showing us the common rules, the uniform limitations, and liberties all human beings live under because they are human, psychiatry gives us a sort of oneness-with-others, a kind of exquisite communion with all humanity, past, present, and future. It is a kind of scientific humanism that frees us from dogma and the tyranny of the mind, a relief from the inhuman strait-jacket or rigid finality of thought.

"Third, psychiatry makes possible a kind of sincere humility and naturalness I've never received from any other study or experience. Perhaps suffering lessens one's delighted conviction in the liveableness of life—I don't know for I've not known much suffering yet. But I know that psychiatry provides the material for a quiet but extraordinarily tenacious kind of humility and a sympathy that is honest and eager.

"And lastly, psychiatry makes it possible to bring to others these things I've mentioned: the light of reason, the oneness-with-others and an attitude of sympathetic humility, and understanding. Also it makes one able to receive these same gifts—and I would count him a poor physician who cannot receive as wisely and thankfully as he gives. So, in short, psychiatry makes possible by teaching and example the exchange of these things so desperately wanted by human beings and they are so healthy and happy when they get them and give them!"[14]

SUMMARY

A method of brief psychotherapy has been described, characterized by early, vigorous interpretation of negative transference and separation anxiety. Its purpose is to restore the patient's function, to show him how his conflicts have led to his self-destructive actions and inhibitions in the past, and to suggest other ways of handling his conflicts. Just as in growing up, the child finds his own way, so the patient must find his. In its most ambitious phase, the treatment attempts to replace the patient's sadistic conscience with a healthier one. At least temporarily, the doctor's model of conscience is offered as a replacement. The replacement of conscience is the most haphazard part of treatment. While the process of introjection can be enhanced by resolving the ambivalence of the patient toward his doctor, introjection cannot be insured. The patient's sadistic conscience is the core of his problem and will continue to plague him in the future unless a healthier introject replaces it.

While the doctor is quite directive in trying to change the patient's conscience, he does not in any way attempt to alter the patient's basic personality. The obsessive is not discouraged from his obsessive character traits, nor the hysteric, from most hysterical defenses. Each person must do his own thing. Patients should not be molded into any set character by the doctor. The striving is for less infantile, less masochistic individuals who function better. One of my patients summarized her ideas about her successful termination of therapy this way. "What I've achieved from the treatment is knowing myself, getting rid of unrealistic guilt, controlling my infantile feelings, achieving the goals I'd set for myself when I began, having activity I take pleasure in, and learning to love, to give, and to share. I guess I deserve credit for doing that, instead of looking for ugly motives behind everything that is good." The results of this method of brief therapy are good, comparable to long-term therapy.

The area where most research is needed is in the introjection of conscience. There lies the key to the cure for emotional illness. The ancient Greek view was expressed by Polybius in the Second Century, B.C.

> There is no witness so dreadful,
> No accuser so terrible
> As the conscience that dwells
> In the heart of every man.

The essence of the Puritan ethic in colonial America was made manifest by the phrase "agonbyte of inwit" (pangs of conscience). For our times, the proclamation is issued from Walt Kelly's cartoon character, *Pogo*, in his paraphrase of Commodore Perry's stirring message from The Battle of Lake Erie, "We have met the enemy, and they are *Us!*" Saul Bellow's anti-hero, *Herzog*, is the current protagonist of our modern masochistic world. We are becoming increasingly aware of the problems of masochism, individually and collectively. Today, we are at the brink of destroying ourselves with devisiveness, paranoia, and thermonuclear weapons. Perhaps the future will yield an answer to the problems of conscience that have plagued man since recorded time. I hope that I have contributed in some small way to that end.

REFERENCES

1. Aldrich, C.: Brief psychotherapy: a reappraisal of some theoretical assumptions. *Op. cit.*, pp. 37-38.
2. Avent, H. H.: How effective is short-term therapy? In Wolberg, L. R. (Ed.): *Short-Term Psychotherapy*. New York, Grune & Stratton, 1965, pp. 7-22.
3. Alexander, F., and French, T.: *Psychoanalytic Therapy. Op. cit.*
4. Bellak, L., and Small, S.: *Emergency Psychotherapy and Brief Psychotherapy*. New York, Grune & Stratton, 1965, p. 4.
5. Brady, J.: Psychotherapy, learning theory, and insight. *Arch. Gen. Psychiat.*, 16:304-311, 1967.
6. Campbell, R., discussant for Stroker, M.: Brief psychotherapy in an outpatient clinic. *Amer. J. Psychiat.*, 124:112, 1968.
7. Edelson, M.: *The Termination of Intensive Psychotherapy*. Springfield, Thomas, 1963.
8. Eysenck, H. (Ed.): *Behavior Therapy and the Neuroses*. New York, Pergamon Press, 1960.
9. Frank, J.: *Persuasion and Healing*. Baltimore, Johns Hopkins Press, 1961.
10. Frank, J.: The dynamics of the psychotherapeutic relationship. *Psychiatry*, 22:17-39, 1959.
11. Gillman, R. D.: Brief psychotherapy: a psychoanalytic view. *Amer. J. Psychiat.*, 122:601-611, 1965.
12. Goldstein, A. P.: *Therapist-Patient Expectancies in Psychotherapy*. New York, Macmillan, 1962.
13. Gottschalk, L. A., and Auerbach, A. H.: *Methods of Research in Psychotherapy*. New York, Appleton-Century-Crofts, 1966.
14. Gregg, A.: In Menninger, W. C.: *Psychiatry in a Troubled World: Yesterday's War and Today's Challenge*. New York, Macmillan Co., 1948, p. XIV.
15. Heine, R. W. (Ed.): *The Student Physician as Psychotherapist*. Chicago University of Chicago Press, 1962.
16. Hollander, M. H.: Selection of patients for definite forms of psychiatry. *Arch. Gen. Psychiat.*, 10:361-369, 1964.
17. Knight, R. P.: *An Evaluation of Psychotherapeutic Techniques, Psychoanalytic Psychiatry and Psychology*. New York, International Universities Press, 1954.
18. Lennard, H. L., and Bernstein, A.: *The Anatomy of Psychotherapy*. New York, Columbia University Press, 1960.
19. Lowinger, P., and Dobie, S.: An evaluation of the role of the psychiatrist's personality in the interview. In Masserman, J. H. (Ed.): *Science and Psychoanalysis*, Vol. 7. New York, Grune and Stratton, 1964, pp. 211-229.
20. Malan, D.: *A Study of Brief Psychotherapy. Op. cit.*
21. Marmor, J.: Psychoanalytic therapy as an educational process. In Masser-

man, J. H. (Ed.): *Science and Psychoanalysis,* Vol. 5. New York, Grune and Stratton, 1962.

22. McGuire, M.: The process of short-term insight psychotherapy. *J. Nerv. Ment. Dis.,* 141:83-94, 219-230, 1965.
23. Report of ad hoc committee on central fact gathering data of the American Psychoanalytic Assoc. *J. Amer. Psychoanalytic Assoc.,* 15:841-861, 1967.
24. Sapolsky, A.: Effect of interpersonal relationships upon verbal conditioning. *J. Abnorm. Soc. Psychol.,* 60:241-246, 1960.
25. Semrad, E., Binstock, W., and White, B.: Brief psychotherapy. *Amer. J. Psychother.,* 20:576-599, 1966.
26. Shoban, E., Jr.: Psychotherapy as a problem in learning theory. *Psychol. Bull.,* 46:366-392, 1949.
27. Sifneos, P.: Dynamic psychotherapy in a psychiatric clinic. In Masserman, J. H. (Ed.): *Current Psychiatric Therapies,* Vol. 1. New York, Grune & Stratton, 1961.
28. Sifneos, P.: Seven years' experience with short-term dynamic psychotherapy. In 6th International Congress of Psychotherapy, London, 1964. *Selected Lectures.* New York, S. Karger, 1965, pp. 127-135.
29. Sifneos, P.: Crisis psychotherapy. In Masserman, J. (Ed.): *Current Psychiatric Therapies,* Vol. 6. New York, Grune & Stratton, 1966.
30. Sifneos, P.: Two different kinds of psychotherapy of short duration. *Amer J. Psych.,* 123:1070, 1967.
31. Skinner, B.: *Science and Human Behavior.* New York, The Macmillan Co., 1953.
32. Skinner, B.: *Verbal Behavior.* New York, Appleton-Century-Crofts, 1957.
33. Sloane, R., Davidson, P., Staples, F., and Payne, R.: Experimental reward and punishment in neurosis. *Compr. Psychiat.* 6:388-395, 1965.
34. Sloane, R.: The converging paths of behavior therapy and psychotherapy. *Amer. J. Psychiat.,* 125:877-879, 1969.
35. Stevenson, I.: Direct instigation of behavioral change in psychotherapy. *Arch. Gen. Psychiat.,* 1:99-107, 1959.
36. Strupp, H. H., and Williams, J. V.: Some determinants of clinical evaluations of different psychiatrists. *Arch. Gen. Psychiat.,* 2:434-440, 1960.
37. Szasz, T.: *The Myth of Mental Illness.* New York, Hoeber Med. Div., Harper & Row, 1964.
38. Tompkins, H.: Short-term therapy of the neuroses. In Usdin, G. L. (Ed.): *Psychoneurosis and Schizophrenia.* Philadelphia, J. B. Lippincott, 1966.
39. Wolberg, L.: The technic of short-term psychotherapy. In Wolberg, L. R. (Ed.): *Short-Term Psychotherapy.* New York, Grune & Stratton, 1965.
40. Wolberg, L.: Perspectives in short-term therapy. In Masserman, J. H. (Ed.): *Current Psychiatric Therapies,* Vol. 6. New York, Grune & Stratton, 1966.
41. Wolpe, J., and Lazarus, A.: *Behavior Therapy Techniques.* New York, Pergamon Press, 1966.

INDEX

264